THE GREAT CRICKETER

'A figure that radiates robust cheerfulness, tireless energy and an unquenchable zest for life. . . .'

THE
GREAT CRICKETER

by
A. A. THOMSON

Illustrated

London
Robert Hale Limited
63 Old Brompton Road S.W.7

First published 1957

PRINTED IN GREAT BRITAIN BY
EBENEZER BAYLIS AND SON, LTD.
THE TRINITY PRESS, WORCESTER, AND LONDON

To
THE OTHER ONE,
SIR DONALD BRADMAN

AUTHOR'S NOTE

To write a book about W.G. is probably an impertinence; without a great deal of help it is an impossibility. This help I have received in generous measure: first, from M.C.C., particularly from H. S. Altham and Miss Diana Rait Kerr; also from G. Neville Weston, who knows more about W.G. than any man alive, John Arlott, G. D. Martineau, L. E. S. Gutteridge and Mrs. Dorothy Middleton. For anecdotes, reminiscences and photographs I am further indebted to Captain Percy Burke, the Rev. A. Doxey, Messrs. Henry Grierson, Patrick Hone, R. L. Ingelsee, Harry Nicholls of Downend, Jack Pride, Alec Rowley, J. W. Scott, Peter Stone, C. A. Wildish, and Miss V. S. Hubert. I have also drawn sustenance from that very human statistician, G. A. Copinger. My sincere gratitude is tendered to all.

CONTENTS

7

LIST OF ILLUSTRATIONS

The Author and Publishers wish to record their thanks for permission to reproduce the following pictures: 3, 5, 6, 7, 8, 19, 22, and 29, the M.C.C.; 9 and 10, Mrs. Beldam; 14, the Editor of *Punch*; 12 and 13, Mr. H. C. Hall; 27 and 28, the *Picture Post Library*; 26, R. L. Ingelsee, Dutch Correspondent of *The Cricketer*; 20 and 25, Mr. Peter Stone; 21, Mr. J. W. Scott; 30 and 31, Miss V. S. Hubert.

THE LEGEND

No legend ever springs from nothing and the legend of W. G. Grace is the best story in cricket, the best story in sport, and, in its own uncomplicated way, the best story of nineteenth-century England. It is a story of almost unbroken success and yet, unlike so many success stories, it is never dull. The story is illumined by the bright light that plays round its principal character, so that in his day and for long afterwards his countrymen saw a picture of him which was clearer and vivider than that of any other public figure in England. No one but Queen Victoria herself, and perhaps Mr. Gladstone, would have been more easily recognizable in the street throughout the land, from London to Sheffield, from Bristol to Manchester. Railway porters frankly abandoned their barrowloads of luggage to shake his hand and he would never refuse you his hand, however grubby, if you were bold enough to ask for it. C. B. Fry's bearded housemaster at Repton was once mistaken for W.G. by a porter at Nottingham station. It was a proud moment in a modest life.

The picture that has come down to us is outstanding for its clarity of outline. Close your eyes and look at it: the burly seventeen-stone figure with its massive chest and shoulders, the best-known beard, even when beards *were* beards, between 1870 and the first world war—perhaps the most famous beard between Shakespeare and Bernard Shaw—the huge feet and, perched in comical contrast at the other end, the ringed red and yellow cap of the most famous cricket club in the world. It is a figure that radiates robust cheerfulness, tireless energy and an unquenchable zest for life and what he most enjoyed in it. The picture was luminous in his lifetime and, forty years after his death, still remains resplendent.

But this picture, clearly though it shines, is only a 'still'. This fourth son of a west-country doctor was not born with a massive figure and a buccaneer's beard. He was once a small boy, modestly fielding, as a small boy should, to his elder brothers' batting in the garden at home; here he was coached by a highly intelligent uncle and counselled by a loving but unsentimental mother. He did not burst upon the larger cricket world until he was all of sixteen; and his beard did not wave very flauntingly until he was twenty. He was a normally sturdy small boy, but in his fifteenth year he had a dangerous bout of pneumonia, which affected him so that he suddenly grew inordinately lanky. He did not gain his gargantuan girth until he was over forty. In 1865, his first regular first-class season, he was seventeen years old, measured six feet tall, weighed no more than eleven stone and worked off his surging energy by winning hurdle races in times which even today can be considered respectable. In memory he is and always will be the Old Man, but when did he become the Old Man? He lived to be elderly, but not old. He was in turn an eager small boy, lifting (but not very high) a straight and not too heavy bat under his uncle Pocock's expert tuition; a gawky big-boned youth, coming up to London for the first time as a fresh addition to an already notable cricketing family; a bright-eyed, muscular young man in the glorious eighteen-seventies rejoicing in his strength; and the middle-aged working doctor, looking down wryly on his increasing waistline, who at the age of forty-seven came back into cricket to outrage the laws of probability by scoring 1,000 runs in May and hitting his hundredth century. He died at the age of sixty-seven in the middle of a European war which baffled and saddened his uncomplicated mind.

The legend fills in a background with strong brush strokes of its own. It recounts, with an appreciative smile, that on some county cricket grounds you could see the notice: 'Admission threepence: if Dr. W. G. Grace plays, admission sixpence.' It states, categorically and picturesquely, that he provided half the bricks in more than half the pavilions in England. It tells how, in the days of his prime, hundreds of hansom cabs would go rattling down St. John's Wood Road when it was known that he was at the wicket; and when he celebrated his jubilee, a quarter of a century later, the crowds at Lord's were thicker than ever. Great Western trains would humbly wait for him at Paddington station, while he talked to a friend. The legend also underlines that immense vitality which would literally run his partners off their feet and seemed to thrive on being in action, batting and bowling or fielding, for the whole of a three-day match. It chuckles over his artfulness that, within the rules, demanded and delighted in, as surely as ever did Mrs. Battle, the 'rigour of the game'. And it builds up a picture of his perennial boyishness, his bubbling exuberance and, as attested by virtually all the contributors to the Memorial Biography, his genuine personal kindness.

That is the legend and it may be that the very brightness of its colours have obscured the man. Sometimes a legendary figure looms so large, that the man himself is lost. Already those who say that sort of thing will be muttering about the Grace myth, or even myths, thereby implying (a) that Grace never existed and (b) that this was highly to his discredit. The legend is so large that young people think of W.G., if they think at all, as a figure, heroic but shadowy, like Hereward the Wake, who could not conceivably compete in cricket today.

These pages offer, not what is called a 'new judgment', a modern phrase well meant, but savouring of impertinence; still less do they present what is now happily called an agonizing reappraisal; they repeat an older judgment: that beyond the glitter of the legend, the man was greater still.

W. G. Grace was, like the great comedy characters of English fiction, much larger than life, but perfectly natural. The outsize opulence of his personality made him akin to Mr. Pickwick or the jolly Ghost of Christmas Present or Tristram Shandy's Uncle Toby or John Jorrocks or the great Sir John Falstaff or, occasionally, that superb comedy character, Mr. Toad from *The Wind in the Willows*. G. K. Chesterton once said that Pickwick was the true English fairy and W.G., that bulky sprite, was a prodigious Puck in a truly English midsummer day's dream.

To every man life must bring tragedy and may bring comedy: tragedy in the death of dear ones and in the gradual loss, as age creeps on, of the strength and skills through which

he has fulfilled himself; comedy in the ceaseless interplay of
incident on character and character on incident and in the
thousand natural quirks and oddities that flesh is also heir to.
W.G. had his tragedies, like the rest of mankind, poignantly
suffered in the loss of a brilliant younger brother and of a
beloved son and daughter. The comedy in his life lay in his own
ebullient character and in the 'beautiful but complicated
English game of cricket' which he stamped with his image and
superscription. He did not invent the game and, indeed, the
heroes of Hambledon lived long before him. Giants like Alfred
Mynn and Fuller Pilch had had their day by the time W.G.'s
had begun. Yet the difference between cricket when he found it
and when he left it was something like the difference between
Stephenson's 'Rocket' and the Coronation Scot. In one of
cricket's best known descriptive phrases 'he turned the old one-
stringed instrument into a many-chorded lyre', and as the most
brilliant of cricket writers has said: 'Through bat and ball,
through a game born in a rustic field, W.G. expressed himself
to the full circumference of him, and at the same time he
enlarged the scope of cricket, until it became, year after year,
the embodiment of the English scene in summer, of English
humour, artfulness, pugnacity and good fellowship.'

All those qualities W.G. had, and exemplified, in abundance.
The humour of the game was largely *his* humour, its artfulness
revolved around stories of *his* artfulness, apocryphal or otherwise; his pugnacity symbolized the sometimes forgotten fact
that cricket was a hard game played with a hard ball; as for
cricket's good fellowship, it is almost impossible to think of it
without a genial bearded face beaming over it.

Because he was a wonder, a nonesuch, a champion—*The*
Champion—and because he was for them the jolly symbol of
the sportsman, the countryman, of everything that went with
green turf and a kindly sun—the English gave him their hearts.
He appealed to them for the straightforward way in which he
would stand up for the rights of Grace, Gloucestershire and
England. They even loved his modest lack of modesty which
could say: 'Yes, I think Arthur is the second-best bat in the
country'. He had a simplicity that was not to be pitied, a

simplicity which almost every Englishman of his day admired and loved. Even to-day when the newspapers record the death of some old cricketer, however humble or obscure, they will light his passing with a headline's momentary gleam: *He played with W.G.*

When the time came to find an inscription for the great memorial gate at Lord's there was difficulty in choosing. The poets sent in their verses and the scholars their Greek or Latin elegiacs but, set against that jovial Jove-like figure, all of them seemed woefully inadequate. Suddenly the phrase came to Sir Stanley Jackson, 'Jacker' of the old days. Not a question was raised, not a word was said against it, and so the gate bears the simple inscription that all cricket lovers know:

TO THE MEMORY OF
WILLIAM GILBERT GRACE
THE GREAT CRICKETER

CHAPTER ONE

SPRINGTIME

Was I not bred in Gloucestershire,
One of the Englishmen?

I

W. G. Grace said that, though he was not born a cricketer, he was born in the atmosphere of cricket. Similarly, though not born a doctor, he was born in an atmosphere of doctoring. He and his father and his four brothers were doctors, all except Fred (G. F.—,) the youngest, who died shortly before obtaining his degree. William Gilbert was the fourth of Henry Mills Grace's five sons, who were Henry, born in 1833; Alfred, born in 1840; Edward Mills, the famous E.M., born in 1841; W.G., born on the 18th July 1848, and G.F., born in 1850 to be a splendid cricketer and a charming person and to die tragically three months before his thirtieth birthday. There were also four sisters who in those days came on, as it were, in crowd scenes, but were not, bless them all, of great cricketing significance.

Dr. Henry Mills Grace was a Somerset man from Long Ashton who, on his marriage in 1831, moved half a dozen miles over the border into Gloucestershire to take up his first practice, thus conferring on one west-country shire, rather than another, an inexhaustible cornucopia of cricketing riches.

The village in which the young couple set up house was Downend, then about four miles out of Bristol, but now virtually joined up in the straggle of modern conurbation. It had a square, gabled church and two pubs, one of which was later presided over by the old Gloucestershire wicketkeeper, Harry Smith.

The Graces belonged to the middle class; not the amorphous mass to which, according to the statisticians, ninety-seven per cent of us now claim to belong, but to that genuine country middle class which, filling its place midway between the much abused rich man in his castle and the slightly idealized poor man at his gate, earned and received the respect of both. It was in fact a remnant of a semi-patriarchal society and it comprised the doctors, lawyers, parsons, schoolmasters, solid farmers and merchants of the region. Their social position was assured; the value to the community of their work, full, strenuous and highly responsible, is not to be questioned.

Dr. Grace had always lived a strenuous life. While a medical student he could only indulge his love of games by getting up at the incredible hour of five in the morning to play cricket with one or two of his devoted fellows on Durdham Downs at Clifton. His work as a country doctor was hard, as a country doctor's work always had been. There were long daily rounds in the gig or on horseback and long rides by lantern light to outlying villages in the cause of more or less radiant motherhood. The early morning saw him riding six miles eastward, W.G. recalled; at midnight he was often six miles to the west. Yet though he often had little sleep and less leisure, he managed to snatch a little time in winter for hunting with the Duke of Beaufort's hounds, and in summer for some kind of cricket. Nothing could turn him from his ambition to raise and unfurl the banner of the summer game in this green and pleasant land of west Gloucestershire. Here he was deservedly fortunate in his sons who, one after another, took to cricket as ducklings take to water at the earliest possible moment.

Above all, he was richly fortunate in his wife, born Martha Pocock, a perfect woman nobly planned to be the mother of mighty cricketers. Moreover, she had a brother, Alfred, and Uncle Pocock turned out to be the almost perfect coach.

Downend House, a place full of memories, is a typical country doctor's house, with a grey stucco front and a porch covered with red tiles. (The porch is not shown in the old photographs.) The garden is short at the front and has two enormous cedars at the side but there must a hundred years ago have been room for a cricket pitch. Here, as soon as his eldest son was born, the doctor laid out his wicket. He also took the leading part in setting up a cricket club at Mangotsfield which was the parent parish of Downend. The new club, which came into being when his son Henry was about twelve, played on Rodway Hill Common, which, standing above the village, had a glorious outlook but a rough surface. The common, with its fringe of gorse and bracken, badly needed levelling before any cricket could be played on it, but Dr. Grace was not merely an enthusiast; he was the cause of enthusiasm in others. A reasonably good pitch was ironed out and a piece about forty yards square was railed off.

In Downend I met a very old cricketer who had played in country games with W.G. long ago. He waved his hand towards the Downend cricket ground, just below the church. 'This wasn't W.G.'s club,' he said. 'It didn't exist when he was young.'

'Then he never played here?'

'Oh, yes, when he was doctoring in Stapleton Road, I remember him bringing a team along. He only made two when Ted Biggs, the postmaster, bowled him. And Mr. Jessop only made twelve.'

We walked round the cricket field, past the stand and the pavilion, which bore a plaque with the legend:

This Pavilion was erected and the cricket ground
purchased by supporters of Downend Cricket Club
in memory of the World's Greatest Cricketer,
Dr. W. G. Grace. 1922.

'It should have been dedicated to Ted Biggs,' said my old cricketer with a grin. 'He was captain of the team for a long time and he did bowl W.G. for two.'

We walked together up Rodway Hill. 'Look over the Common,' he said. 'It's proper Grace country. Over to the left there's Kingswood Hill, where Henry did his first doctoring and behind you there's Chipping Sodbury, that's where Alfred went to live. We've just come up from Downend where the family started and it's a pity we can't see Thornbury, which was E.M.'s territory—in fact, there's a Dr. E. M. Grace there now—or we'd have had our eye on nearly all of them.'

Looking out over the Common I thought of the match played here in 1858, when W.G. was ten years old, between Redland and West Gloucestershire, which had been swallowed by the Mangotsfield club, but left its name behind. Before the game began, an intoxicated spectator was found lying practically on the pitch and, polite requests having failed to shift him, Alfred Grace, the boxer of the family, was deputed to carry out the removal. This took exactly two minutes; the enemy departed, and the players, a little surprised that any fight should take place *before* a match, began their game. It was an even contest and the home side, set 101 to win, had reached 84 for the loss of five wickets, when a raucous yell heralded the return of the original drunk, who had brought an escort of lesser drunks with him to demand his rights. It was a boring interruption, but Alfred knew his duty. In all good will, he went and knocked his man down for the second time. This should have satisfied the aggressor, but his friends rallied to his aid with sticks and stones, and the battle commenced. The two teams, surrounded by this angry mob, armed themselves with bats and stumps and charged the foe, shoulder to shoulder.

The fight went on for half an hour and it was only when the local magistrate, whom Dr. Grace had ridden off to fetch, began to read the Riot Act that the enemy started to break up and sneak away. But the match had to be abandoned and W.G. never forgot it. They had needed only 17 to win.

My old cricketer, who had not heard this story before, nodded appreciatively. 'Ah,' he said, 'they were always fighting at Mangotsfield . . .'

He told me about a match he had played in sixty-odd years ago. That game, too, had been abandoned.

'It was a Frenchay man,' he said, 'hit a ball up into the poplar trees and started to run. When they'd run six, we shouted "Lost ball!" "That it ain't," said he, "I can see it stuck in the branches." So they kept on running. In fact, they ran twenty-eight and were too puffed to run any more. We offered 'em six, we even offered 'em twelve, but they would have twenty-eight or nothing, so we pulled up the stumps. What would you have done?'

Dr. Grace, I feel, would have dealt firmly with such a situation. He was a steady and persevering captain, taking batting, fielding and his own left-handed donkey-drop bowling extremely seriously. He was not aggressive by nature but, like all the Graces, and particularly E.M. and W.G., he was ever determined to stand four-square for the rights of his family and his side. He did not think you a cricketer at all unless you could catch and throw-in and, though he was keen on every kind of practice, he made certain that once a week sides should be picked and a game seriously played under full match conditions.

The earliest of the Grace family stories concerns the wager match between Thornbury, assisted by one or two Graces, and a Bristol eleven. There were two games. The first of them was easily won by the Bristol side, for whom Henry and Uncle Pocock were playing. In spite of this, the Thornbury captain issued a challenge for a return match with a bet of £25 on the issue. Dr. Grace was furious when he heard about this, for he thought cricket and betting should be kept apart, but he promised to play for Thornbury and entered into the contest with rugged determination. On the day of the match the Bristol captain demanded, rather laughingly, that the stakes should be deposited. When Thornbury had dubbed up, it was discovered that the Bristol captain had forgotten to bring his money along, and Dr. Grace firmly insisted that the Bristolians should put up their watches and spare cash instead. Then came the match. It was one of those games that happen often enough in fiction, but less often in fact. The doctor went in first and stubbornly batted right through the innings; then, through cunning bowling, helped by an icy wind and a worsening wicket, he lured the enemy to their fate. The result was against all the probabilities, but it happened and it was a long time before the merciless banter about this match came to an end in the Grace family. There was always a good deal of chaffing in the Downend household and, if you were a Grace, it was no use being too sensitive.

The Pococks were in their way a more strikingly interesting family even than the Graces. The father, George Pocock, was a highly intelligent and eccentric schoolmaster, whose main in-

terests in life were religion and box-kites. His religion was like
everything else about him, magnificently sincere and slightly
incongruous. He erected a tent or 'itinerant temple' in places
where the inhabitants were unlikely to be regular churchgoers
and there preached to the rough colliers, and 'lately reformed
Sabbath-breakers and thieves.' 'As little or no refreshment can
be procured in such a wilderness,' his 'tent notices' announced,
'the friends will do well to bring the requisites for tea with
them, and any of the cottagers, many of whose huts are become
very decent, will gladly provide them with water . . .'

The itinerant temple had no bell, but villagers were called to
the service, by the voice, loud and clear, of the preacher's
daughter Bessie—we shall meet Bessies again in the united
families—who began to sing as the trap that carried her and her
father approached the village.

'Granfer' Pocock's passion for box-kites was equally fervent.
He invented a kite-drawn carriage (shades of Mr. Dick!) in
which he incredibly drove from Bristol to London, knocking off
chimney-pots as easily as though they were bails and terrifying
the wives of toll-keepers who felt (perhaps with prophetic truth)
that only the devil could so swiftly propel carriages along the
roads of England without horses. Besides, there were four
imps of hell, impersonated by the younger Pococks, sitting
silent and sinister in the carriage-seats. There was another
occasion when the kite-carriage came up with the more dignified equipage of the Duke of York, postilions and all. From the
Pococks came yells and hallooing and, though the postilions
naturally refused to give way, it came about that, as soon as
they came to a wider part of the road, the kite-carriage shot
past, established its lead with rude gestures, and then, having
scored its point, politely fell back again.

There was one experiment of this innocently diabolical old
gentleman the thought of which, even now, makes the blood run
cold. So great a faith had he in his various kites that he allowed
his daughter Martha to be suspended in her chair and carried
across the terrifying chasm of the Avon Gorge. It is a shattering
thought that the very existence of the greatest cricketing family
the world has ever seen once literally hung by a string.

Martha Pocock, however, survived this awful ordeal to grow
up, marry her doctor and become a tall, strong, imperious
woman, as the mother of five such sons as hers had need to be.
Her portrait shows her, standing erect, in a voluminous crino-
line dress of heavy, shiny material and her features, framed in
long corkscrew curls, are firm but not unkindly. Like her sister
Bessie, she was musical and owned a harp, which she sometimes
used to play, sitting under a medlar tree in the garden. She was
a member of the Downend church choir and took her part in
the anthems, 'rendering' two solos on the very day before her
youngest baby was born. She was noted for the dignified but
friendly attitude which she preserved towards her neighbours
and the doctor's patients, and her outlook on the important
things of life, e.g. her family and cricket, was serious but not
over-solemn. The mother of the Graces might well have been
named, without serious mistranslation, the mother of the
Gracchi.

She watched and fostered the talents of each of her brood
unsentimentally and sometimes sternly. She must have
attended successfully to their daily welfare for they grew up
strong and well-adjusted lads, but the records tell us little of
this. One of the most cherished documents in cricket history is
the letter in which she recommended E.M. to the captain of the
nomadic All England Eleven and told him with the grave can-
dour of a major prophetess that she had another boy growing up
who would do better than his brother because his defence was
sounder.

To the end of her days her cricketing sons not merely
cherished and adored her but deferred to her cricketing judgment. When they were playing at Clifton, or other grounds
near home, she sat in the stand and watched them from the
boundary, never failing to criticize them severely when criticism
was due. When they were far away, they would write or even
telegraph their scores to her. The scrapbooks she compiled of
their scores were almost *Wisdens* in themselves, and W.G.
thought the world of them. When she died in 1884, theirs was
no ordinary loss. E.M. and W.G. were playing against Lancashire at Old Trafford when the telegram arrived. At once A. N.

Hornby, the Lancashire captain, a character not on the whole noted for imaginative sympathy, stopped the match and these two burly and boisterous men went home, stricken, to attend their mother's funeral.

II

When W.G. was born in 1848, Henry was fifteen, Alfred eight and E.M. seven. It is an odd fact that, while Downend House is officially regarded as W.G.'s birthplace and the family were undoubtedly living there at the time, his sister Annie, Mrs. Skelton, told the curate of Downend in the eighteen-nineties that W.G. was, in fact, born at Clematis House, a little way up the road. This house was in earlier days the home of the curate and it may be that the curate's wife looked after Mrs. Grace in her confinement, but why on this occasion the wife of the village doctor should have been absent from her (and his) home, a few doors away, remains a mystery.

In any event, by the time W.G. was born, cricket on the lawn at Downend House was already in being. Fifty years later W.G. remembered touching a bat when he was two years old. That would be in 1850, the year that Fred, the youngest of the Graces, was born. It was also the year when the growing family moved across the road to a larger house, The Chestnuts, which no longer exists, except as an economic bomb-site: that is, it was pulled down to make room for a cinema, but the cinema has not been built. When the house was pulled down, the cricket master of Wellingborough Grammar School bought the front doorstep and had it reset in the doorway of the school pavilion to be an inspiration to all who passed over it. W.G.'s earliest biographer, W. Methven Brownlee, has left a description of The Chestnuts, 'a square plain building in those days, ivy creeping all over, with a pretty flower garden and numerous out-houses.' It had a lodge which the Doctor used as his surgery. The Graces showed their individuality by dropping the 't' in the middle and spelling the word Chesnuts. There was a large tulip tree in front and a long orchard beyond, with a wood and a deep pool beyond the wall on the right. Dr. Grace at once set about cutting down some apple trees in the orchard so that a better pitch could be laid out. The following year the pitch was ready and, as the summers of the early fifties glided by, Dr. Grace and his son Henry, who had now qualified in medicine, would come home to lunch after a hard morning on their rounds with another duty besides eating. Every day they would work at the pitch, first at laying, cutting and rolling and then in practice.

In 1854, the year of the Crimean war and the earliest season that W.G. could remember, he saw his first real cricket match, when William Clarke's travelling All England Eleven came to Bristol to play a local Twenty-Two, led by Dr. H. M. Grace. The game was played in one of the fields behind the Full Moon Hotel, Bristol. These fields have long ago been built over, but as little as twenty years ago there were old men who remembered as boys seeing Tom Sayers fight one of his bare-knuckle fights in one of them. W.G., who watched the game sitting by his mother's side in the pony-carriage, remembered little about it except that most of the players wore tall hats. A thing he did not observe was that one of the umpires at this game was 'kind and manly' Alfred Mynn, the genial giant who, up to a short while before, had by his outstanding skill and personality dominated English cricket just as in years to come it would be dominated by that small boy now sitting in the pony carriage. There were famous players in the All England Eleven—Parr, Caffyn, Julius Caesar, Willsher and the warm-tempered Yorkshireman, Anderson—and there were three members of the Grace contingent in the home side: Dr. Grace, Henry and Uncle Pocock. The All England Eleven, whales against minnows, were naturally victorious.

The next year they came again. Clarke had had some trouble with his eyes and did not play in this game but, watching from the boundary, he saw two more Graces added to the original three: Alfred, taking a few days off from his medical studies, and E.M., now a diminutive but perky lad of fourteen, brought back from school at Long Ashton to strengthen the side. E.M. was disappointingly out leg-before to a ball that hit him in the chest, but William Clarke was impressed by his agility at long-stop and, in recognition of this, presented him with a bat, which had a spliced handle with a strip of whalebone down the centre. He also gave Mrs. Grace a book, 'Cricket Notes by W. Bolland, with a letter containing Practical Hints by William Clarke.'

These were the memorable days of practice at The Chestnuts, days lit by eager emulation and bounded by firm rules: a quarter of an hour's batting practice for the grown-ups, with five minutes each for the youngsters who would already have had plenty of strenuous fielding practice. Nothing shows more clearly the modest place held by Woman in the Victorian conception of athletic sport than the fact that the sisters must have performed their humble daily stint in the field with hardly a 'credit', while, most unjustly, immortality has been conferred upon the three canine fieldsmen, Don and Ponto, who were pointers, and Noble, a sagacious retriever. All four of the Grace sisters grew up to live highly estimable lives: two, Alice and Annie, married doctors and one, Blanche, married a clergyman; but, despite all legends to the contrary, they were not cricketers. If one of them bowled an occasional 'dolly' to the youthful Fred, that was the extent of their efforts.

In Bernard Darwin's short *Life of W.G.* he gives an enchanting picture of the three dogs at work, darting after the ball into the nearby wood and splashing through the waters of pool and stream. They could stop the ball with their chests or catch it, first bounce, in their mouths. Ponto could stop a hard shot better than most human fieldsmen but showed a true conservative's hatred of E.M.'s batting innovations. E.M. would pull ferociously at any ball, wherever it pitched, and this, some have thought, was due to his having originally had to play with a man's bat that was plainly too big for him.

Uncle Pocock disapproved of E.M.'s cross-bat, while sympathetically diagnosing the reason for it, and turned to the little W.G. as one who could be taught to wield a straighter bat from the first. This admirable uncle, a lithographer by profession, was himself a remarkable character. A skilled rackets player, he did not take up cricket seriously until he was twenty-three; he then discovered himself to be a correct batsman, a teasingly accurate bowler and a natural coach. His enthusiasm was boundless. Living on the far side of Bristol he would walk a

dozen miles (to Downend and back) just for the sake of a game
or even of a practice in the orchard.

His coaching was both sound and imaginative and, as he
saw W.G. grow from a baby into a sturdy small boy, he looked
on him with a shrewd, prophetic eye. The younger boy took his
especial fancy, partly because W.G. was an eminently teachable
child (which E.M. obviously was not) and partly, perhaps,
because Uncle Pocock saw E.M. growing up as a ferociously
unorthodox 'puller' who thought nothing of raking a good-
length ball on his off-stump over the square-leg boundary.
Uncle Pocock was determined that little W.G., at least, should
be nurtured in the true faith of the straight bat and the left
shoulder forward. . . . I have heard Sir Leonard Hutton, a
hundred years later than Uncle Pocock, give the same counsel:
'Whenever they tell me a young lad is coming on, I don't look
to see if he has pretty strokes or makes a nice lot of runs: I
watch to see if his defence is sound.'

'Use a bat suited to your height and strength,' urged Uncle
Pocock, 'and if you stand properly and play straight, you ought
to be able to keep the ball from hitting your wicket.' So W.G.
learned the firm upright stance shown in most of the portraits
that we know. He also learned to keep his eye on the ball from
the instant it left the bowler's hand. *I had*, W.G. afterwards
confessed, *to work as hard at cricket as I ever worked at my profession,
or anything else*. And he agreed that he was doubly fortunate in
having 'a good tutor and a strong gift of perseverance . . .'

By the time he was nine, he had mastered the technique of
the defensive straight bat and was now learning to play forward
as well as back. 'Do not allow the bowler to stick you up,' said
Uncle Pocock, 'or it is all over with you . . .' But I doubt if at
any time after he was ten years old, W.G. really allowed a
bowler to 'stick him up'. Forty years later he was advocating
his own version of the old counsel: 'Get at the beggar before he
gets at you!'

Uncle Pocock lived to the age of eighty-four and lies buried in
Downend churchyard. It could be said, without irreverence,
that he had seen of the travail of his soul and was satisfied.

III

Cricket in the Downend district did not stand still, waiting for W.G. to mature. Mangotsfield, by agreement, swallowed up the neighbouring club of West Gloucestershire while annexing its more imposing name. W.G. was ten when he first played for the club, a workmanlike side which contained not only his father, uncle and three elder brothers, but his cousins, William Rees and George Gilbert, the former of whom was also his godfather. These two young men, for the two months of their holidays, greatly strengthened the side by their skill and enthusiasm.

When W.G., a tall, leggy boy of just under ten, came to play for the club, his godfather was impressed by the solidity of the youngster's defensive play and presented him with a bat which had two virtues: it was suitable in size and weight to the boy's strength, and it had a cane handle. Despite the acquisition of this treasure, W.G. did not make any good scores in that year or the next. Success was to come on the day after his twelfth birthday. In a match against Clifton, after E.M., with some assistance from Uncle Pocock, had softened up the bowling, he took the cane-handled bat in with him at No. 8 and scored 35 not out, 'very patiently and correctly, they say.' He added 15 in the morning and no one knew that here was a landmark in the history of cricket. W.G. had made his first half-century.

The next two years did not see any great achievements: they were useful formative years, nevertheless. At home there was hard practice on the orchard pitch at The Chestnuts with its pole-and-canvas wicketkeeper—practice which lasted throughout a March-to-October season. His schooldays were comparatively short and he at least emulated another great Englishman by absorbing little Latin and less Greek. E.M. went away to Kempe's School at Long Ashton, but most of his cricket was played with West Gloucestershire, and there is little record of achievements at school except a story that once, in righteous indignation at being given out leg-before-wicket, he took the stumps away.

As for W.G., he first went to the dame school in the village, kept by Miss Trotman, then in succession to two other small private schools, one belonging to Mr. Curtis at Winterbourne and the other to Mr. Malpas at Rudgway. One of the Rudgway masters, Mr. D. Bernard, afterwards gave up teaching for medicine and married W.G.'s sister, Alice. W.G. was good at sums and collected marbles, birds' eggs and snakes. In becoming the school's marble champion he was aided by Mr. Bernard who, as Methven Brownlee rather mischievously asserts, would bribe the brother of the girl he was courting by transferring to his hoard piles of confiscated marbles. W.G.'s birds' eggs did no one any harm but his snakes caused a good deal of alarm and despondency at home. Out of school, when not playing cricket or football, he learned to shoot and follow hounds on foot. Fred, the nearest brother to him in age, was his constant companion in moderate mischief. At fourteen W.G. left Rudgway and went on with his studies under the coaching of John Walter Dann, who was to become curate of Downend and husband of Blanche Grace.

These were the days when Henry had left his father to set up in practice in the neighbouring village of Hanham and, naturally, took charge of the cricket there. Sometimes young W.G. would go over and play for his brother's side and there was a match against the nearby village of Bitton which long remained an occasion for laughter in the Grace family. As Henry and W.G. were throwing their cricket bags into the trap at Downend, E.M. nonchalantly strolled up and threw his in, too.

'It's no use, Ted,' said W.G. 'They won't stand three of us.'

'I haven't had a burst for a week,' said E.M. 'I'll risk it.'

When they reached the ground the secret came out, for the Bitton men greeted E.M. like an old friend, while Henry and W.G. swore that if they had thought for a moment he was going to turn out for the other side, they would have let him walk, cricket bag and all. There followed a fierce, not to say fratricidal, match and in the end Bitton, who had had much the better of it, were left with only ten runs to get to win. One of that breed of spectators which existed a hundred years ago just as it does today, called out: 'Come on, come on, I haven't seen a decent hit all day!'

'I'll soon put that right,' retorted E.M. and, going in first, set out to rub off the deficit in the first over, if not off the first ball. This was apparently one of Henry's nice easy ones, ideal for the hitting of sixes. Somehow it evaded E.M.'s almighty swing and removed his bails. He returned to the tea-tent, muttering the contemporary equivalent of: 'Was my face red?' The eight Bitton men who had been getting ready to go home were summarily ordered to remove their jackets and return to action, but it was too late. Four wickets fell without any score. Someone blindly hit a three and then, owing to the excited aberration of the long-stop, three byes were added. That was the end of the scoring. The remaining wickets fell to W.G., and Bitton, their pride tumbling, ball by ball, into the ridiculous, were all out for six. Henry and W.G. were sufficiently Christian at heart to let their brother travel home in the trap, but for years afterwards they could damp even the exuberance of an E.M. by a whisper of the word, Bitton.

IV

In his fifteenth year W.G. suffered a serious attack of pneumonia, which at one time put his life in danger. When he recovered he began to grow taller at an alarming rate, so that, although his elder brothers remained a stocky lot, he became an authentic six-footer. Just before his fifteenth birthday he had his first taste of real powder and shot when on Durdham Down he played for the Twenty-Two of Bristol against the All England Eleven. Here were the great names; up till now he had heard and seen them: Stephenson, Anderson, Julius Caesar and the rest. Now he was pitted against them in the flesh and was called on to bat against those wholesale slaughterers of rustic sides, Tear 'em Tarrant and John Jackson, whose epitaph is for ever enshrined in the noble elegy on Alfred Mynn— 'Jackson's pace is very fearful . . .' W.G. played these terrors without terror and when Tinley, All England's cunning lob bowler, came on, carted him impertinently for six. Altogether W.G. made 32 off England's fastest or most cunning bowlers. Ajax had begun to defy the lightning. And, to make the game doubly memorable, the humble Twenty-Two beat the proud Eleven by an innings.

The person who had the greatest faith in him was his mother. In telling George Parr that W.G. was sounder in his back play she had spoken the truth, but the fact is that E.M. would never consent to be a defender. With him it was attack or nothing. There was in all the Graces a streak of amiable ruthlessness and perhaps E.M. had a little more of it than the others. With malice towards none, he would virtually run on amok among the local bowling and so massive were his scores and so un-orthodox his methods that in the early eighteen-sixties there were rumours of a movement designed to prevent him from playing at all. In 1862, when he was just twenty-one, his father was asked to invite him to play at Canterbury for All England against a XIV of Kent. Dr. Grace stood out to obtain better terms for the family, as the Graces always did, demanding that if the young man agreed to play in the first match, they should make his journey worth while by asking him to play in the second. This was quite something to ask, but no Grace ever minded asking for what he wanted and when Mr. Fitzgerald, the M.C.C. secretary, consented, E.M. was wired for at once. He arrived on the Sunday evening a little tired from travelling all day after having scored a couple of hundred in a Gloucester-shire village match on the Saturday afternoon. In the first Canterbury game he made a duck and 56 but in the second he unleashed the fury of his powers from the first ball sent down. Not content with scoring 192 not out, he took five wickets in his opponents' first innings and ten in the second. In his son's house I have seen the ball, now adorned by an inscribed silver plate, with (and upon) which these feats were performed. E.M. was uncurbed and uncurbable; a murderously punishing bats-man, a cunning lob bowler and 'the best point that had ever been seen'.

v

The year 1864 saw another landmark in the young W.G.'s progress. While still only fifteen with a serious illness not far behind him, he was asked to change the side on which he had played the previous year and appear at Lansdowne against the local Eighteen for the All England Eleven, now captained by the blue-eyed, ginger-whiskered George Parr, the 'Lion of the North', who had taken over the management of the touring team from William Clarke. The previous winter Parr had led his men on a tour in Australia and E.M., who had been a successful member of the side and its only amateur, had not yet returned. W.G. was placed at No. 6 in the batting order, a reasonably high place for a youngster, and he was not nervous, because he had played before against the notorious pair, Jackson and Tarrant. He was unlucky to be run out by his partner, John Lillywhite, after having made a comfortable 15, but he did not grieve too much. He had played for the All England Eleven.

Ten days later he played his first game in London. It was his first visit, but he did not spend his time gadding about the capital, for cricket was his only objective. As a protégé of his brother Henry he had gone up to the Oval to play for the South Wales Club. Club allegiances were somewhat shadowy in the 'sixties and enthusiasts would travel fast. Anywhere in the west country, even in Wales, some member of the Grace family could get a game, even though none of them was actually a native of Cardiff or Newport. No sooner had the brothers reached the Oval than the old family solidarity was called into action. The South Wales captain asked Henry if he would mind the boy's being asked to stand down for the second game of the tour, which was to be played against the Gentlemen of Sussex at Brighton, as he had the offer of a very good player.

'The boy was asked to play in both matches,' Henry flared out, 'and he shall play in both matches or none; and I only hope every member of the team will do as well as I expect him to do.' W.G. made 5 and 38 at the Oval and nothing more was said about his standing down. The match at Brighton took place a few days before his sixteenth birthday. W.G. was anxious, as always, that the family name should shine. Henry was not playing—perhaps he stood down himself for the 'very good player'—and E.M. was still somewhere on his way home

'Downend House, a place full of memories, with a grey stucco front and two enormous cedars at the side. . . .'

W. G. at 25. 'A bright-eyed, muscular young man, rejoicing in his strength. . . .'

E. M. and W. G. 'E. M was, always excepting W. G., the most remarkable of the Graces. . . .'

'Summer is golden and seemingly endless. There is no cloud in the sky to tell us that it cannot last for ever. . . .'
Players shown left to right: R. G. Barlow, W. Scotton, W. Barnes, A. N. Hornby, A. Lyttelton, W. G. Grace, A. G. Steel, Lord Harris, G. Ulyett, W. W. Read, A. Shrewsbury, T. W. Garrett, P. S. McDonnell, S. P. Jones, A. C. Bannerman, H. J. H. Scott, F. R. Spofforth, G. Giffen, G. E. Palmer, J. M. Blackham,

from his tour in Australia. A rumour was already circulating that this mighty traveller might land in time to be able to turn out in the Brighton game and W.G. hoped that he would, 'if only,' as he said, 'to give me heart.' There had even been a newspaper paragraph which specifically stated that the *Rev.* Mr. Grace, who had batted so well in Australia, was expected. W.G. said afterwards, chuckling grimly, that they had heard E.M. called many names, but never the *Rev.* and the very thought of that *Rev.* 'gave him heart'.

When South Wales won the toss the lanky, loose-limbed W.G. was sent in at the fall of the first wicket. The second did not fall until the score had almost reached 200 and then it was not W.G.'s. He was at the crease all day and when, first thing in the morning, he chopped a wide ball on to his stumps, he was last man out and his score was 170. Sussex had to follow on, made a better show in their second innings, and left South Wales 134 to win. There was not quite time to get the runs, but W.G., with 56 not out, made a courageous effort. The next highest score was 13. The South Wales captain, perhaps with contrition in his heart, gave him a bat. Blade and handle were in one piece of wood, but W.G. valued it, as he said, because it marked the beginning of his long scores.

In first-class matches that year his average was nearly sixty and he had made over a thousand runs. He was even modestly pleased with the comment in Lillywhite's *Companion*: 'Mr. W. G. Grace promises to be a good bat: bowls very fairly.' It was like saying that Nelson might one day make a sailor, but it was perhaps a wiser and less unsettling comment than a promising young player gets today.

VI

The year 1865 may be called W.G.'s first real season in first-class cricket. At no time has a boy of sixteen played so regularly, or has one family produced so many talented players. All the Graces were good cricketers, at least three of them were potentially great ones. E.M. had come to be reckoned in the highest class and now for some years had ranged the land like a roaring lion, seeking what bowlers he might devour. Fred, now fourteen, was coming along at a speed even greater than that of his older brothers. The baby of the family, Fred had not had quite the same amount of practice as the others, for by the time he was given the freedom of the orchard the two eldest brothers had left home, and at first he could find only the boot-boy and the nursemaid to bowl at him. But, within the limits of maternal good sense, he was his mother's favourite, and, when she took his education in hand, he began to make swift progress. By the age of fourteen he was one of the best-known club cricketers in the district.

In this year W.G. was a long, lean lad of over six feet in height, weighing eleven stone, not a great weight for a six-footer. At this period he was a fine runner and hurdler. On the cricket field he was judged a magnificent performer in the deep with an accurate throw-in from the longest distances. His bowling, too, was a valuable asset to any side. It was a different kind of bowling from the stuff that elderly gentlemen now alive may have seen him send down, a slow avuncular donkey-drop as insidious in alluring honest men to destruction as was the sirens' song long ago. In those early days W.G.'s bowling was straight fastish round-arm stuff, and it took wickets by accuracy rather than guile.

In the eighteen-sixties 'first-class' cricket was uneven in quality, though occasionally rising to heights of magnificence. In quantity it was small and was to remain so for many years. There was no county championship and few county elevens as we understand them today. The chief of these were Notts, Surrey, Yorkshire, Kent, Middlesex, Sussex and, as now seems surprising, Cambridge, county of Tear 'em Tarrant and of Carpenter and Hayward, famous father and uncle of famous son and nephew. The Gloucestershire county club so earnestly striven for by the father of the Graces was not to take firm shape until five years later. A rising young player's opportunities, then, lay in the various representative matches, such as North v. South or Gentlemen of the North v. Players of the South or M.C.C. against a particular county. The sides in these repre-sentative matches were usually much stronger than would appear in the equivalent of such games today. In his first game of this kind it was as a bowler that W.G. shone. Playing for the Gentlemen of the South against the Players of the South, he was stumped before he had scored, but he bowled without a rest through both the Players' innings and by sheer persistent accuracy took thirteen wickets for half a dozen runs apiece.

In this year, too, he played in his first Gentlemen v. Players match and, as Sir Pelham Warner says in his fascinating history, *Gentlemen v. Players*: 'The advent of one player, the now immortal William Gilbert Grace, completely turned the tables. . . . In no representative matches has any player had such an all-round record as W.G. in Gentlemen v. Players.' In the previous twenty-seven years the Gentlemen had won only seven games; in the next eighteen years the Players won only the same number. With the coming of W.G. the long ascendancy of the Players ceased. Here began a chapter that might be called 'The Overlordship of W.G.' and though the Players won the first match (at the Oval) in which he played, they lost the second, at Lord's. From then on, till the end of W.G.'s playing life, the professionals' triumphs were few. Up till then, the sides had been fairly equal in batting strength, but the Players were infinitely more deadly in bowling. Now the batsmen in the Gentlemen's team were joined by one who was fearless of the 'fearful' Jackson on the worst of wickets and could both attack with force and defend with concentration. Furthermore, he was a bowler who cunningly used his head. All three Graces could at all times field superbly and bowl effectively.

In that first game of 1865 W.G., going in at No. 8, made 23 and 12 not out and took seven wickets for 125. This was a modestly promising start and, though no one knew that it was a historic match, it saw the first Gentlemen v. Players game not only of W.G., but of the formidable warriors Jupp and Humphrey and of that crafty professional bowler, Alfred Shaw, with whom W.G. was to fight many a keen-witted duel in the days to come. In the Lord's game the Gentlemen's victory owed a good deal to two fine bowling performances by E.M., who had already established himself in the Gentlemen's side as a powerful all-rounder. W.G., who went in first with his brother, made three (run out) and 34, which, as the Gentlemen were set only 77 to get to win, turned out to be top score. One of his hits went through an upper window of the Tavern.

The Players' victory in the keenly fought Lord's match of 1866 was their last for eight years. The Graces were to see to that. Again E.M.'s bowling was the Gentlemen's liveliest asset. W.G., going in at No. 3, made 25 and 11, and once more his bowling seemed to matter more than his batting. The Oval game went gloriously the other way. Summarily dismissed by some awkward bowling from Wootton, the Gentlemen in their follow-on made a fighting recovery and, when the Players went in again to score two hundred, they scarcely reached half that total. W.G. took seven of their wickets and the long dominance of the Players was over.

His greatest achievement of the year, however, was not his bowling feat, but an innings played for an England Eleven against Surrey at the Oval. He seems to have taken Polonius's advice to 'see that the opposer may beware of thee', because England won by an innings and 300 runs and the county was not so much defeated as demolished. After this game no other county played England single-handed for another twelve years. This was his first hundred in authentic first-class cricket and was genially dedicated to the proposition that if you are going to score one hundred you might as well make it two while you are about it. He went in at No. 5 and, hitting every ball hard and truly, carried out his bat for 224, the biggest score until then ever made at the Oval. His earliest biographer says that when the innings was over the cheering was such as no mortal being had ever heard on a cricket ground, extending as far as Mr. Spurgeon's Tabernacle. On the second day of the match W.G. was 'kindly' let off to run in a 440 yards race over twenty hurdles at the Crystal Palace, a race which he won in the then highly creditable time of one minute ten seconds. Of the amiable leniency which permitted this absence from duty he afterwards said with retrospective ingratitude that if he had been captain he knew what he would have said and it would not have looked pretty in print . . .

His second massive century of the year was also compiled at

the Oval, five weeks after his eighteenth birthday. This was for the Gentlemen of the South against the Players of the South and he himself reckoned it a better display than the earlier one, because it was made against the formidable bowling of Willsher and James Lillywhite, who were then at the peak of their careers. His cavalier treatment of their bowling, his placing, timing and hitting, were seen to be of a quality that had never been reached before. His 173 not out, made out of 240 while he was at the wicket, conformed to what was to become the frequent W.G. pattern in that he made considerably more than half his side's score. During the innings he broke his bat and, exchanging the casualty for the bat which had been presented to him by the Surrey club, incontinently hit two sixes off Lillywhite.

Some measure of the quality of W.G.'s batting may be taken by considering the roughness of the pitch. The surface at the Oval was dangerous, if not as lethal as that at Lords, and it was here that the iron prizefighter, Jem Mace, said to the gnarled and battered Surrey wicketkeeper: 'Pooley, I'd rather stand an hour in the ring than five minutes behind those stumps.' Yet even so early in his career on such a pitch we see W.G. managing not merely to defend his stumps and his person, but to score, with a variety of strokes, off almost every ball.

Here, just eighteen years old, he reaches the rich promise of springtime.

Summer is a-coming in.

CHAPTER TWO

SUMMER

*'At his high noon he was a superb example of manhood, every
muscle quick in him, no superfluity, his brow classic and his
eye keen and fine . . .'*

NEVILLE CARDUS

I

SUMMER sometimes enters with a cold May after a balmy April
and for W.G. the 1867 cricket season was not so bright as that
of the year before. For one thing, he had begun to study, as his
father had once done, at the Bristol Medical School and for
another he was taking odd days off from both work and cricket
to try his skill at various athletic meetings. As for cricket, a split
finger and a sprained ankle at one time or another hampered
his batting and for six of the best weeks of the summer he was
put out of the game by an attack of scarlet fever.

But germs could seldom subdue a Grace. Though he was
batting under various handicaps, nothing seemed to interfere
with his bowling and he never again had quite such fantasti-
cally low figures. In sending down 200 overs, half of which
were maidens, he took thirty-nine wickets for just over seven
runs apiece. If thirty-nine seems a small number of wickets, the
records show that only George Wootton, the Notts left-hander,
and James Southerton, the man of many counties, took more.
The tale of W.G.'s bowling was studded with feats like his eight
for twenty-five for the Gentlemen against the Players at Lord's.
In the Lord's match of 1865 he had gone in first and now, after
a short break, he became the regular No. 1 in the batting order,
a position from which it was virtually impossible to dislodge
him for over thirty years.

In 1868 W.G.'s normal life fell into the pattern it was to
follow for the next few years. In the winter months he would
stick fairly closely to his medical books and lectures, devoting

his spare time to beagling and shooting and making a passing
acquaintance with Rugby football. He found it difficult to
keep out of *any* game, but gave up rugger almost at once. The
story is that in his first game he came into head-on collision with
a big bony fellow, taller and heavier than himself. It was not
that he minded hard knocks, but he feared risking an injury
that might interfere with his cricket.

In the spring he would collect prizes in athletics for most of
the track events up to the half-mile, competing not only locally,
as at Bedminster, but as far afield as meetings of the London and
Blackheath Athletic Clubs. He did not by any means win every
race he entered for, but he won often enough. When he gave up
racing he had won over seventy cups and medals. He had some
terrific tussles on the track with his brother E.M. Once he
'poached' a couple of yards in the hundred from E.M. (and the
gun) and won by a foot. 'E.M.,' he said, 'wouldn't speak to me
after this for a time.' But E.M. got his own back. W.G.'s best
distance was the 200 yards and E.M.'s the 100. One year each
beat the other at his own game and E.M. won the 200 by sheer
stamina and determination. Once when W.G. went up to
receive an indecent number of prizes, the civic head of Bristol
addressed the large body of competitors whom W.G. had
beaten: 'Never mind, gentlemen, don't be discouraged. He
will grow old and stiff one day.' But, as we shall see, he never
really did.

Another awe-inspiring picture of W.G. the hurdler comes
from his chase of a pickpocket at a Berkeley Hunt point-to-
point meeting. The thief had snatched a lady's purse and, as
his victim hailed a policeman, set off across country. W.G.
went after him, leaping over hedges and ditches, until the thief,
as unlucky a hare as was ever beagled, doubled back and rushed
for mercy into the arms of the policeman who had been following in lower gear.

With the beginning of the cricket season W.G. left no doubt
as to which game he loved best. He had fully recovered from the
effect of his illness and that year suffered from no fever except
the feverish desire of bowlers over the country to dislodge him.
All over the cricket fields of England the sun shone and it was a

batsman's year. W.G. made five centuries and every one of
them was a beauty in its own right. In the Gentlemen v. Players
at Lord's he scored an undefeated 134 out of the 193 made while
he was at the crease, and B. B. Cooper, who made 28, was the
only other batsman to reach double figures. The ground, W.G.
said afterwards, was 'very bad and difficult'. Even Pooley, that
man of granite, shamefacedly begged for a long-stop and many
good-length balls flew over the stumper's head. W.G. thought
this was one of the best innings he had ever played and he was
undoubtedly in a position to judge, for the pitch was perilous
and the bowling good; furthermore, he was still batting in the
era when every hit had to be run unless the ball actually landed
inside the pavilion or outside the ground altogether. Even when
boundaries were introduced their object was not so much to
help the batsman as to prevent spectators from being injured
by galloping fieldsmen.

His next centuries were captured on what was to become his
happy hunting ground at Canterbury. Playing in the game
known as South of the Thames v. North of the Thames (which
today sounds like an explosion between two Gas Boards), he hit
130 out of 284 and 102 out of 195, thus becoming the first
person to score two hundreds in a match since the feat had been
performed at Lord's by that skilful but scandalous character,
William Lambert, fifty-one years before. Lest it should be
thought that in this game W.G. was merely piling up easy runs
against inferior opposition, it must be recorded that, despite
W.G.'s efforts, the North, for whom that superbly muscular
Christian, Canon M'Cormick, made 137, won the game by
69 runs. In this match occurred one of those slightly grim
incidents which were bound to occur when someone called
Dr. Grace was in the vicinity. R. Lipscombe had his thumb
put out of joint by a hard hit, and, said W.G.: 'My brother,
E.M., had it in again in a jiffy.' Poor Mr. Lipscombe, the heart
goes back nearly a hundred years and bleeds for him; he was
only the first of many to suffer, at the hands of a Grace, such an
efficient but painful remedy.

There is a belief that W.G. in this year might possibly have
gone up to Cambridge, a prospect which must have set flutter-

ing the hearts of cricketers in Cambridge and, consequently, in
'another place', too. It seems probable that if W.G. had expressed a desire to go to one of the older universities, his father
would have argued against it, even to the extent of putting his
foot down. Old Dr. Grace had himself worked hard and played
hard while he studied and he may well have thought Oxford
and Cambridge to be light-minded places where neither study
nor sport was treated with due seriousness. As it turned out,
W.G. went on playing cricket all over the country and treated
his studies in perhaps more leisurely fashion than would have
been allowed at Cambridge.

The year 1869 saw his twenty-first birthday and he signalized
his attainment of man's estate with a flourish of trumpets. His
toll of nine hundreds in the year was exactly half that exacted
by Denis Compton in the cloudless summer of 1947; yet, when
you consider the viperishness of the wickets in the late 'sixties,
the hostility of the bowling, and the paucity of fixtures, you see
that W.G. does not suffer severely by the comparison.

He was elected a member of the Marylebone Cricket Club
and, being nothing if not grateful, he turned out against Oxford
University on a chilly May day and hit up another of those
centuries that formed more than half his side's score. Once
more for M.C.C. against Surrey at the Oval he carried his bat
through the innings for 138, while against Notts in the only
Lord's match of the year that lasted the whole three days—a
tribute to the horrors of the Lord's wicket— he scored 121 out
of 210 in a fighting effort to break through to victory in the
fourth innings. When W.G. was out, however, the rest of the
innings was rolled up like a hearthrug by J. C. Shaw, one of
Grace's friendliest 'enemies'. It must have been a finely contested game. Richard Daft made a not out century, though a
rather tedious one, and W.G. later noted in mild surprise that
if an opponent made a hundred, he himself would frequently
follow the example. 'This was more frequently the case,' he
added modestly, 'when Daft gave me a lead . . .' In other
words, anything Dick Daft could do, W.G. at twenty-one could
already do better, and Daft was a recognized champion among
English batsmen.

There was a high-scoring game between Gentlemen of the South and Players of the South at the Oval in which W.G. knocked up an almost contemptuous 180, but his visit to Sheffield for South *v.* North brought him into conflict with distinctly heavier metal. His 122 out of 173, with B. B. Cooper once more as his only partner capable of collecting 10, was a superb achievement by any standard. Here, too, was the beginning of the ferocious but friendly warfare that he was to wage with the Yorkshire Titans, handsome George Freeman and rollicking, Rabelaisian Tom Emmett. As long as he lived, W. G. claimed that Freeman was the best bowler he had ever played against. 'How Freeman bowled!' exclaims the chronicler. 'And, oh, how Grace hit!' Freeman bowled him twice, the second time for a mere seven, with a ball that 'hit the foot of the stumps with terrific force and spun like a top'.

W.G. finished this happy season with two happy matches at Canterbury. In the first innings of the earlier game he was bowled neck and crop third ball. 'Imagine Patti singing outrageously out of tune,' said the *Daily Telegraph* in awestricken tones; 'imagine Mr. Gladstone violating all the rules of grammar, and you have a faint idea of the surprise created by this incident . . .' If the young W.G. ever got a duck, someone had to pay for it. In the second innings of this game he hit a fiercely compensatory century and in the next match he crowned his year with a masterly 127. It was all done with apparent ease and one newspaper, lapsing a little rashly into personalities, called him 'the most good-humoured of young giants . . .'

II

In one of A. A. Milne's delightful cricket stories there is a sentence which runs: 'I am now approaching the incredible.' To write of W.G.'s exploits in the eighteen-seventies is to move among facts which would seem like the wildest fiction if they were not so firmly documented. History has reckoned 1870 a momentous year. In it Charles Dickens died, the Dickens who had written immortally of the cricket match between All

Muggleton and Dingley Dell; the Dickens who, in the beautiful picture which hangs at Lord's, showing cricket at Gadshill, is seen bowling the first ball of a charity match played on the tree-girt meadow behind his house. He liked nothing better than to undertake the duty of scoring in local matches. It is sad that he did not live to see the major cricket triumphs of one who by his very rampageous boisterousness was in spirit a true Dickens character. In 1870, too, the first great Education Act was passed. In its summer W.G. continued his career as a Dickens character in the flesh and his determination to educate the bowlers of England.

Those cricketers with whom W.G. played in the 'seventies were outstanding performers in an outstanding period. If he raised himself head and shoulders above the others it was not that they were mediocre, but that he was exceptionally gifted. In an age of giants he was a bigger giant still. In the ranks of the Gentlemen he found batsmen of the calibre of R. A. H. (Mike) Mitchell, a master at Eton, a splendid coach and in batting the most elegant stylist between Fuller Pilch and L. C. H. Palairet; W. Yardley, the first man to score a hundred in the Varsity match, a free and audacious hitter who would boldly compete in rapid scoring with W.G. himself; A. N. Hornby, the hard-hitting Lancashire captain who could run every partner, except W.G., off his feet; and C. I. (Buns) Thornton, who put Scarborough on the map and by his enormous hitting nearly knocked it off again. (James Shaw once woke from a fearful nightmare, exclaiming: 'I dreamt Mr. Thornton hit one slap back at me!') There were fine batsmen among the Players, like Richard Daft, W.G.'s greatest contemporary rival, and Ephraim Lockwood, who two years earlier had been brought into the Yorkshire side as a last-minute substitute and made a historic début at the Oval. The bowlers were even more distinguished. George Freeman, whom W.G. thought the best fast bowler he had ever played against; the fast left-hander, J. C. Shaw, who more than once got W.G. out for a duck but was made to pay dearly for such impertinence; and Tom Emmett, also a fast left-hander, erratic but frequently deadly, not to mention Allan Hill, another York-

shireman with a swift, beautiful action. There was also
Alfred Shaw, the most cunning of all slow bowlers before
Wilfred Rhodes, who in his career performed a feat that no
other bowler ever approached: that is, he bowled W.G. more
than twenty times. No one can maintain that W.G.'s great
scores in the glorious 'seventies were made off indifferent
bowling.

The game in 1870 that gave W.G. the century with which he
was again to cap one by Richard Daft was remembered for his
swiftly-scored 117 not out in the first innings, while, once more,
only one partner made double figures. The second innings
brought him a duck, bowled by J. C. Shaw with a ball that
broke his middle stump clean in two. (Harsh punishment fell
on Shaw for this act of *lèse-majesté*.) The match is more tragically memorable for the ball that struck young Summers of
Notts on the temple, causing his death two days later. The ball
probably hit a small pebble, shooting violently upwards and the
horrid impact on the victim's head was heard all over the
ground. This was the ultimate proof of the literally lethal
wickets on which W.G. achieved his mighty performances of
the 'seventies. From that time, no doubt owing to the unhappy
fate of Summers, a heavy roller was used and the pitch at
Lord's began slowly to improve.

In the Gentlemen *v.* Players match at the Oval W.G. took
his revenge for a first innings failure with a hard-hit total of
215 which for a long time remained the highest score of the
series. He afterwards admitted that the Gentlemen robbed
themselves of victory in this game by making too many runs in
their second innings and that the Players were allowed to escape
through a tactical error in timing. 'For some occult reason,' he
commented, 'we did not have lunch in those days until two-
thirty.' Occult is good. Fred Grace played in this game and
bowled well, but, as in his first and only Test match, scored no
runs at all.

Rubbing his hands, so to speak, W.G. went straight on to the
Lord's Gentlemen *v.* Players game and on his twenty-second
birthday, hit up 109 out of 197 as if he had hardly had his pads
off. He was, as he said, giving the Players another treat. Fortunes

swayed and swung more violently than usual in this game and
the Players, set 154 to win, were still 24 behind, with three
wickets to fall, when the clock struck seven. Amid noisy excitement Lillywhite was bowled by C. K. Francis. Then Fred,
bowling very fast, tumbled out the last two men, and the
Gentlemen had won by four runs.

The year 1870 is also entitled to cricket fame as marking the
founding, or at least placing on firm foundations, of the
Gloucestershire county club. This had long been the dream of
the father of the Graces and happily he lived to see it. For
several years he had been trying, with less help than his efforts
deserved, to place his county on an equal footing with the
'great' counties of Nottinghamshire, Yorkshire and Surrey. At
last success crowned his efforts. In June 1870 Gloucestershire
played their first county match proper, against Surrey, on
Durdham Down where over forty years before the old doctor,
as a young student, had got up at five in the morning to practise. There is an old local saying, 'As sure as God's in
Gloucestershire', and, without insisting too much upon divine
intervention, it can at least be said that from that day to this,
from the Graces to the Graveneys, with Jessop, Hammond and
Barnett in between, Gloucestershire has brought colour, light
and a flaming kind of glory to every corner where the sun shines
on cricket.

From this time, then, W.G. began to make his centuries for
Gloucestershire: the first, 143 against the poor (in both senses)
Surrey bowlers at the Oval, and the second a quite staggering
172 against M.C.C.—did he, for their confusion, wear the red
and yellow cap?—at Lord's. It is a slightly fantastic fact that,
batting on a wicket which a thunderstorm had turned into
'mud and sawdust', he and his opening partner, C. S. Gordon,
made themselves responsible for 225 runs out of 276. There
were four ducks and the next highest score was Mr. Extras
with 13.

W.G.'s best innings of the season, however, was not a century,
but 66. It was played at Lord's for M.C.C. against Yorkshire
and the wicket was still as murderous as only the Lord's pitch
in 1870 could be. The heavy roller had not yet subjugated its

terrors. In an article in the periodical *Cricket*, George Freeman wrote of it:

> 'Tom Emmett and I have often said it was a marvel the doctor was not either maimed or unnerved for the rest of his days, or killed outright. I often think of his pluck on that day when I watch a modern batsman scared of a medium ball that hits him on the hand. He should have seen our expresses flying about his (W.G.'s) ribs, shoulders, and head in 1870 . . .'

In this glorious decade the proudest years were 1871 and 1876, with 1873 intervening. Those six years saw the maturity of W.G.'s powers; the perfecting of a noble unity between brain, eye and hand. Runs flowed from his bat, as from a cataract, profuse, prodigal, and, as bowlers must have thought, punitive. Many of his centuries were double centuries, because he set no limit to his unbridled greed for runs and simply did not know where to stop.

He was richly generous in more ways than in just 'giving the Players' a treat. No cricketer has ever been so much in demand as W.G. for a professional's benefit match and certainly no one has ever given so freely of his opulent best to that kind of good cause. If he knocked the beneficiary's bowling about to the tune of a couple of hundred runs, that was only his fun. If he were out for a duck, as happened in the first innings of at least two of these games, the crowd and the beneficiary shared his chagrin, but woe betide the bowlers in the second innings. His revenge was as richly imaginative as Monte Cristo's and their earlier success had to be paid for with exorbitant interest.

In 1871 that happy British institution, the Bank Holiday, was inaugurated by Act of Parliament and for over thirty years W.G. went on dispensing joy to Bank Holiday crowds. In this year, too, turnstiles were introduced at Lord's and W.G. celebrated their coming by hitting 181 for M.C.C. against Surrey.

The first of the benefit games of 1871, Single *v.* Married, was played at Lord's on behalf of Edgar Willsher, the Kent fast

bowler, and W.G. carried his bat through the innings of 310 for
189 not out. The second, North *v*. South, was played at the
Oval for the benefit of H. H. Stephenson, 'one of the best speci-
mens of English professional players who ever stood in front of
or behind the stumps.' To the crowd's consternation, W.G. was
given out l.b.w. for nought to James Shaw, who must have felt
terror-stricken at the success of his appeal. One almost wonders
that he did not appeal against it. In the second innings W.G.
exacted retribution by amassing an enormous score. The only
adjective worthy to borrow to describe this innings is the French
abracadabrant. Out of the first 100 runs, he hit 70, of 200 he had
made 150; at 300 he was over 200, and when he went at 426,
his score was 268. (His liveliest partner scored no more than
36.) At the end of the game Stephenson presented him with an
inscribed ring, and with how many pounds sterling W.G.'s
drawing power had presented Stephenson it is difficult to
compute.

One Gentlemen *v*. Players game was played at Brighton and
set aside for the benefit of 'that jolliest of cricketers, John Lillywhite'; this game went almost exactly the same way. James
Shaw, poor wretch, bowled W.G. first ball in the first innings,
and had to watch him score another of his monotonously
masterful double hundreds in the second. This match was the
scene of one of the classic episodes. After suffering his duck,
W.G. apologized to Lillywhite who, so far from accepting any
excuses, handed him two sovereigns, demanding back sixpence
for every second innings run scored. As W.G. at the end of the
day's play walked towards the pavilion with 200 not out on the
board, Lillywhite ran after him and politely requested five
pounds on account. When W.G., looking comically glum,
handed over the fiver, Lillywhite took the money, laughing.
'I'm quite ready to cry quits now,' he said, 'if you are.' And so
was W.G., for, as he recounted: 'I was in batting fettle.'

It was after this season that the title 'Champion' began to be
attached to him, a title never before bestowed on any cricketer
except Alfred Mynn. This was the time, too, when an admirer
presented him with Alfred Mynn's pads as a votive offering,
reverently intimating that 'only he was worthy to wear them'.

W.G.'s centuries that dry, sunny season glittered like a diamond necklace: 146 for Gloucestershire and 181 for M.C.C., in two games against Surrey, the latter being the 'turnstile' match; 162 in his first game at Fenner's, where he met for the first time that fast and furious hitter, C. I. Thornton. He contributed the usual monumental offering at Canterbury against Kent; and, playing for Gloucestershire, he scored the first century made in a county match at Trent Bridge. When W.G. had been dismissed for a mere 79, Richard Daft said: 'You ought to have made a century; it hasn't been done here before.' And W.G. replied: 'Never mind, I'll do it next innings.' He then proceeded on his way towards a flawless 116 out of 163. His match total was just under 200 out of 350. This is not the place to discuss averages, and it will be agreed that averages are not everything, but at least it can be said that Grace's batting average for the season was considerably higher than twice that of the next best, the remarkably successful batsman, Richard Daft.

In this year died Dr. H. M. Grace, father of the brotherhood, a man to whom cricket everywhere, and not only in the west country, owes an incalculable debt. He had followed the old Spartan rule of playing hard and working hard and, despite his devotion to cricket and hunting, he never neglected professional duty. He once stayed for three days and three nights by a patient's bedside and was finally helped home on feet so swollen that his boots had to be cut away. His death was probably hastened by his determination (*a*) to ride to hounds with a heavy cold upon him and (*b*) to follow this heavy day in the field by once more sitting up all night with a patient. That was the Grace spirit: a trifle perverse, perhaps, but magnificently unswerving.

He is buried near the west door of the church at Downend, where, within a small green area, almost all the Graces, except W.G. himself and his own family, are buried. Dr. H. M. and his wife, with their youngest son, lie all together and the stone that covers them describes him, with more truth than the average tombstone, as 'beloved, respected and deeply regretted by all classes.' His greater monuments—*si monumentum requaeris*—

W. G. in the field at Lord's. 'There came a time—he was fifty-one years old—when his hands were too far from the ground. . . .'

LORD'S IN DANGER. THE M. C. C. GO OUT TO MEET THE ENEMY.

In 1891 by an Act of Parliament the Manchester, Sheffield and Lincolnshire Railway were authorised to build tunnels from Marylebone Station running under the Eastern fringe of Lord's Cricket Ground. This proposal was strongly opposed by the M.C.C., but finally they gave part of the freehold of the Practice Ground for a larger area occupied by the Clergy Orphans School on the condition that the Club were granted a ninety-nine year lease of the ground immediately over the tunnels

China plate designed to celebrate W. G.'s 'century of centuries'

are the fame of the Grace family and the Gloucestershire county club. One of his minor legacies, recounted by W.G., is his recipe for picking an eleven: bring up long-stop to leg-slip and you have a method which might be commended today to selectors at any level.

'First, I must have two good bowlers, also two good change-bowlers, a wicketkeeper and long-stop. The rest, as long as they can field, will make up a fair team.'

For any other cricketer than W.G. 1872 would have been an outstanding year; for him, it was not quite so brilliant as the year before or the year after. His centuries numbered only six, but they were mostly scored against the best professional bowling. There were two more 'treats' for the persecuted Players, who numbered in their ranks the two Shaws and Martin McIntyre; and there were two hundreds against York-shire, who had Freeman, Tom Emmett and Allan Hill, the best trio of fast bowlers to be found in any county of the period, not to mention Roger Iddison, a master of insidious slow-motion lobs. At Lord's W.G. returned to the pavilion for refreshment with his score at 97 not out and, going back to the wicket—'whether I had too much or too little luncheon I forget'—hit a four off Iddison's first ball, missed the second and was bowled neck and heels by the third. At Sheffield, where he forgivingly appeared to help in Roger Iddison's benefit, he and his opening partner, T. G. Matthews, made just under seven-eighths of the score between them. This was his first appearance at Bramall Lane.

'He's all right playing against these south country chaps,' Tom Emmett had said, 'but wait till we get him up at Sheffield.' And it may well have been as W.G. reached 150, including two successive square-leg hits that went out of the ground up Har-wood Street and never came back again, that Tom uttered his classic *cri de cœur*: 'Him? He ought to have a littler bat!' Furthermore, just to prove that hitting hundreds was not his only accomplishment, W.G. also ran into 'pretty fair form' with the ball, taking eight for 33 and seven for 46. No wonder Tom called him a nonesuch. In his score were two sixes, one five and eleven fours and eighteen threes, all run. Even the sixes had

4

to be run for, until the fielding side grudgingly agreed to call:
'Lost ball.'

There was also that heart-warming 170 not out, made on a
cold, damp day at Lord's for an England Eleven against a combined Notts and Yorkshire side. In this W.G. literally ran his
partners off their feet and caused poor Bob Carpenter, now a
staid old gentleman of forty-three, to utter the almost equally
famous heart-cry: 'It's no pleasure batting with Mr. Grace,
you spend all your time running *his* runs.'

W.G. had some fun, though it was not strictly first-class fun
for a United South Eleven against a Twenty-Two of Glasgow.
An unknown bowler, McAllister by name, gained fleeting
eminence by getting rid of the English side for 49, but Grace's
second innings century embraced six heaven-kissing sixes; one
descended into a cab, and another hit a 'sweet inoffending
young lady' in the crowd. Her fiancé, who was fielding near the
wicket at the moment, was unable to go to her comfort, but at
lunch-time he escorted her into protective custody. Even in the
reputedly safer place to which she had been moved, however,
the next towering six sought her out and hit her again. She
must have thought, poor girl, that the villain still pursued her...

Later that summer an article in the comic paper *Fun* reflected
the slightly dazed state of public feeling in a series of facetious
suggestions for handicapping W.G. down to the level of the
common man.

'That W. G. Grace shall owe a couple of hundred or so before
batting.'

'That his shoe-spikes should be turned upwards.'

'That he shall be declared out (l.b.w.?) whenever the umpire
likes.'

'That he shall always be the eleventh player.'

'That he should not be allowed to bat at all.'

III

In the August of 1872 W.G. went off, with eleven others, on a
light-hearted cricketing tour of Canada and the United States.
The side was captained by R. A. Fitzgerald, then Secretary of

the M.C.C., who recounted their adventures in an amusing volume, *Wickets in the West*. There were some fine batsmen in the team, including Alfred and Edgar Lubbock, A. N. (Monkey) Hornby, the Hon. George (afterwards Lord) Harris, and C. J. Ottaway, one of the heroes of Cobden's Match. Despite the competition of their talents, W.G. took a greedy share of the runs scored, for he made over 500 in all while none of his distinguished colleagues reached 150. He would have taken most of the wickets, too, if his captain had allowed him to bowl all the time.

After a fairly horrible voyage, the tourists landed and went on to enjoy a gay holiday, winning most of their matches against odds. When they were not engaged in cricket, they spent their time in shooting, fishing and banqueting in semi-royal style. They visited Niagara Falls, played the ladies of London, Ontario, at croquet, and exercised much ingenuity in declining the gifts forced on them by their hosts. W.G. had to refuse a couple of bear-cubs which, he felt, would have been out of place at the Chestnuts. The tour is best remembered for two historic matters: for W.G.'s celebrated after-banquet speeches and for a couple of slightly macabre games on the American side of the border. The banquet speeches embrace the best-known of all the W.G. stories. Charged at Montreal with the reply to the Champion Batsman of Cricketdom, W.G. rose and said: 'Gentlemen, I beg to thank you for the honour you have done me. I never saw better bowling than I have seen today, and I hope to see as good wherever I go.' This framework he adapted at various subsequent banquets to praise 'Better batting', 'better wicket', 'prettier ladies'—this was mightily applauded— and, rising to a sublime climax, 'better oysters'.

Speeches at banquets were frequent. Appleby, who had fallen off a log in a lumber camp and narrowly escaped drowning, was called on to respond to the toast of the Navy almost before his clothes were dry. W.G.'s family at home were alarmed by *The Times* account of the Ottawa match which was headed: 'Grace Ill with Cholera', but the next news they heard was that he had made 142 in the next match. The attack had not been fatal.

At least one commentary on the Montreal match has come down to us, showing that the transatlantic tradition of brighter sport reporting was already on the march:

'W. Grace is a large-framed, loose-jointed man, and you would say that his gait was a trifle peculiar, but when he goes into the field you see that he is quick-sighted, sure-handed, and light-footed as the rest. He always goes in first and to see him tap the ball gently to the off for one, draw it to the on for two, pound it to the limits for four, drive it to heaven knows where for six, looks as easy as falling off a log.'

In the Montreal game W.G. made 81 by fierce hitting and was out to a catch by a small stout fieldsman. The ball hit him in the midriff, bounced out into his hands and remained there. The crowd rushed on to the field and carried the winded hero off shoulder-high.

When the tourists crossed the border into America they played two rather more harassing matches, which are described with some relish in *Wickets in the West*. The Twenty-Two of Philadelphia numbered some fine players among their ranks and they made the Englishmen fight for every run. Even W.G., who was more cunning than any batsman who ever lived at placing the ball between twenty-two fieldsmen, could muster only 14 in the first innings, and these he felt he had earned by the sweat of his brow. On the last day the Englishmen were left on a crumbling wicket to get 33 to win. They lost one wicket for 1, two for 8, and three for 15. It was a fast bumping bowler named Newhall who was doing the damage with his 'rib-roasters'. The fourth man out was W.G., who had battled an hour for 7 and, in spite of all his experience against closely-packed battalions in the field, still found it hard to get the ball through. When he was out the crowd went wild with excitement and, the chronicle says, 'the air was darkened with head-gear of every hue'. Six wickets were soon down for 29. So taut was the strain among those watching that, said Fitzgerald, it was agony to answer a question and almost insulting to human nature to demand a light for a cigar. . . . After a fortuitous leg-

bye had momentarily eased the tension, there was a deathly
half-hour in which not a single run was scored and then
Appleby, lashing out with all of a fast bowler's fortitude, hit a
full-toss for four and the game was over, except that a madly
cheering crowd made the visitors come out on to the balcony
to receive three cheers for Grace, Gloucestershire and the
British flag.

The last match of the tour was played at Boston on a rain-
soaked mud-patch. W.G. felt that he did not bowl quite so
effectively, as he took only thirteen wickets for 35, while
Appleby slew seven for 3 and was taken off. The shades of
night were falling fast when the Englishmen, with five wickets,
but not W.G.'s, left standing, still needed 22 to win. The
players went on with the game, if only from memory, though the
fieldsmen were splashing about in mud, and finally, after the
visiting captain had been knocked almost insensible in the
darkness, it was agreed to call it a night.

IV

In 1873 W.G. enjoyed his second 'great' year. His batting was
uniformly of a quality never seen before and his bowling was
far more than merely effective. For the second time he scored
over 2000 runs and for the first time he took a hundred wickets.
This was the first time that he, or anybody else, had done 'the
double' and it was looked on at the time as something of a
miracle, as indeed it was. Every kind of bowling spent itself
on the broad middle of his bat like waves on a cliff. In com-
piling his eight centuries he made the Players suffer twice, once
at the Oval with 158 and once at Lord's with 163. When he had
made 30 in the first of these games he played a ball from Tom
Emmett hard on to his wicket but, amid groans from the
Players' sympathizers right round the field, the bails stuck on.
Tom had every excuse for feeling that W.G. lived for only one
purpose: to break his (Tom's) heart. To celebrate this escape
W.G. hit 25, all run, off Tom's next dozen deliveries.

The other big spoils of the year were ravaged from the
Players of the North, the Players of the South, and an Eleven

of the North. Added to these was one of those frequent hundreds (160 not out) which he scored for Gloucestershire against Surrey. Time and again he, or he and one partner, hit more than half the total score. At the old Prince's ground, where Cadogan Square now stands, he set upon the Players of the North and made 145 out of 237. E.M. contributed 26 and hardly anybody else made anything at all. Against the Players of the South his was the sixth wicket to fall after he had made 134 out of 185 and then, just to keep the family name before the bowlers, Fred, who had always been a powerful hitter, scored a hurricane 74 not out. For the South against the North W.G. made 192 out of the 294 runs that came from the bat, staying at the crease till the end of the innings, while none of his partners scored more than 40. For any side, against any side, he towered, a Brobdignagian figure, above friend and foe alike.

v

On 9th October 1873 W.G. was married at St. Matthias Church, West Brompton, to Miss Agnes Nicholls Day, a daughter of his first cousin, whose family home was in the Clapham Common district. The Rev. John Walter Dann, who had been W.G.'s tutor and was now his brother-in-law and Vicar of Downend, officiated, and Arthur Bush, the Gloucestershire wicketkeeper, was best man. There seems something particularly fitting in having a wicketkeeper for a best man. One feels he would let nothing past him.

Scores of 'poems' had been written in the previous few years on W.G.'s exploits and one of them ended with the stanza:

> *We'll wish him a cricketer's luck, love,*
> *In life, a long innings and stout;*
> *By Fate never bowled for a duck, love,*
> *Or by time prematurely run out.*
> *May he muff none of Fortune's best catches,*
> *And—eh? that's your sex to a T—*
> *May he win in the sweetest of matches,*
> > *Our W.G.*

Here then was 'the sweetest of matches'. It would be interesting to know how W.G. conducted his courtship. Was he
shy and gruff, as he had undoubtedly been when a little
younger? Did he adapt one of his famous Canadian speeches?
'I never saw a prettier lady than I see now and I hope . . .' At
any rate, he was successful in his wooing. 'Happy, happy he,'
says the early biographer in lyric mood, 'who can say he has
found one who is in touch with him in work and sorrow, who,
in a thousand ways, has made life a charm, and revealed all
that is implied in the words Home, sweet Home.'

In less fully floral language, it is probable that the couple
were extremely well matched. In the present age when no
public figure is allowed a private life, some may find it hard to
believe that private life ever truly existed. Personal relation-
ships have now become so cluttered up with a pestilential jargon
that I may appear to be using a foreign language when I say
that here were two people who married and for life retained
each other's affection and respect. They had no greater joy
than their children's successes and no greater sorrow than the
loss of two of them. Yet these are true facts. Mrs. Grace was
variously described by her contemporaries as sweet, gentle,
womanly and sympathetic, and for those who are distressed by
such adjectives I would add that she was a highly competent
wife and mother and knew her business, which was nobody
else's business, extremely well.

A fortnight later, best man and all, W.G. and his bride set
out on the honeymoon which was to be part of an Australian
tour. There had been two previous tours by English teams, but
the second of these, in which E.M. played a lively part, had
taken place ten years before. The Australians were eager to see
an English side again and it was in answer to an urgent cable
that W.G. set about selecting his team. There were twelve of
them, including himself—none of your seventeens and eighteens
as today—and he took with him the best team he could lay his
hands on at the time. He would have liked a stiffening from
some hard-edged north-country bowlers like Appleby, the
Shaws and Tom Emmett or a couple of aggressive-spirited
batsmen like A. N. Hornby and William Yardley; nevertheless,

his second best was very good. In his Twelve there were some
sturdy west-countrymen: Fred, who had become the next best
all-rounder in the country to himself; W. R. Gilbert, his cousin
and one of the heroes of the old West Gloucestershire days, and,
of course, Arthur Bush, his wicketkeeping best man.   For
bowlers he had, in addition to himself, James Lillywhite,
McIntyre, Oscroft and Southerton. Jupp, the Surrey batsman
who was to be his first-wicket partner, seems to have been
celebrating up to the last moment before leaving and nearly
missed the boat.

Cricketers on early tours endured some stormy voyages,
though they were at least spared the sufferings of modern
touring teams, who find newspaper correspondents, hungry for
scandal, peering at them through every porthole. Otherwise,
amusements on board ship were much the same as today. W.G.
actually started a diary, and, considering the interest of one or
two early entries, it is a pity that it was not kept up, but even
W.G.'s staying power wilted during a voyage of fifty-two days:

October 24th. Not at all right; never turned out—sympathy
below.
25th. Dinner on deck; beginning to crawl.
27th. Arrived at Gibraltar; piano on deck; small dances.
30th. Tremendous sea caught ship, and broke two or three
hundred plates and saucers.
November 1st. Malta; supped at the United Service Club.
Made speech. On board again. Leapfrog and boxing;
nearly killed one of the team.

The Englishmen played fifteen matches in Australia, mostly
against odds, and almost every game carried with it a civic
welcome (with brass band), a mayoral banquet and a fairly
bad wicket. Ten of their matches were won and the fact that
Lillywhite and Southerton took 320 wickets between them at
less than six runs apiece shows the main cause of their victories.
W.G. and Fred headed the batting averages with 39 and 33;
the rest were a long way behind. Of the three matches they
lost, one was their first, against an Eighteen of Victoria, for

whom W.G.'s old friend B. B. Cooper hit up a big score. Forty thousand people paid half-a-crown each to see this game. During practice beforehand, W.G. was batting at the nets. A young man from the crowd bowled him a simple ball or two and then slung one down like a shot from a gun. 'Who bowled that?' demanded W.G., as he heard the rattle of the stumps behind him. But the bowler had melted away into the crowd. But not for ever. His name was Frederick Robert Spofforth. Another game lost was played against a Twenty-Two of Stawell in a blinding light on a grassless pitch amid a plague of flies worthy of the Book of Exodus. One ground had just been ploughed up for the occasion and another was so deeply rutted that a ball would disappear as into a rabbit-hole. Of one of the other games Lillywhite wrote: 'Mr. W. G. Grace won by seven wickets.'

In the second innings of the return game against Victoria at Melbourne the home team, for the first and only time of the tour, fielded eleven-a-side instead of eighteen and the skilful placing of W.G. and his partner Jupp proved a spectacle such as local spectators had never witnessed before. W.G., who made 126, gave a sumptuous exhibition of every stroke in his repertory, which was twice as large as any other batsman's, and caused a Melbourne journalist to describe him as 'W. G. Grace, an extraordinary run-getter, a perfect wonder, and worth going ninety miles to see every day of the week. . . . A freak of nature, a cricket phenomenon.'

The tour had not been specifically arranged for the comfort of the travellers and, in addition to the gruesome condition of some of the grounds, there were between matches some voyages of fearful roughness from Melbourne to Sydney or back again. These trips in 'miserable little coastal steamers' were 'calculated to cause the severest stomachic disturbances', and it is pleasant, in the interests of pure humanity, to record that Mrs. W.G. was not subjected to the cruel sea, but stayed on dry land with friends in Melbourne. Some of the landward journeys, by coach over rough bush-track, were nearly as hazardous.

W.G.'s prowess in the field was everywhere respected and admired, but some of the Australian papers thought him legalis-

tic in small matters. Australians enjoy an argument far more
than does the average Englishman and perhaps they were surprised that W.G. should answer back. No doubt some of the
umpiring was a little sketchy, as when, at Castlemaine, the
eager Mr. Bush had an obvious stumping disallowed because,
the umpire alleged, the tip of his nose was in front of the
wicket.

It is by no means certain that W.G. started all the arguments
but, being a Grace and being 'in', he would not give way when
he thought he was right. So, despite the torchlight processions,
the bands and the banquets, a little of the spirit of warfare
occasionally crept into the cricket. The *Lillywhite* comment on
the tour, which is supposed to have been written by Fred, the
mildest-mannered and most sensitive of the Graces, said: 'The
trip, on the whole, was an enjoyable one, as far as seeing the
Colonies and meeting good friends; but in a cricketing point of
view it was *not* a good one. We were met in a bad spirit as
though cricketers were enemies.'

Certainly clashes, which were possibly a little less hostile than
the *Lillywhite* article averred, sometimes occurred on the field of
play. This was understandable when you remember the roughness of the grounds. At Kadina W.G. had the pitch swept and
gathered up almost as many basketfuls of stones as remained
after the miracle of the loaves and fishes. The ball, worn rough
by such a rugged wicket, W.G. kept as a lopsided souvenir after
Martin McIntyre had taken sixteen wickets for five runs with it.
It is equally certain that, once the day's play was over, hostilities
were over, too, and every kind of entertainment was lavished on
the visitors. This they received with a maximum of goodwill;
the only creatures who cannot have welcomed them were the
fish, fowl and four-footed animals, from rabbits to kangaroos,
who suffered from the all-round exuberance of W.G. and his
sporting hosts. There was practically nothing on four legs, two
legs or no legs at all which did not form part of their monster
mixed bag. My own sympathies are with the innocent
kangaroos but the outlook in a primitive pioneering country is,
no doubt rightly, entirely different.

The tumultuous welcome given to the tourists in the up-

country districts must have seemed like successive scenes from
one of Bret Harte's fictional mining camps or from a documen-
tary Western film: the posse of welcoming horsemen, the
caracoling trumpeters, the torchlight cavalcades, the gargantuan banquets of which it was said in retrospect: 'The sun
shone hotly; the visitors batted tremendously; Ballarat fielded
abominably, and all drank excessively.' At Ballarat, in baking
heat, they played on a dusty pitch surrounded by trees, which
in anticipation of the current Caribbean custom, were heavily
laden with spectators. One of these W.G. brought down with a
big hit, as neatly as if he had been an opossum, but, happily,
without fatal results. The local people spoke in awe of W.G.'s
tremendous driving and it was chucklingly reported that one
fielder went so far out at long-on that he was captured by bush-
rangers and never seen again.

W.G., inexhaustible in his strength and energy, took everything, including seasickness, in his stride, batting, bowling,
fielding, dancing, sailing and shooting with equal enjoyment
and unquenchable gusto. The newspapers treated him as
though he were some jolly convulsion of nature, such as a flood,
earthquake or volcano that happily did nobody any harm.
When they called him 'the best batsman in the world', they
knew they were praising only one of his many attributes. But,
whatever they said about him, W.G. just laughed his schoolboy
laugh. Neither praise nor blame had any effect upon him.
Without self-consciousness he accepted all that came along as
one gigantic, rather serious lark.

VI

After a strenuous summer at home and an even livelier winter
abroad, W.G. might, had he shared the normal human weak-
nesses of the race, have been a tired man. As it was, he came
back to his native land as though he had but one wish, a longing
to get at the English bowlers again. 'Married life and the trip
to Australia,' says the chronicler, 'must have agreed with
Grace.' A few days after landing he went down and made
259 for E.M.'s team, Thornbury, against Clifton in a game in

which Fred and he carried the score from 2 to 298. In first-class
cricket he made eight centuries, which was tolerably masterful
in a season not considered one of his great ones. In the
Gentlemen *v.* Players game at Prince's he extracted his usual
hundred from the old enemy. This was the mildly notorious
match in which Fred, who had made 93 not out in the first
innings, played a ball back to Lillywhite who might have taken
a dolly catch if W.G.'s bulky form had not intervened. Now in
his twenty-sixth year, W.G. was filling out. There was a fully
choral appeal for obstruction. Both umpires rejected the
demand and, though Fred was out soon after having made no
more than a dozen runs altogether, the Players felt that in some
dark mysterious way they had been robbed of a just verdict,
particularly as W.G. went on to make one more imperturbable
hundred. *Wisden,* in describing the game, lapsed from its usual
objectivity into sympathy with the Players, 'whose misfortune',
it said, 'was that nearly every appeal by a Gentleman was
decided affirmatively and the Players' appeals were mainly
met with "not out".' Twenty years later W.G. described the
incident, perhaps euphemistically, as 'one of the remarkably
few instances that have occurred during my long career as a
cricketer of a difference of opinion between my opponents and
myself . . .' Perhaps he should not have rubbed salt in the
Players' wounds by taking seven wickets in their second innings.

There were, too, the customary centuries against Yorkshire
which had now become almost automatic and about which
nobody but the bowlers could complain. In the Sheffield game,
which was played for Luke Greenwood's benefit, W.G. made
167, well over half his side's total, and then shared all the Yorkshire wickets in both innings with Fred. In the return game at
Clifton the Yorkshire batsmen were once more slaughtered to
make a Downend holiday. E.M. came in to the side for this
game and the three brothers hit 259 unrelenting runs out of
Gloucestershire's 303. At the end of the innings the abject
Yorkshire bowlers must have hated the sight of the whole
family. W.G.'s other hundreds were prodigally scattered about
the country: one at Brighton, another at Prince's and two at
Canterbury where for a mixed Gloucestershire and Kent side

he came within six runs of making a century in each innings. This, he said, calling philosophy to his aid, was fairly hard luck.

The following year, 1875, was damp and chill and some critics foolishly prophesied that this would repress W.G.'s noble rage and freeze the genial current of his soul. Not so. Though his centuries were fewer they were made in the appropriate places. Whoever escaped the slaughter, it was not fitting that either the Players or Yorkshire should be let off. His 152 (run out) against the Players at Lord's was hailed as 'the exhibition of the year', and his quasi-annual hundred at Bramall Lane (111 out of 174, and stumped at that) added liberally to the benefit of old uncle John Thewlis. All through this season in which, because he had made only 1,500 runs, his batting was said to have faltered, his bowling, backed by E.M. at point and Fred at long-leg, proved a continuous menace to batsmen. There were few first-class games in which he did not take ten or a dozen wickets and his bag of wickets for the season was 191, the largest he ever obtained. This was one of the rare years in which, at least by figures, he failed (though only just) to show himself as England's best batsman. On paper, in practice and by any standard that could be devised, he was indubitably England's best bowler.

VII

W.G. was in some sense to do superlative things right up to the time of his retirement, but never again did he recapture the glory of 1876, the unchallenged year of Grace. By most standards, 1895 was a wonderful year, but at least part of the wonder lay in the fact that he was by this time forty-seven years old. This year of 1876 was his centre and summit, his perfect golden day of high summer, and in this season it was seriously said: 'Modern cricket, in fact, seems to have resolved itself into a match between Mr. Grace on one side and the bowling strength of England on the other.'

The year was also a notable one in English literature, for, besides a play by Tennyson and a volume of verse by Swinburne, it saw the publication of *Daniel Deronda, Beauchamp's*

Career and *The Hunting of the Snark*. But W.G. pursued a different quarry.

Oddly, the year's triumph was slow in maturing. May was moderately unproductive and no century was seen until 14th June when, at Brighton, another of his favourite grounds, he hit another 104 against Sussex. The Lord's Gentlemen *v.* Players was a historic game, not so much for W.G.'s 169 and Fred's furiously hit 68 not out, but because it was the first Gentlemen *v.* Players match of the lad from Nottingham about whom W.G. was later to say in authoritative admiration: 'Give me Arthur.' Young Arthur Shrewsbury, who turned up at Lord's in a small billycock hat, was run out early in the first innings and bowled by W.G. in the second but this was no true portent, for he was, like W.G. himself, to be a pillar of the series for another quarter of a century. Another century in July was W.G.'s contribution at Nottingham to a North *v.* South game for the benefit of his old and friendly enemy, Richard Daft, who had begun his career as a Gentleman, followed most of it as a Player, and then, several years later, became a Gentleman again. Another old enemy was that most accurate of bowlers Alfred Shaw, who in the first innings of this game bowled 38 maidens, 23 of them in succession.

The momentous month of August 1876 is now upon the horizon. W.G. began on the old Argyle Street ground at Hull in a game for the United South *v.* the United North with one of those one-man performances which must have made the scorers wonder why he ever bothered to have any partners at all. While W.G. played superbly against hostile bowling, Pooley was making 14 and the next highest score was 4. Thus W.G. made 126 and ten others made 28 between them. In this innings he made several hits into the grounds of a nearby lunatic asylum and lifted one colossal drive into a passing railway truck, and thereby into history for the confusion of modern cricket brains trusts.

And here begins the story of the 11th to the 18th August, eight days which shook the cricket world. On 10th August he went down in blazing sunshine to his well-loved Canterbury to play in a twelve-a-side game for the M.C.C. against Kent. He spent the first day modestly, painstakingly leather-hunting while Kent piled up a huge score on the foundations of a finely hit century and a half by Lord Harris. (This was the first time, I think, that the batsmen's names were hoisted on to the scoreboard and the acolyte distinguished himself by dropping an 'H' and designating his lordship as ARRIS.) Next day, doubtless worn out by their exertions, M.C.C. collapsed and had to follow on after tea with the hopeless task of getting well over 300 runs to save the innings defeat. W.G., as always, was rather anxious to get home to Downend that Saturday night and so hit out in his free style, not being much oppressed by any particular urge to stay in. But so true was the wicket, so hard (though never reckless) was his hitting that in forty-five minutes he had scored his hundred and at close of play was 133 not out.

Next day, as he recalls, he was 'busy'. Runs flowed from his bat in a turbulent torrent. Partners came and went until, very near the call of time, he was caught for 344 out of a total of 546. William Yardley, who spent the whole time in the field against him, confessed that, in every sense, it was the hottest time he was ever likely to experience—in this world, at any rate. This score of 344 beat by 66 runs the record for a first-class match set up fifty-six years earlier by William Ward, the great amateur batsman and benefactor of Lord's.

W.G. did not get his Saturday rest and spent most of his Sunday in the train on the stifling cross-country journey to Bristol, but by Monday morning he was ready to turn out at Clifton for Gloucestershire, to win the toss, roll up his sleeves and under a hot sun put his old friends from Nottinghamshire to the sword with a score of 177. He called this innings the filling in the eight-day sandwich, not because it was meatier, but because, as in railway refreshment rooms, it was smaller than the other two slices.

He had not far to go for his third game, which was played at Cheltenham. There is a story that the Notts men, travelling back to Trent Bridge after their hammering, met the Yorkshiremen coming down from the north on Cheltenham railway station and gave them a graphic account of what W.G. had been doing.

'Maybe you're reight,' chuckled Tom Emmett, 'but afore we'd let him knock us about like that against Yorkshire, we'd shooit him. Even t'Big 'Un couldn't do it three times.'

But in those eight days the Big 'Un could do anything. He was insatiable and inexorable. He could win the toss, bat all the first day, and after the unexpected rain had stopped on the second day, go on to hammer the Yorkshire bowlers not merely into exhaustion but into insubordination. As he had approached the wicket at the beginning of his innings, he had said genially to Tom Emmett: '*You'll* have to get me out today. I shan't get myself out!' Nor did he. The bowlers suffered total subjugation. They toiled, they sweated and then they mutinied. When their captain, Ephraim Lockwood, an amiable but hardly commanding personality, asked Allan Hill to come back and bowl, he begged to be let off.

'Make him bowl,' cried Tom Emmett. 'Tha'rt captain.'

'Bowl him thi-sen, Tom,' retorted Allan. 'Tha'rt frightened.'

Whereupon Tom picked up the ball and delivered in succession three of the widest wides that even he had ever sent down. In Yorkshire they like to pretend that Tom then bowled his opponent with a 'sostenutor'. But the grim fact remains that at the end of the innings W.G.'s score stood at not out 318, the highest individual total in county cricket until A. C. MacLaren broke the record twenty years later. In eight days W.G. had made 839 with an average, as he liked to boast, of 419½.

In July a game, not technically termed first class, took place at Grimsby between United South and a local Twenty-Two. Before the match the Grimsby captain complained that the eleven brought by W.G. was not strong enough. This was a little hard, seeing that, besides W.G. himself, Fred Grace and their cousin W. R. Gilbert, the side contained Jupp, Humphrey, and the redoubtable Pooley. It was also a factual error.

At the end of the first day the visitors had scored 217 for two (W.G. 136 not out, Fred 39 not out). There were twenty-two fielders and W.G. played unmercifully on the weakest of them. He wore brown pads—were these Alfred Mynn's?—and at the end of the second day he had made 314.

A tribute to the presence of twenty-two fieldsmen and to

'His beard, that banner with a strange device, was for nearly forty years part of the English landscape. . . .'

'I hate defensive strokes—you can only get three off them. . . .'

'You cannot take nearly three thousand wickets in first-class cricket without being a formidable attacker. . . .'

Left: A favourite picture of W. G.'s, showing his bubbling vitality and unquenchable boyish zest (Notts v Gloucestershire at Trent Bride, 1898.)
Right: From the sightscreen at Trent Bridge W. G. watches his colleagues at practice. A moderate day: he was lame and made only 168

W.G.'s almost superhuman endurance lay in the fact that his
innings, when everybody else was out, contained 158 singles.
Only the centre of the ground was closely cut and, time and
again, W.G.'s hits were slowed down in the long grass.   His
innings also contained four sixes and twenty-one fours, but the
ceaseless stream of singles was the true sign of stamina.   There
was one break in the flow, however.   Towards the end of the
second day a telegram arrived, announcing that Mrs. W.G.
had been safely delivered of her second son.   Right through
W.G.'s life there were certain occasions thought worthy of
champagne.   This was one of them and he invited both sides to
toast the new child of Grace.   In Grimsby they still swear that
W.G.'s final score was not what appears in the records.   When
the last wicket fell at 681, W.G. came towards the pavilion and
called up to the scoring-box—there was, of course, no running
indication of individual scores:

'What did I get?'

'Three-ninety-nine,' the scorer called back.

'Oh, make it four hundred,' laughed W.G.

And the scorer, who believed that something should be done
to celebrate an innings of 399 and the birth of a happy baby,
replied: 'All right, then, you certainly deserve it!'

And that is how W.G.'s score appears in all the records as
400 not out.   Or so they will tell you in Grimsby.

Again the writers for the comic papers showed their awe in
protective facetiousness.   The periodical *Funny Folks* gave a
burlesque account of a cricket match:

'W.G.'s first stroke was a clean square hit to leg for 34.
At three o'clock two more went down with sunstroke while
umbrellas were supplied to those remaining.   Score 1,142.   At
half-past three W.G. ate an Abernethy biscuit and anchovy,
but declined drinks.   Thermometer 98.   Bowlers changed
every five minutes.   Fielders now reduced to eight men—the
score at 1,366. . . .   W.G. carried out his bat for 2,001 by as
fine an exhibition of all-round cricket as we would wish to see.
He had been at the wickets exactly twelve hours, and
declared himself in readiness to go in the next day, but the

Wapshots declined. I forgot to say that eleven bats were broken during the match.'

VIII

W.G. would have been more (or less) than human if he could have 'kept it up' in 1877. This was a quiet season but by no means a poor one. He had 'not a bad commencement' in May with a glorious and characteristically generous 261 for South v. North at Prince's in a benefit match for the Cricketers' Friendly Society. In a game at Lord's for a combined Gloucestershire and Yorkshire Eleven against the Rest of England he made 52 in the first innings and 110 in the second. Two points in this match gave him pleasure. One was the deep satisfaction derived from a tremendous six hit right out of Lord's into Dark's garden and the other was the happy thought that this century happily celebrated his twenty-ninth birthday.

Though his batting average in this damp summer was much lower than the previous year's—40 instead of 62—he still headed the table and Ephraim Lockwood was the only other batsman who made a thousand runs; at the same time his bowling was more destructive than in any season, before or since, except 1875. Gloucestershire, who had shared the championship with Notts in 1873 and won it outright in 1876, were again the leaders, and in fact owed more to W.G.'s bowling than to his batting. There was one game between Gloucester and Notts in the two innings of which he bowled an unconscionable number of maiden overs, taking seventeen wickets, the last seven without having a run hit off him. This was the match in which batsman after batsman succumbed to the irresistible temptation of hitting one of W.G.'s guileless deliveries out of the field. It did not, of course, go quite out of the field but, instead, into the greedy hands of Fred or his cousin, William Gilbert, at long-leg. It was such a dolly of a ball, pitched short and outside the leg-stump, that the batsman fell under its 'unknown and fatal influence' and simply had to hit at it. As each man went forth to the wicket the Notts captain, Richard Daft, warned him sternly against the trap. In they went and out they came. Finally Daft himself went in, smothered his first ball sternly and then, under some fatal compulsion, hit his second in the exact manner in which he had shown his men not to do it. Up went the ball, high and hard and, when at last it came down, it descended on Fred like a blessing. Daft, who did not himself suffer fools gladly, must have suffered acutely that afternoon.

IX

The cricket year of 1878 was an important date for several reasons: W.G., a married man with two children, was genuinely concentrating on his medical studies and was even considering giving up cricket altogether. This was the year of the first visit to England by an Australian side and the result was electrifying. These hard, unrelenting men carried all, or almost all, before them and it is certain that, however firmly W.G. may have intended to retire, the thought of these Australians ravaging the land without personal interference from him played its part in keeping him in cricket, studies or no studies.

The Australians were formidable foes. Captained by David Gregory, the leading member of a distinguished family, they had some good batsmen and at least three tremendous bowlers. They suffered in their first game from the wretched English weather, for, having travelled by way of San Francisco and New York, they wore silk shirts and had not brought sweaters with them. They arrived at Plymouth, unheralded and unsung, and in their first game they suffered even more from the bowling of Alfred Shaw and Morley. Then came the blow that shook the very pillars of English cricket.

On 20th May they arrived at Lord's in a horse-drawn brake and tumbled the pride of the M.C.C. in the dust, or rather, because the ground was wet and puddly, in the mud. The M.C.C., out for 33, went down before F. R. Spofforth like corn before the reaper. This was the young man who had once bowled W.G. at the nets in Melbourne and his policy of 'Disguise in action, surprise in effect' brought him six wickets for four runs. England hit back sharply to dismiss the enemy for 41, but they fared even more lamentably at their own second attempt. W.G., who in the first innings had hit a four off the first ball and been caught at short-leg off the second, was clean bowled for a duck and the deadly bowling of Spofforth and H. F. Boyle sent the rest of the side back for 19. Spofforth took four wickets for 16 and it was now Boyle's turn to perform miracles, capturing the remaining six for 3. In getting the dozen runs needed to win, the Australians lost Bannerman, beaten by a vicious breakback from Shaw, but they had no further trouble in their task and a few minutes later they had won the game, and won it in one day, against a representative batting side of the highest class. The Lord's crowd took the tourists to their hearts and *Punch* wryly lamented:

> *The Australians came down like a wolf on the fold,*
> *The Marylebone cracks for a trifle were bowled;*
> *Our Grace before dinner was very soon done*
> *And Grace after dinner did not get a run.*

The Australians went on to exact many victories from their foes, though they were beaten by Yorkshire, by a Cambridge team acclaimed as possibly the greatest of all University sides and by a Gentlemen's eleven which, mainly by means of the cunning slow bowling of W.G. and A. G. Steel, defeated them heavily. W.G.'s 25 was top score.

The Australians put out every effort when they played Gloucestershire at Bristol and won by ten wickets a low-scoring game in which Spofforth, who was no batsman, made the top score on either side. This defeat was the first ever inflicted on Gloucestershire at home. The warhead of the Australian attack was Spofforth, a lean, rangy, slightly saturnine man, nicknamed the 'Demon'. He was fastish, aggressive and diabolically clever in his powers of deception and intimidation. Of all the Australian bowlers he was the one who was to fight the fiercest duels with W.G., who called him, now that George Freeman had retired, the greatest bowler in the world. At a time when W.G. was acknowledged lord of all the bowlers, Spofforth never bowed the knee to the master. He, at least, had complete confidence in his own talents. 'Others were petrified by the thought of what he would do to their bowling,' he asserted, 'but not me.'

Perhaps it was the patriotic conviction that *someone* would have to deal with Spofforth, this frowning symbol of the ruthless foe, which made W.G. finally decide that, come what might, he must still play a little more cricket.

The season saw two mildly amusing episodes. The first concerned Midwinter, the Gloucestershire all-rounder, who had gone out to Australia as a young man and returned to England with the visiting side. It seems that Midwinter, an outsize but peaceable citizen, had amiably promised to play for either side when he was free, but there was bound in time to be a clash. One morning when Gloucestershire were due to play Surrey at the Oval, it was discovered to the Graces' indignation that the recreant Midwinter was down to play for the Australians at Lord's. Hell knows no fury like a Grace deprived of what he conceives to be his just rights and, boiling with wrath, E.M. and W.G. set off in a cab to claim their man. By other accounts it was Arthur Bush who accompanied W.G. but I prefer the E.M. version, because the story has the authentic E.M. flavour. What they said, and what the Australians said, has never been set down in an agreed text, though there must have been eloquent exchanges, but in the end the Graces drove back in triumph with their prisoner. Midwinter, who does not seem to have said anything or indeed to have wanted anything but a quiet life, did not play in the Gloucestershire *v*. Australians match. It would have been as much as his life was worth.

The year also witnessed W.G.'s visit to Dublin as President of the Field Sports Section of the British Association.[1] He and Fred had been twice to Ireland before on a short tour with the United South Eleven and in 1874 had both delighted Dublin crowds by making quick hundreds. W.G. was credited with breaking a window in a club a long way from the ground and, although this did not actually happen, the legend stands.

When the British Association held its annual assembly in Dublin, W.G., in his official capacity, made what was described as 'a learned and not unamusing' address on the contribution of

---

[1] *Cricket in Ireland* by Patrick Hone. Kerryman Press.

cricketers to the progress of science. 'My lords, ladies and gentlemen,' he began: 'I have to congratulate the British Association on the acquisition of a Field Sports Section. There is nothing more closely allied to sanitary subjects than field sports generally and cricket in particular, and I have no hesitation in saying that a keen study of the game in early youth, followed by moderate indulgence during manhood, is as favourable to *mens sana in corpore sano* as it is to the advancement of science and art . . .'

The whole thing, as set down, is intelligent and almost witty and suggests powers of eloquence foreign to the Grace of the two-sentence Canadian speeches. If the contemporary account in the Dublin press is to be believed, this oration was followed by a paper, read by E.M., on 'The relative merits of Curvilinear and Rectilinear Bowling', while Fred, announced as the distinguished author of *An Infallible Recipe against Shooters*, congratulated Ireland on being the first country to bring cricket seriously before the world. Everybody, including the Irish journalists present, seems to have had a happy time.

x

In 1879 W.G.'s long war of attrition with the medical schools ended with honour to both sides. He became a Licentiate of the Royal College of Physicians, Edinburgh, and a Member of the Royal College of Surgeons, England. In the most hallowed of all the Gracian phrases, he had 'got his diploma'. This dallying with the examiners had meant that he did not begin cricket early in the season. The summer of 1879 must have been the wettest between Noah and 1954. The previous winter had raged from October well into May. During that winter several cricket matches were played on ice and as May set in, with all its rigours, cricketers must have felt that the same slippery surface was still beneath their skates.

W.G. himself did not turn out at all until he came to Lord's at Whitsuntide to play in a match arranged for Alfred Shaw's benefit. Those who have accused W.G. of excessive artfulness, particularly in Gentlemen *v.* Players matches, should remember

that he would go to almost any length to play in the Players'
benefits and to do well in them. He was always at his brightest
in games of this kind. Another of his early biographers said:
'To score largely and thus please the beneficiaire, the public and
himself was his laudable hope . . .' Shaw's benefit was ruined
partly by rain and partly by Shaw himself, who was so ill-
advised as to take eight wickets for 21 runs.

During the season there were three good centuries in county
games: against Surrey, Notts and Somerset. There was also
some remarkably effective bowling, including a seven for 37
against Lancashire and a six for 16 against Middlesex. It was
certainly not his fault that his county failed to win the
championship.

Two years before, the M.C.C. committee had, at the instance
of its President, the Duke of Beaufort, started a national testimonial to W.G. in consideration of his 'extraordinary play and
his great services to cricket'. Word went out to all the clubs in
the country and the response was warm and wide. The M.C.C.
gave a hundred guineas and the Prince of Wales was a sub-
scriber. A complimentary match between Over Thirties and
Under Thirties was played at Lord's in July and, at lunch time
on the second day, a presentation was made in front of the
pavilion. The gift consisted of a 'handsome' clock, valued at
forty guineas, a pair of bronze ornaments in the shape of
obelisks, and a cheque for £1,458.

As the Duke of Beaufort was abroad, the presentation was
made by Lord Fitzharding and Lord Charles Russell. The
former confessed that the original idea had been to buy a
practice for Mr. Grace, but, having talked the matter over, they
had decided that Mr. Grace was old enough to take care of
himself (laughter and cheers). Lord Charles said in part:

'I am an old cricketer and the enjoyment I have had in the
cricket field for many years past has been in seeing Mr. Grace
play the game. I look upon cricket and love it as a sport of
the people, open to all, from the prince to the peasant, and
am delighted to see that it is increasing year by year in
popularity, and in some respects also it is being better played.

I agree with some friends that we have seen better bowling than we see now. You must not be surprised, then, to hear me say that I have seen better bowlers than Mr. Grace, but I can say, with a clear conscience, that I have never seen anyone approach him as a batter, that I have never seen a better field. But he might be the good bowler that he is, the fine field, and the grand batter, without being a thorough cricketer; more than usual dexterity and agility of limb are required to play cricket—the game must be played with the head and heart, and in that respect Mr. Grace is very prominent. . . .

'You all know the miserably tame effect of the ball hitting the bat, but whether acting on the defensive in playing a ball Mr. Grace put every muscle into it, from the sole of his foot to the crown of his head; and just as he played the ball so he played the game—he was heart and soul in it. I have never heard the bell ring for cricketers to go into the field but he was first into it. . . . I must hazard an opinion that H.R.H. is grateful to Mr. Grace for having afforded him an opportunity of showing his respect for the one great game of the people; requiring in those who play it the national essentials of patience, fortitude and pluck, and fostering the respect for law and love of fair play which are characteristics of the Englishman. And now, sir, in conclusion, let me have the pleasure of addressing you as Dr. W.G.; you have entered upon a liberal profession, you have adopted the healing art. My best wish for your future is, that your right hand may never forget its cunning, and that in time to come you may be as successful in alleviating pain and promoting health as most assuredly in time past you have been in promoting and satisfying to the full the enjoyment of all those who take delight in the grand game of cricket.'

So there you see W.G. being treated with the semi-reverent affection normally reserved for a public character on the point of his retirement after a lifelong career. And this was less than a week after his thirty-first birthday.

CHAPTER THREE

AUTUMN

I

THE first game that can be called a Test Match was played in Melbourne in March 1877 between Australia and an all-professional side, captained by James Lillywhite, Junior. As we have seen, there was an exciting and even devastating visit from an Australian side in 1878, but no Tests were arranged. Today we sometimes complain that cricket, like so much else, is over-organized, but complete lack of organization can raise sharper difficulties. There was an almost terrifyingly haphazard quality about cricket organization during the 'seventies and the season of 1880 might have passed without a national encounter if a game had not been belatedly arranged in September.

The fact is: the Australians had come uninvited, and had received no particular welcome. There had been what was euphemistically called 'an unfortunate incident' during the Australian tour of Lord Harris's team in 1878–79 when a mob of some thousands invaded the pitch at Sydney for the purpose of doing violence to one of the umpires, if not to the whole visiting eleven. This was the occasion when A. N. Hornby seized the leader of the invaders and carried him bodily off into custody, while George Ulyett and other professionals snatched up stumps to defend themselves and their captain. The 1880 visitors to England, however, were cricketers and not Sydney larrikins and their good sportsmanship and skill in the field greatly impressed English spectators everywhere. Scruples therefore were overcome and a game was arranged at the Oval for the 6th, 7th and 8th September. (Lord Harris, who had rather sportingly accepted the post of England's captain, commented rather grimly that heavy pressure was needed to haul some of the leading amateurs back from the Scottish moors and that, when they did appear, they were sadly out of practice.)

It was, then, against the visitors of 1880 that the first Test match on English soil was played. W.G. was the first man picked; indeed, for almost the next twenty years he 'picked himself' and when he was dropped after his comparative failure in the Nottingham Test of 1899, he may be said to have dropped himself. For nearly the whole of the intervening period he remained the scourge of opposing bowlers, asserting over them a physical and technical superiority which only Sir Donald Bradman, in his shorter heyday, ever matched.

Early in the season W.G. played for an England eleven against the Australians at Lord's and, most fittingly, scored the first run recorded by the new automatic scoreboard. In May and June he did yeoman work for Gloucestershire, though he made only one century, a courageous 106 against varied Lancashire bowling. There was an exciting finish to the game with Surrey at Cheltenham; fortunes quivered like a fever patient's chart and finally Gloucester were left 52 to get to win in 45 minutes. Fred Grace was, with humorous disloyalty, laying five to one against the possibility of his side's victory; and E.M., who had always gone in first, fiercely buckled on his pads to give young Fred a lesson. To E.M.'s scandalized amazement he saw his cousin, W. R. Gilbert, also buckling on his pads and a moment later W.G. and Gilbert were striding out to the wicket.

'There they go,' growled E.M., 'the slowest couple of run-getters in England.'

The runs were scored—almost splashed on to the board—in twenty-five minutes, Fred paid up and looked pleasant, and Shuter, the Surrey captain, had the cheque framed.

The match of the season was, after all, the Test match against the Australians, which, as it transpired, was worth waiting for, even until September. This was the only Test in which the three brothers played, or indeed could have played, together. England had a strong batting side, despite the lack of practice of the sportsmen torn from their partridges. It must have been a heartening sight to see W.G. and E.M. stride out to a pitch bathed in the bright sunlight of late summer to open England's innings. E.M. by his own forceful methods hit up a useful score and there were honourable contributions from

Lord Harris, A. P. Lucas and the brilliant Lancashire all-
rounder, A. G. Steel. But while the other batsmen came and
went, W.G. went on as though the limits of space and time had
never been. His score reached 152, his hitting was, according to
the critical authorities, 'severe and safe', and he gave the utmost
pleasure to the largest crowd that up to then had ever watched
a cricket match.

Besides W.G.'s splendid century and a half, this first English
Test contained two other historic happenings. One was W. L.
Murdoch's heroic fighting innings of 153 not out after the
Australians had had to follow on nearly 300 behind. He had
bet W.G. a sovereign that he would beat his score, mighty
though it had been, and he wore the sovereign on his watch-
chain for the rest of his days. So gallantly determined was his
resistance in this game that instead of suffering an innings
defeat, his side set England 57 runs to win and made them fight
desperately for every single. The other heroic deed was performed by Fred Grace, who got his second duck of the match in
a courageous effort to hit England out of trouble, but took from
the bat of Bonnor what has come to be regarded as the most
famous catch in the game's history. Bonnor, who stood six-foot-
six in his socks and was one of the most powerful men ever to
wield a bat, hit a slow ball from Alfred Shaw with a Vulcan-like
swing. Up and up the ball soared, a dot against the sky where,
at the top of its curve, it seemed to hang. The batsmen ran one,
ran two. . . . Now it was coming down and it landed in hands
which had been brought by Fred Grace's racing speed and
superb judgment into precisely the right position close on the
pavilion boundary. At least, in a treasured second-hand volume
of mine, the author states that it was near the pavilion. Pen-
cilled in the margin, however, is the comment of a previous
owner: 'Nonsense. Vauxhall End. *I was there.*' Sir Home
Gordon, who saw the match at the age of ten, agrees with my
pencilling commentator and says that the catch was taken, after
Fred had run a colossal distance, in front of the second gaso-
meter. The distance between the wicket and the spot where
Fred stood was found on measurement to be 115 yards. This, I
think, settles the matter in favour of the Vauxhall end; if the

ball had gone the other way, it would have landed in or behind the pavilion. Fred told William Woof a day or two later—it was during a United South game at Stroud, the last game in which he ever played—that the Bonnor catch was the only one about which he had ever felt 'funky'.

II

Within a fortnight all cricket lovers were saddened to hear that Fred Grace had died. He was three months short of his thirtieth birthday and in the prime of manhood. The cause of his death was congestion of the lungs, brought on by a chill. After the Test he had gone up to Stroud to play for the United South against the local Twenty-Two. After this game he returned to Downend and was on his way to Winchester, but was taken so ill that he had to stop at Basingstoke. According to the generally accepted story, he aggravated the chill he had caught by sleeping in a damp bed. It seems a tragic foolishness that this could have occurred in a family that contained six doctors, including Fred himself.

Fred was the most clearly charming of the Graces; he was not so relentless as E.M. or so awe-inspiring as W.G. An especial enchantment surrounds the memory of those who died young, uncondemned by the years. The brilliance of his cricket and the attractiveness of his personality have come down to us over three-quarters of a century. He was a gay, audacious hitter all round the wicket, an eager fast bowler and an impeccable fieldsman, generally at long-leg. With Fred a-roving in the long field, E.M. creeping in at point and W.G. purposefully sidling across to mid-off for catches off his own bowling, a batsman must have lived a fevered and precarious life.

Fred developed early into a tall, handsome, muscular lad. If you look at his photograph and try to picture it, in imagination, without the mutton-chop whiskers of the period, you will see that his features were very like his mother's. At sixteen, he was not merely playing first-class cricket, but was standing up to professional fast bowling without a tremor. His free-hitting style was more obviously attractive to the eye than that of either

of his famous brothers, though he did not, of course, have
W.G.'s unbreakable concentration and tempered-steel defence.
Like all the Graces, he hated missing a game, and managed to
intersperse his medical studies with cricket played for Gloucestershire or for the United South, a side which he captained and
managed. Always after W.G., he was the most successful of the
cricketers who toured Australia in 1872–73 and, though no one
can say how far he would have gone, his potentialities were
plainly of the very highest. His temperament was gay and in-
stinctively friendly and, without ever seeking it, he gained
popularity wherever he went. We can still hear with the mind's
ear his gales of laughter when the luncheon-tent collapsed on
W.G. and left him indignantly complaining: 'I wish you'd clear
this nonsense away and let me get on with my lunch.' It was
motherly affection, and something more besides, that made his
mother say: 'His many gentle virtues, added to his noble
character, endeared him in an extraordinary way to us all. To
know him was to love him.'

My own Downend cricketer told me he remembered Fred's
funeral vividly, though he could only have been seven years old
at the time. There must, he said, have been three or four
thousand people present and the conduct of some of them, pushing and jostling to catch a glimpse of the coffin, was ill-
mannered and unruly. The line of mourners and friends seemed
infinitely long and by the time the coffin reached the graveside
the end of the cortège was still near the white gates of The
Chestnuts. He recalled, just as W.G. recalled of his first All
England eleven, that the members of this great cortège all wore
top hats.

Fred was the youngest and best beloved of the brethren and
the success of his brief career gave a pleasure, poignant in retrospect, to all who had been his companions, but to W.G. more
than to all the others. The death of Fred was especially tragic
for W.G., who loved him as Joseph loved Benjamin.

III

Some quiet years followed for W.G. In 1881 he was busy in his profession, and played in only a limited number of first-class games. Nevertheless, though he had had little practice, he gave the Players another 'treat' in an exciting Gentlemen v. Players match at the Oval which the former, after a lively struggle, won in the end by two wickets. In this game he made exactly 100 in an innings which was reckoned the best seen in London that year. His 182 against Notts at Trent Bridge was a record score, though not held for very long, for the ground; and, although he appeared so infrequently, he managed to come second in the season's batting averages. It had now for a dozen years been almost impossible to imagine him as other than first.

The year 1882 is notorious, if for nothing else, for England's historic rout by the Australians at the Oval and for the legend of the Ashes that rose from it. To some it seemed an even more disastrous defeat than that of Majuba which had occurred the year before. It was a moderate cricketing year for W.G., who was still giving up most of his time to doctoring and, while he dealt firmly and confidently with several minor epidemics, he failed to preserve himself from a severe attack of mumps. Even today the thought of mumps struggling for existence in the inmost recesses of that fierce dark beard puts strain on the imagination. The scorebooks show that for the first time since 1867 he made no centuries in first-class cricket, though in minor games he scored half a dozen, one of which was completed, to the common danger, in semi-darkness.

Naturally it was the Australian visit that moved English cricket lovers to excitement. The tourists comprised a more powerful side than ever before and there were giants among them: furious hitters like Bonnor and Massie; Murdoch, hero of the 1880 match and W.G.'s great rival as a batsman; George Giffen, already acclaimed as the 'Australian W.G.' and at least his potential rival as an all-rounder; and Alec Bannerman, the stubborn stonewaller, who for hours at a time would 'sit on his splice', like patience on a monument, smiling at the bowler's grief. Their bowling strength was varied and vital, and above all there was the Demon, Spofforth, who, bowling in even deadlier manner than four years before, seemed hostility's own self. There was only one Test match and it did not take place

until the end of August. Some games are easily forgotten. Some
are historic. Some pass into legend, like Cobden's match in
1870 or Jessop's match in 1902. The Oval Test of 1882 has been
described by more writers and with more eloquence than any
other game that was ever played. In an essay called 'The
Greatest Test Match', Neville Cardus has written an imaginative reconstruction of the game which is a descriptive master-
piece, even for him. H. S. Altham's *History of Cricket* gives one of
the vividest accounts of a game ever set down on paper.
England dismissed Australia for 63 on a wicket which, as we
should now say, was taking spin, but, on going in, they fared
almost as wretchedly as their opponents and failed to establish a
lead of more than 38. Again Australia struggled in the toils and
England were asked to make a mere 85. It seemed an easy
enough task, but the question was one that worked both ways.

As the fielding side came down the pavilion steps, Spofforth
was heard to mutter with diabolical determination: 'This thing
can be done.' Hornby and Barlow were out early, both clean
bowled by Spofforth, but when the score reached 50 without
further loss, and with W.G. and Ulyett apparently installed in
comfort, it seemed as if the thing could *not* be done. But
Murdoch at this point changed Spofforth over from the Vauxhall end and thenceforward he bowled his malevolent break-
backs with the dark bulk of the pavilion behind his arm. Ulyett
was snapped at the wicket, W.G. was caught off a mishit at
mid-off, and after that came the deluge. Wicket after wicket
fell until the score was 75 for nine. With C. T. Studd, who had
not yet received a single ball, at the non-striker's end, out strode
Peate, the contemporary Yorkshire slow bowler, one of the class
whose presence from then till now has been virtually com-
pulsory in an England eleven. The tension of the moment has
been excitingly depicted. One spectator fell down dead;
another gnawed pieces out of his umbrella-handle, and the
scorer's hand trembled so much that he could not write
properly. Peate was a great bowler, the spiritual ancestor of
Peel, Rhodes, Verity and Wardle, but his views on batting were
eccentric. Perhaps he was happy-go-lucky. Perhaps he was
paralysed with fright. Perhaps he was convinced that two

shrewd blows would be enough. And so, most unhappily, they were.

Off the first he hit a gruesomely streaky two, the second shaved his stumps and the third bowled him neck and crop. England had lost by 7 runs. ('What did you do that for, Ted?' 'I couldn't trust Mr. Studd.') Incidentally, Mr. Studd, who could not be trusted, was the most successful batsman of the year. When Peate was out, the spectators were for a moment stunned into silence and then, in all the generous excitement of an Oval crowd, they rushed on to the turf to carry off Spofforth and his fellow-heroes shoulder-high. He had taken fourteen wickets in the match and his last eleven overs had yielded four wickets for 2 runs.

And W.G.'s comment had a ring of classic irony: 'I left six men to get 32 runs, and they couldn't get 'em.'

The year 1883 was another doctoring year, when W.G., because of a professional engagement, was not even free to turn out in the Gentlemen v. Players game at the Oval which had the distinction of ending in a tie. (One wonders what engagement, short of a royal accouchement, could then have been reckoned so much more important than a Gentlemen v. Players match?) The game at Lord's in which he played, was won fairly easily and he made a powerful and aggressive century against Lancashire, a side never easy to score against. Otherwise, the season held few excitements. He had now reached the age when critics were beginning to say that he was not the man he used to be. He did not mind. He was one of the few men about whom it could not be said that he never was.

The following season the Ashes were regained, though in no spectacular manner, from visiting Australians who were not quite so well armed at all points as were their forerunners of 1882. This time three Tests were played, and of these England won one and two were drawn, both in Australia's favour; the last game tended to be dragged out in a manner more often complained of now than then. The first was what is slanderously called a typical Old Trafford match in which rain rendered one of the three days a total loss. The second game, played at Lord's, brought a victory with a north-country

Phil May's famous *Punch* cartoon. 'Why, oh, why', demanded W. G., 'does square-leg wear stumping gloves?' to which Phil May r eplied: 'To keep his hands warm'

W. G. with two Somerset paladins, the elegant L. C. H. Palairet and the hard-hiting H. T. Hewett

flavour, which was ensured through the superb batting of A. G. Steel and the superlative bowling of Peate and Ulyett. The Oval match finds a special niche for itself in the W.G. story because it was the Test in which he kept wicket. The long Australian innings of 551, buttressed by three centuries, one of them a double one, went on and on. Finally it reached the point when Alfred Lyttelton surrendered his stumping gloves to W.G., who had already fielded in every other position. Lyttelton then proceeded to capture the last four wickets with lobs, one of them a catch at the wicket by W.G. Perhaps because it was a genuinely doubtful catch or because the victim was his Australian-Gloucestershire colleague, Midwinter, W.G. was always a little apologetic about it.

Though he did not trouble the Australians severely in the Tests, he made three separate hundreds against them in other games: for Gloucester at Clifton; for the Gentlemen of England at the Oval and for the M.C.C. at Lord's. In this last game, after a punishing 101 from the bat, he took seven wickets for 11 runs each and showed that he was still England's most effective all-rounder, despite the challenging advance of the highly talented A. G. Steel. What was even more remarkable was that W.G. started the season rather feebly and afterwards performed most of his more spectacular feats under the handicap of a damaged hand and/or a strapped-up leg.

In this year occurred another family loss, the death of the Graces' mother. The death of Fred, four years before, had been a cruel blow to her, and latterly the famous pony carriage had been exchanged for a wheel-chair. Seldom has there been so undemonstratively but so firmly devoted a household and it was around this loving, unsentimental mother that the Grace world revolved. No Victorian mother of nine children can ever have had an easy life. The thousand and one amenities open to the modern housewife's choice were not for her. Her sons were wilful, boisterous and intent on their own pursuits, yet they told her their troubles and even telegraphed her their scores, sought her maternal counsel on a variety of problems and placidly accepted her rebukes for the errors and bad strokes she had recognized. ('How often must I tell you, Willie, not to play it that way?') Richard Daft said she knew ten times more about cricket than any lady he ever met, while old George Anderson of Yorkshire said she could throw a cricket-ball seventy yards, and though this was not strictly true, she must have known how to handle a ball.

Most of W.G.'s biographers stress the fact that the Graces were, above all things, a clan. One of them even offers this as an indisputable proof of Scottish ancestry. Though they could dispute warmly enough among themselves, the moment an attack was threatened from outside, the ranks were closed and claymores flashed out against the common foe. Mrs. Grace knew nothing of women's emancipation and would, I think, have viewed the idea with amused scorn, but she ruled her realm with a firm hand which none resented. Her régime was the perfect matriarchy. In return her sons gave her unswerving allegiance. They would depute one of their number to escort her to a concert or see that her pony-carriage was in a position for her to watch a Meet and, if the ice on the old quarry was safe, they would skate behind her chair, pushing it along in front of them.

She had always been a regular spectator at Clifton and, though delighted to see her sons' big scores, was intelligently critical of their technical errors. Her interest in the game was not assumed as a pretty pandering to male foolishness: it was genuine and utterly free from affectation. She had her prejudices: it is said that she disliked left-handers. But she obviously liked her sons to do well. We can well imagine her pleasure at receiving such a telegram as:

Handed in at Dublin 7.49 p.m. Received at 9.15 p.m.
 From   *To*
  W. G. Grace,   Mrs. Grace,
   Dublin   Downend
Self one hundred and forty not out. Fred one hundred and three; two hundred and ninety, four out.

This must have been in 1874 when the United South eleven toured Ireland to the delighted amazement of the natives. It also shows—ah, progress, progress—that telegrams travelled a good deal quicker in 1874 than in 1957.

One pictures W.G. and E.M. sombrely travelling home by train from that abandoned match at Manchester; and then the depleted but loyal family standing at the green graveside, where Fred had been buried four years before. Father, youngest brother and now mother had been laid to rest. Sorrow and their love for her formed for those that remained an unbreakable bond. It would have seemed to them, had they known, wholly fitting that hers should become the only woman's name to find a permanent home in *Wisden*.

IV

In the eighteen-eighties less nonsense was written about cricket, if only because less was written. There was no 'personal' journalism in the modern sense and there were no suggestions in the press, now familiar to us all, that a Test match was a cross between a tuneless opera for twenty-two prima donnas and a free fight among neurotic gangsters. If a headline confided that Dr. Grace had made another good score, that was the nearest it approached to sensation. Language was temperate and even the word *amazing* contained a hint of surprise. Journalism of such an old-fashioned sort may now be reckoned dull, but it had its advantages, if only because understatement is preferable to competitive overstatement. Yet even in those more decorous days critics existed who felt they were on a good wicket if they could only keep on alleging long enough that W.G.'s powers were failing. Methuselah's detractors might have felt the same, if they could only have lived long enough. Unfortunately for the critics, 1885 was one of the years in which W.G. leaned back and genially hit them for six. This was his most successful season since the greatest, nine years before, and there was something of almost classic dignity in the comment in Lillywhite's *Annual*:

'For twenty-one years W. G. Grace has stood alone as the best all-round cricketer, and even now there is no one to rank as his superior. It is eminently satisfactory to all who know Mr. Grace's unbounded enthusiasm for the game, of which he has been such a magnificent exponent, to find that he is still, after nearly a quarter of a century's hard work, the noblest Roman of them all.'

He did not start his bigger scores until fairly late in the season, but after a punishing 132 in late July at Huddersfield against Emmett, Ulyett, Peate, Peel and Bates—the most militant cohort of bowlers in England—it appeared that there was no holding this youthful thirty-seven-year-old. Runs once more poured from his bat in the old torrential style, like water over Niagara, and he galloped towards the tail-end of the season with consecutive scores of 104, 19 not out, 221 not out (this was against Middlesex, when, as he confessed, he had won the toss for a change and, incidentally, was up all one night in the middle of his innings with a difficult maternity case). The other two scores were 68 and 174. The last of these, hit up in a light-hearted Gentlemen v. Players match at Scarborough, was the most masterly and dominant. He was pleased to admit that he was 'in particularly fine form' and actually made his 174 out of 263. Only one other batsman scored 20. Of those last five innings with their aggregate of 586, he said, with a momentary lapse from modesty: 'This gave the *remarkable* average of a trifle over 195.'

An uncle of mine saw him play at Harrogate in a match between an England Eleven and the team which Alfred Shaw and Shrewsbury had taken to Australia the previous winter. It was a low-scoring game and W.G. made 51. He made them, however, out of 52 and my appreciative relative described the innings as 'a fair bobby-dazzler'.

Only five bowlers took a hundred wickets in this season and W.G. was one of them. But, as he might well have reminded them, none of the others scored over 2,000 runs.

v

The Australians were at this period coming over to England

every other year and in 1886, although an applauding welcome
greeted them on arrival, they were in performance a poorer side
than any of their predecessors. Weather, wickets and their own
sketchy fielding were against them and Spofforth, the familiar
'Demon', broke a finger in stopping a guided missile from Lord
Harris and was out of the game for a critical month. Among the
old heroes were Palmer, Garrett, Giffen, their most versatile all-
rounder, and Blackham, Australia's most illustrious wicketkeeper, lynx-eyed and bushy-bearded. More successful than
any of them as a batsman was a newcomer, S. P. Jones.

England won all three Tests, two of them by an innings.
There was some deadly bowling by Barlow and Briggs of
Lancashire and Lohmann of Surrey, while majestic centuries
were scored, first by Shrewsbury, in the finest innings of his long
Test career, and then almost as a matter of course, by W.G.
The Champion pursued the Australians, as Saul of Tarsus pursued the early Christians, with threatenings and slaughter; on
no ground were they safe from him. Once more he was not
satisfied with less than three centuries. For the Gentlemen of
England at the Oval he made 148 in a game which brought
injury to two or three players on both sides; for his county he
made 110 in the second innings after failing to reach double
figures in the first. The Oval Test, in which 'the poor Australians did not have much of a show', brought W.G. a score of
170, which remained an English record in a home Test for
thirty-five years. In this innings he started carefully, supported
in slow-motion by the notorious Scotton, whose rate of progress
resembled a glacier's, and the total had reached 170 before
Scotton was out for 34. W.G.'s individual score had also
reached 170 out of 216 when he was snapped at the wicket.
Never had bowling been more authoritatively mastered.

In the more relaxed atmosphere of September at Scarborough he came within a couple of boundaries of scoring his
fourth century of their tour against the Australians. It was
historically one of their lean years and, as we know, such a
period was not to last for ever, but, on his form at the time,
W.G. would have subjugated far better bowling.

This was another of the happy years in which W.G. achieved

the double feat of making a thousand runs and taking a hundred wickets. It was, in fact, his eighth 'double'. Moreover, though Walter Read and Shrewsbury were ahead of him in the batting averages, his aggregate was higher, and his 122 wickets were captured at comparatively small cost.

VI

The year of the great Queen's Jubilee was 1887 and W.G., partly in loyalty and partly to commemorate M.C.C.'s centenary, chose its almost cloudless summer to stage a celebration of his own. Here was another season studded with centuries; indeed it was to be his most prolific year between the sensational 'seventies and 1895, his golden autumn's finest hour. If 1895 was his St. Luke's summer, 1887 shone on him direct from St. Martin. There were no overseas visitors to pillage and he did not mete out so much punishment to the Players as usual, but there was a hundred for M.C.C. against a strong Cambridge side, during which he hit a ball into the upper part of the pavilion at Lord's. Furthermore, five centuries were, almost as a matter of routine, registered for Gloucestershire. As almost always, they were made in the teeth of good bowling. Lord Hawke used to claim that W.G. had a slightly devilish liking for Yorkshire bowling and in the game at Gloucester he castigated a versatile attack. Ulyett, Bates, Peel and Emmett were all striving their hardest and he pounded them impartially. His totals were 92 and 183 not out, and of these he murmured a little plaintively that if his runs in them had been better arranged they would have allowed him to bring off the double event of a century in each innings. This feat he achieved 'by the skin of his teeth' a couple of months later against Kent, whose by no means negligible attack was led by Wootton, Alec Hearne and Martin. Along with E.M. he contributed 171 (E.M. 70) to a total of 277 and then in the second innings, in a little less than the comparatively short time that was left to play, he hit up 82. There was a quarter of an hour still to go and in fourteen out of the fifteen minutes that remained he scored 17 more by the sweat of his brow. No one sent him down the one easy delivery that kindly convention suggested and with two balls to go he was still 99. Then with a powerful sweeping pull, more characteristic of E.M. than of his more prudent self, he hit the last ball but one of the day high over square-leg's head for four and the game was over.

Against Middlesex he scored yet another of those hundreds (ninth out for 113 in a total of 174) when only one other batsman could muster 20 and only two made double figures. There was, too, against Notts, a not out 113, scored on a turning wicket after Gloucestershire had been compelled to follow on. This was an innings to which one batsman managed to contribute 30 and seven others made 15 between them.

Frequent, almost monotonous scores such as these pose the reasonable question: how, in a given innings, did W.G. so often succeed in scoring more than all the rest of his side put together? Was it his continued and overwhelming superiority or did he, in modern phrase, merely 'hog' the bowling? I have no doubt in my own mind of the answer. He delighted in scoring every run he could off every ball he received and in making his partners run for them, but any deliberate 'farming' was reserved for the stages of the game when genuine tail-enders were in need of care and protection. A glance down the batting order of the Gentlemen's or powerful M.C.C. elevens of the period would show that he had partners whose quality, even if not so high as his own, was very high indeed. It is, for example, inconceivable that a batsman of the ebullience of E.M. would have allowed *anybody* to keep on 'stealing' the bowling from him. E.M. would have seen him damned first. Aggressive hitters like William Yardley and Walter Read and tough and thrusting rugger players like A. N. Hornby and A. E. Stoddart would not willingly have played second fiddle to any other batsman on earth. The true fact is that W.G. was the best of the lot, but they were a very good lot.

Though W.G. did so well, his county fared badly. If anything could have saved Gloucestershire from lowliness in what was for them an unhappy season it would have been the exploits of W.G. with both bat and ball, for he scored over 2,000 runs, a high proportion of them for the county, and performed several remarkable bowling feats in a batsman's year. Not for the first time, he was rather unfortunate to miss his hundred wickets; this time by a mere three. Four years before he had missed the target by six. He crowned the season at Scarborough with a glorious lark for, when the cricket had finished prematurely, he turned out in a football match, arranged at short notice between M.C.C. and Yorkshire. Never content to be a passenger, he 'made' the two goals by which his side led at half-time, then changed over from Association to Rugby rules and scored the winning try. For a bulky general practitioner of forty this was, as the journalists of the period were in honour bound to describe it, no mean feat.

VII

England were successful in two of the three Test matches played in the wretchedly dank and cold year of 1888. The Australians brought over two superlative bowlers in Turner and Ferris, but their batting on soft pitches was weak. W.G., though he did little to bring about England's Test victories, saw to it that the Australians were not robbed of a taste of his quality in other games. As it happened, in the first Test at Lord's, his 24 out of 63, played on a bad wicket in worse light, was the highest individual score in the four innings, and, though this was the game that England lost, it was certainly not his fault. For the Gentlemen of England at Lord's he hit a commanding 165 out of 250. In the first of the two county matches against the tourists he made 51 and took four wickets for next to nothing at a vital point in the game; in the second he was out once more when only those two fateful boundaries short of another, and most brilliant, century.

In May, while the weather was reasonably fine, he piled up a double century for Gloucestershire against Sussex at Brighton, admitting afterwards that he was slow about the business, and getting out, hit wicket, in sheer exasperation to one of Walter Humphreys' lobs, which were underhand in every sense of the word. There was a heavy-scoring game in which W.G. may reasonably be said to have pulverized the Yorkshire bowling.

Tom Emmett, the old warrior, had now retired, but Ulyett and
Peel, men of the highest international quality, remained there
to take what punishment was coming to them. W.G. scored
148 and 153, only two others making double figures in each
innings. 'This,' he opined, 'I may fairly call my champion
match.'

In this year of bowlers' harvests, W.G. was by far the heaviest
scorer. Once more he missed the double event by a mere trifle,
making nearly 2,000 runs and taking 93 wickets. With the least
touch of extra luck in these fecund middle years he might easily
have raised his total of 'doubles' from eight to ten or eleven. In
his career W.G.'s tale of 'doubles' does not flatter him, for there
were three seasons when, with plenty of runs in his locker, he
took over 90 wickets, and at least two when, with the bag of
wickets safe, he 'stalled' at round about 970 runs.

For W.G. 1889 and 1890 were moderate years and 1891,
mainly because of an injury to his knee, was a positively poor
one. In the first of these three years the size of the over was
increased from four balls to five, an innovation of which most
bowlers approved, but the change did not bring W.G. any
special success. In this wet season he took fewer than half the
wickets he had taken during the even wetter year before, and in
the two following years his captures fell to only 61 and 51. In
two of these lean years his batting aggregates were a little lower,
but only in 1891 did his batting seriously go off. At Lord's
against Middlesex in 1889 he played a grimly defensive 101 for
his county after Gloucestershire had somewhat abjectly followed
on. In the return game at Cheltenham he carried out his bat
for 127 and forced Middlesex, in their turn, to follow on. In
point of fact, Middlesex did some furious hitting in their second
innings and when Gloucestershire went in again, they were hard
put to it to make a draw of the game.

W.G. always enjoyed end-of-season life at Scarborough with
its lighthearted atmosphere, on and off the field. In the South
v. North game he went in for a second time, when the South
followed on, and proceeded to hammer out 154 while his partner, the quick-scoring Bobby Abel, played a more modest part
than was usual for him at the other end. In the 'eighties new

personalities had been rising in the batting world: Shrewsbury,
A. G. Steel, Walter Read and Bobby Abel (the Guv'nor), but
to none of them would W.G. cede pride of place.

W.G.'s sporting activities were not strictly confined to the
cricket field. His energies found further outlet in an evening's
dancing. Imagination blinks at the picture of W.G. galloping
like a charge of heavy cavalry round Scarborough's biggest ball-
room, particularly as his favourite dance was the polka and the
very thought adds point to the venerable lines:

> *You should see me dance the polka,*
> *You should see me cover the ground . . .*

But in strict fact W.G. was as light of foot as of heart and pretty
girls practically queued up for the privilege of being his
partner.

W.G. seldom complained of ill-luck on the field, and even
then he did it with a kind of rueful good humour, which vented
itself in a low rumble of fairly harmless grunts and growls.
There were, however, at least three occasions in 1890 when he
might well have plucked his beard out by the roots in exasperation, for while he made a sound not-out century against Kent in
May, he missed the hundred by a hair's breadth on three
separate occasions. An archangel might ruffle his wing-feathers
with resentment if he were given out leg-before-wicket at 98.
This happened to W.G. at Dewsbury, a place where misfortune
has frequently been known to descend upon the righteous, but
this innings, so near and yet so far from personal triumph, made
certain that victory was snatched from Yorkshire's grasp at the
last moment.

At Old Trafford on a vile wicket he battled his majestic way
against bowlers as fierce as Mold and as cunning as Barlow
towards his hundred and at 94 was gleefully caught by Hornby,
the old Monkey. Lancashire robbed him again in the return
match, in which, after scoring 90 in his own vigorous style, he
was out to a catch so good that it was positively sinful. He had
so far in his career made ninety-three centuries and might well
have claimed to have scored three near-misses.

The customary tour by an Australian team in 1890 brought victory to England in the only two matches played. The third, at Manchester, was completely washed out by rain. Looking out over the rain-soaked turf, W.G. laughed a trifle apprehensively: 'They'll have to send the lightweights out to field. A man of my weight would sink in that . . .' At Lord's, W.G. in the first innings was sensationally caught and bowled by C. T. B. Turner for a duck, but in the second, when his side were set 135 to win, he took charge of England's destiny in an almost arrogant manner and, with his 75 not out, gave both a foundation and a steel framework to victory. In the sharply contested final Test at the Oval he came near to getting the pair which he had avoided, and was to avoid in first-class matches, all his life.

This was the last year in which W.G., along with E.M., who was now nearly fifty, delighted their admirers at Bristol with the sort of century opening partnership in which they had revelled twenty years before. In Gloucestershire's Bank Holiday game of 1890 the happy pair put on 117 and never again did they have so prolific and profitable a partnership.

Little need be said of 1891, which was W.G.'s and Gloucestershire's unhappiest season. He suffered from a severely strained leg, but the damage did not happen till late in the season, and cannot bear the full weight of his ill-success. There was not a single century and once or twice, in a mood which, at first sight, suggests lack of confidence supremely difficult for his admirers to credit, he pushed himself down the batting order. As a matter of fact, the lack of confidence was not his, but his colleagues', for when he was out at No. 1, they faltered, and he temporarily demoted himself in an unsuccessful effort to add some stiffening to the middle.

His most valuable achievement that year was not a brilliant innings, but the discovery of Jack Board, the gardener's lad who was to become one of the finest wicketkeeper-batsmen in the country. Board himself has left an account which has a kind of moving simplicity of his initiation in a South v. North match at Lord's. He received a wire from W.G. in London, telling him to call on Mrs. Grace at Stapleton Road. She gave young Jack £2 for his journey from Bristol to London and told him to

pay no more than eighteenpence for the cab between Paddington and Lord's. All his life Board remembered how, when he
arrived at Lord's W.G. took him by the arm, led him to the
professionals' room and introduced him to the men who were
henceforward to be his companions and colleagues. After the
game, in which the youthful stumper had to stand up to Lohmann, Sharpe, Ferris and Martin, the most awkward bowlers of
the day, W.G. took him in his own cab to Paddington. 'He
travelled with me,' said Board, 'and I rode through the streets
of Bristol with him to his home. W.G. was W.G. in those days.
His name was a household word the world over. I felt somebody. There was a lot of pride in me . . .'

VIII

The following winter W.G. made his second trip to Australia.
This time he was eighteen years older. So, for that matter, was
Australia, which had become a slightly more sophisticated
country than it had been when he had visited it before. For one
thing wickets were greatly improved, particularly by the introduction of Bulli soil; for another, many of the journeys, once
followed by a lurching coach, were now covered by railway
extensions. Accommodation, too, was a little less primitive than
when the proprietor of a shanty-hotel had cheerfully greeted
him: 'Pleased to meet yer, W.G., but we can't do you Sydney
style, no bloody bathrooms and suchlike.'

'That don't matter,' W.G. had replied equally cheerfully,
'we Graces ain't no bloody water-spaniels!'

He took with him a side bristling with accomplishments.
Arthur Shrewsbury was unfortunately missing, but with this
exception and one or two others he was able to head a ministry
of almost all the talents. With A. E. Stoddart and Abel to
support him in batting, Gregor McGregor to keep wicket like
an urbane panther, and a whole variety bill including Lohmann, Briggs, Peel and Attewell to bowl, he should have had a
reasonable hope of bringing home the Ashes.

With W.G. as captain and Alfred Shaw as manager, the tour
was arranged under the patronage of Lord Sheffield, and a

special cap was designed for the occasion with broad stripes of red, yellow and deep purple, fronted by a crown and the letter S. The total cost of the jaunt was £16,000 and as the receipts came roughly to £2,000 less, his lordship, according to Shaw's account, was that much out of pocket. For his services to the tour W.G. was given a fee of £3,000 and expenses, which seems an excessively large sum of money for an amateur to have received. To this it could be replied (*a*) that there was never any secret about the transaction, (*b*) that nobody seems to have seriously objected or claimed that W.G. had forfeited his amateur status and (*c*) that all cricketing Australians considered the money well spent, for interest in cricket, which had begun to wilt a little, started to blossom again the moment W.G. stepped ashore. H. F. Boyle, the great Australian bowler of earlier days, said bluntly that in a Test match W.G. was worth five men.

In the second match of the tour, which was played at Melbourne, against Victoria, he made 159 not out in the old majestic manner. This was his only really massive score of the journey, but he made many useful ones and topped the batting averages both in eleven-a-side games and those against the odds. He appears to have enjoyed almost every moment of the tour, though he had more than one vigorous tussle with the umpires, some of whom, in his probably correct opinion, lacked basic cricket knowledge. Some chroniclers of the tour have thought it odd that, this being so, he should afterwards have confessed to such enjoyment. For myself, I think that he had sufficient in common with his Australian hosts to enjoy the tussles, too, and he certainly never bore malice. He never let the sun go down upon his wrath, though there were some colourful sunsets while it lasted.

His idea of a joke, as all who knew him have maintained, was elementary, if occasionally elemental. George Giffen has told how during the first Test a fast ball just 'shaved the paint off' W.G.'s leg stump. W.G. wagged his beard mournfully and took three sad steps in the direction of the pavilion. Instantly a wild shout went up. Twenty thousand enthusiasts were on their feet, clapping and yelling. Then W.G. turned towards his

crease and took up his batting position again as though nothing
whatever had happened. 'Then the crowd are silent and crest-
fallen, for a rise has been got out of them, and they don't like it.'
W.G. loved to bait the barrackers, whose repertory of witticisms
has not widely increased in the past sixty years or so. When
W.G. stood suicidally close to Alec Bannerman, the very sultan
of stonewallers, a barracker shouted: 'Look out, Alec, he'll pick
your pockets.' Sixty years later that barracker's legitimate (or
possibly illegitimate) descendants shouted similar counsel when
Tyson and Statham were bowling to a closely-packed leg-field.

England lost this first stubborn game by 54 runs, possibly
through sheer over-confidence. This was shown by their premature attempt to score rapidly, while the Australians were
more wisely content to dig in and take their time. The second
game was also lost partly through over-confidence and partly
by what appears to have been a tactical mistake on W.G.'s part.
When England started their second innings in poor light, he put
himself in at his usual position of No. 1, because he deemed that
the wicket would deteriorate, and that he had better make runs
while he could. This was one of his rare errors of judgment, for
after he was out, the wicket grew better instead of worse, and
he was left with the knowledge that if he had gone in later the
result might have been different. This game, at any rate,
brought another triumph for the Australian tortoise over the
English hare. The steadier side had won on its solider merits
and the Australians were delighted with this 'victory of the
pupils over the masters'. That England won the third Test (at
Adelaide) by an innings and 230 runs counted for little, because
the Ashes were already lost.

Whatever had been the results of the tour, and, apart from
the losing of the two Tests, they had been excellent, the
Australian press and public seldom failed to acclaim W.G. as
the focal point of all interest. He was by far the greatest draw
an English visiting side had ever brought to Australia and,
denizens as they were of a land of strange creatures, they
revelled in his bulk and his buoyancy, his consuming energy,
his doughty independence in controversy and, above all, his
appearance of being a bigger and more highly-coloured

character than anyone or anything they had ever met. As
fellow-citizens of the kangaroo, the emu and the ornithoryn-
chus, they appreciated creatures that were 'rich and strange'.
Tributes to his overpowering personality came forth in rich
Australian style. They said he had 'got no older, but a tremendous lot fatter'. It may not have been literally true that his
bristly black beard stretched 'nearly to his waist' or that, when
bowling, he rolled up to the crease with a 'lumbering action like
a Clydesdale colt' or that his hands were like 'vast carpet bags'.
But that is how he seemed to his livelier admirers. 'Great Scott,'
exclaimed one of them. 'He could get £2 a week and his tucker
merely to walk about in the grasshopper districts to kill off the
pest.'

IX

The next years of the early 'nineties—1892, 1893 and 1894—
cannot by any means be reckoned among W.G.'s great years,
but neither were they poor ones, like 1891. For much of the
time he was hampered by knee trouble, which prevented
indulgence in short runs. This, no doubt, was why in 1892 he
failed to make a single century. Nevertheless, he failed by only
a single run. There was a 99 against Sussex at Gloucester that
was as authoritative as any but the most regal of his earlier
centuries. The Gloucester scoreboard of those days did not
indicate the individual total run by run and W.G., without
knowing it, remained for several overs at 99. Then he hit out
and was caught and bowled off a skier.

'Why ever didn't you tell me?' he demanded of E.M. when at
last he saw his score. 'I could have scored off any of those balls.'

'Ay,' said E.M., 'and if I'd told you, you'd have been the first
to grumble.'

When the long-delayed hundred came at last in June 1893,
it was made for M.C.C. against Kent and was W.G.'s first on
English turf since 1890. Spectators at Lord's agreed that, as
entertainment, it had been worth waiting for. W.G. showed all
the old zestfully punitive powers, making 128 out of 189; in
a stand of 127 the share of his partner was 35. This was the year

when W.G. Junior, born in 1874, had a trial with Gloucestershire but, though his school records had been outstanding, he did very little. Indeed, during the three or four seasons in which he put on flannels for his family's county, there is not much in the scorebooks that does justice to what were, after all, his considerable talents.

The number of W.G.'s centuries had now reached ninety-five and in 1894 he added three more, two against his favoured whipping boys of Cambridge University and the third in the extra Gentlemen v. Players match which for a time was forming the main feature of the Hastings Festival. The game took place in mid-September and W.G. 'had to leave some capital partridge shooting' in order to play. After getting the Players out cheaply on a muddy wicket, W.G. went in on an improving one and scored 131 out of 247, going in first and, as often, being last out. Somewhere in this innings a ball from Mold, the Lancashire 'chucker', cannoned off his pad on to a stump, without removing the bails. This was not so much a 'peculiar slice of luck', as W.G. called it, as, considering Mold's ferocious pace, a minor miracle. Most batsmen of the time felt they would rather be hit with a blacksmith's hammer than with a ball from Mold. It was during one lunchtime of this game that he received a telegram: 'Please say to settle bet if you ever made century against Australia.' As W.G. handed the telegram round, Sammy Woods undertook to reply and sent off a return wire: '*What do you think you cuckoo.*'

In the Cambridge game at Fenner's, W.G. took with him his son, now a Cambridge undergraduate, to open the innings, and sadly saw him snapped at the wicket for nought. After that he proceeded systematically, in company with the slower Chatterton, to take the score from 6 for one to 256 for two. At Lord's, in a game of gargantuan scoring, W.G. Junior was again in the M.C.C. side and again, now batting at No. 5, he was caught at the wicket for nought. But in the second innings the Cambridge bowling was collared as bowling had seldom been collared before in a first class match at Lord's. While W.G. was remorselessly punishing the bowling at one end, first J. T. Brown and then a slim young Indian named K. S. Ranjitsinhji played swift, beautiful cricket at the other. When it was W.G. Junior's turn, he did not fail a second time but made a sound half-century off the tired bowling. W.G. went on with later partners to make 196, which was his highest score at Lord's and the highest total of that season anywhere. Even such a long innings did not quell his irrepressible energy for, as soon as it was over, this forty-six-year-old came out impatiently into the field again and took four wickets for 33.

And all this time the stage was being set for what was to be the most wonderful of all W.G.'s wonderful years.

CHAPTER FOUR

INDIAN SUMMER

*'Think of it! On the field for every ball bowled, 330 runs for
once out, and a man of close on forty-seven!'*

H. S. ALTHAM

I

No cricketer in his forty-seventh, or any other, year has surpassed the exploits of W.G. in 1895. He scored a thousand runs
in a cold, uninviting May. He reached his hundredth hundred,
a feat never before achieved or even conceived by any other
batsman. And, a fact that delighted him most of all, he saw his
son, W.G. Junior, make two useful scores in the Varsity match.

There was no promise of triumph and good fortune in W.G.'s
first innings of the season, which amounted to exactly 13. This
was scored for M.C.C. against Sussex on 9th May and it was
K. S. Ranjitsinhji, playing in his first county game, who caught
him in the slips when he had reached the unlucky number. In
W.G.'s second innings Ranji, who had himself batted
dazzlingly, failed to repeat his first innings catch. When W.G.
had made 14, Ranji missed him and was thenceforward obliged
not only to watch him progress towards his ninety-ninth hundred without the ghost of another chance but to put up with the
Old Man's ponderous leg-pulling. Ranji, whom one had not
envisaged as a bowler, at last took W.G.'s wicket, but not until
he had made 103. On the last day of the match when Sussex
had been set 405 to win, Ranji played a semi-miraculous innings
of 150 of the kind which, over the next dozen years, was to add
to sober English cricket a touch of oriental magic. Then, with
the first ball that he sent down, W.G. clean bowled him. That
was something, but it did not happen before Ranji had in the
match scored 227 for once out. Furthermore, he had, despite
his one lapse, fielded brilliantly, and taken six wickets at fairly

98

small cost. Even in W.G.'s wonderful year, a new star was seen to be swiftly rising and the next greatest cricketer of the age was making his glittering entry. In the words of the late Poet Laureate, who had died only three years before:

> *There's a new foot on the floor, my friend,*
> *And a new face at the door,*
> *A new face at the door.*

II

W.G.'s next game, which was against Yorkshire, gave him two merely moderate scores and then on the 16th, 17th and 18th May came the match with Somerset at Bristol which was to turn the nation's attention from the problem of whether Lord Rosebery or Lord Salisbury should be Prime Minister. It might have been difficult to explain to an intelligent foreigner why the population of this island, with plenty of worries of its own, should worry whether a stout, bearded middle-aged gentleman should hit a stuffed leather ball with a cane-handled willow-board a greater or lesser number of times. But this is a strange island and the possibility of W.G.'s hundredth hundred set a large number of human emotions alight with excitement.

The match began with no particularly shining prospect, either for W.G. or for his county. Somerset, given a scintillating start of 200 by Palairet and Fowler, did not quite live up to this early promise, and Gloucestershire were lucky to dismiss the rest of the side with only another hundred added. When stumps were drawn on the first evening two Gloucestershire wickets had fallen quickly and W.G.'s score was 38 not out. A man who watched every ball of this game said that the first half-hour of W.G.'s innings showed utter mastery. The Somerset bowlers, especially Woods, displayed every weapon in their armoury, but W.G. was valiant and unconquerable. His timing was wonderful, his defence impregnable.

The next morning was dry but bitterly cold, even for an English May, and the first ball sent down saw the start of the great stand between W.G. and the slight, graceful Clifton schoolboy, C. L. Townsend, which was to bring about something hitherto undreamed of in cricket history. As news began to filter down into the town that W.G. was attacking the bowling (and the record) with confidence, crowds began to flock to the ground from all over Bristol and the surrounding country. Cricket-lovers, half-happy and half-apprehensive, were coming to witness their hero's triumph or disaster; the others were keenly curious to gaze on this extraordinary phenomenon, this bulky middle-aged man endowed with the zest and energy of a boy.

As the score mounted, there was no diminution in the big batsman's energy and artistry. The day continued bitterly cold and as we recall that at times big white snowflakes dappled the Doctor's dark beard, we feel inclined to ask: 'Where's your Hermit's Derby now?' At last W.G. entered what were now, if never before, entitled to be called the 'nervous nineties'. One of the scorers thrust his hand out of the score box with two fingers upraised, not in a prophetic victory-sign, but to show that now only two runs were needed. Curiously, there was someone who was at least as nervous as W.G. was ever likely to be. This was S.M.J., the great Sammy, Woods, not normally known as a sensitive plant, who had in these last few overs developed an unwonted diffidence. C. L. Townsend who, after all, was there at the time has said: 'This was the only time I ever saw W.G. flustered. . . . Poor Sam Woods could hardly bowl the ball and the Doctor was nearly as bad.'

One sympathizes with Sam, of course. Suppose something went wrong? Suppose, horror of horrors, he accidentally got his man out? This fate the previous season had befallen Bobby Abel who had dementedly got himself out off the 'gift' ball offered him at 99. Sam, when his own normal sunny self, was the most violently hostile of fast bowlers. Now he trotted up and sent down a slow full toss on the leg side and W.G., to Sam's almost tearful relief, drove it hard and true for four. The thing had been done.

The crowd cheered wildly and hats and walking sticks were flung into the air. In those days nearly everybody wore a hat, which was handy for flinging. The fielding side, who did not

then normally greet each fifty as they do today, with the hand-
clap of conventional courtesy, joined spontaneously in un-
inhibited applause. W.G. raised the peak of his cap towards
both sides of the ground and then settled down with renewed
concentration to the serious business of getting the second
hundred. Young Townsend was batting beautifully, too, and
betting men were speculating whether W.G. would get his
second hundred before C.L. got his first. W.G. won by a short
head and when the storm of cheering broke out again, a figure
was seen walking solemnly from the pavilion to the wicket
bearing on a tray the 'special occasion' bottle of champagne and
glasses. One story says that it was E.M. who brought it out, but
it is more probable that he, sitting in the pavilion and wishing
to heaven he were out in the middle, had sent it out in charge of
one of the brothers' Century Club friends. Play was suspended
for a few minutes while the fielders drank the Champion's
health. It is a solemn thought that various authorities disagree
about the size of the bottle. Some say it was a magnum. Others
say there were two of them. A third contention, that of a Bristol
journalist, swears that it was a jeroboam and that this huge
bottle remained on the mantelpiece of a friend of his until, at
the latter's death, it was impiously thrown away. It is strange
that people should still be arguing about the size of a bottle
brought out to a cricketer, and a moderate drinker at that.
Among Britain's Prime Ministers, there are three or four, including Walpole and the Younger Pitt, who were notable
drinkers, but nobody now quarrels about the size of their
bottles.

In *Wisden* for 1957 there is a record of the cricketers who have
in their careers scored a hundred hundreds or more. These, in
addition to W.G., number thirteen and include the incomparable Sir Jack Hobbs, whose total is 197, and every one of
them has been an outstanding cricketer. To score a hundred
centuries is a remarkable feat for a batsman in the present age
who is fortunate to enjoy a long playing career uninterrupted by
war or serious personal injury. In 1895 the thing seemed a
miracle. And, considering the varied strength of the bowling,
the erratic quality of the pitches, and the continuous wear and

tear upon human physique and human concentration, so it was.

The solemnity of the ritual or, perhaps, the mere sight of the champagne helped, as Dr. Johnson might have said, to concentrate W.G.'s mind wonderfully, but the break had an unsettling effect on Townsend who was disappointingly given out l.b.w. when only five runs short of his hundred. After his departure, W.G. found no further serious partners. Apart from Townsend and himself, only two out of the whole eleven reached double figures. As he rolled on in majesty towards his third hundred, they kept leaving him at short intervals, like the guest from the poet's 'banquet-hall deserted', until finally even *his* concentration faltered and he was ninth out, having amassed 288. This was an astonishing innings even for W.G. Somerset's wicketkeeper, the Rev. A. P. Wickham, who had crouched there all day in his faded Harlequin cap, said that in the whole of that immense innings W.G. allowed the ball to pass the bat only four times. Modern batsmen might well ponder this staggering fact every day of every season from 1st May onwards.

Even then W.G. had scored nowhere near a thousand runs in May. He compiled a pleasing 52, but no more, for the Gentlemen of England against Cambridge University and then something in the Gravesend air must have put the idea into his head. For M.C.C. he fielded all the first day against Kent's big score of 470 and batted all the second day for a monumental individual effort of 257, first in and last out, almost world without end. But, so far as this match was concerned, even a score of that magnitude was not enough. On a wicket which had every reason to be rather worn, Painter, with a little help from Roberts, tumbled the Kent men out. There is an extraordinary story about this Kent second innings which is only, in fact, less extraordinary than the truth. The tale is that W.G. carelessly tossed the ball to Murch, the normal opening bowler, but let it slip, so that it rolled towards Painter, who picked it up and at once prepared to mark out his run. The only drawback to this fascinating story is that Murch, after getting a duck on the second day, had been allowed to go off and carry out a previous engagement elsewhere. (Remembering W.G.'s views on this form of desertion, one wonders how this absence came to be allowed.) It had been freely prophesied in the newspapers that M.C.C. would lose the game, and when they were set 104 to get in an hour and a quarter, the newspapers seemed to be right. A wicket fell almost at once, but that was all. When W.G. was joined by Painter, he did not so much 'farm' the bowling as seize it by right of conquest. When the winning hit was made after just under an hour, W.G., unfatigued and indefatigable, had made 73 not out. He had fielded the first ball sent down and hit the last one for four, and never been off the field, while play was in progress, for the whole of the three days' game. He was even lucky to get away in the end, for he was pursued from the ground to the station by an uncontrollable mob of juvenile admirers.

These 330 runs scored on the 24th and 25th of the month made a substantial advance towards the thousand runs, but then came a setback. W.G. would never, if he could help it, miss a benefit for a fellow-player and he went off to the Oval to join an England eleven against Surrey in Walter Read's testimonial match. Excited, slightly awe-stricken crowds came along to cheer the batsman who had twice made 250 in the last ten days, but, alas, Tom Richardson bowled him when his score was only 18. What was worse, Surrey maddeningly collapsed, and the game was over before he had the chance of a second innings. This was hard on W.G. and cannot have been much fun for Walter Read. The dream of a thousand runs in May seemed to have faded.

It was now the 30th of May. Only two days of the Gloucestershire and Middlesex match at Lord's remained and there were still 153 to be got, but W.G. set about the task with a kind of mathematical efficiency. His first duty was to win the toss and then dig himself in. This he proceeded to do in determined but leisurely fashion. It was not that he played more carefully than usual; he was always vigilant, even when scoring rapidly. Now it was clear that he intended to take every ball, fast, slow or curly, more unmistakably than ever before in the middle of the bat. By lunch-time he had made only 58, which would have been reasonably quick scoring for any batsman nowadays but was slow for him. After lunch he accelerated his pace. It was

not a matter of 'having a go', a thought which he would have
scorned as 'chancy'; it meant that he had taken the complete
measure of all the bowling on view, including the slow curvilinear stuff of E. A. Nepean which he treated almost respectfully
all the morning. He then went hard and systematically at it
until he reached 99. At, but not until, this point he was offered
the customary complimentary long-hop, which he coolly turned
to leg for a complimentary single.

Another 53 runs remained to be added and still he went on,
remaining calm and commanding while the tension round the
boundary tightened. At 149 there was one more friendly long-
hop and, as it received its *coup de grâce*, the long, clamorous
tumult of applause took on that abandoned quality which
mingles hero-worship with sheer delight and relief with both.
He made 16 more runs than were strictly necessary, was bowled,
and came back to the pavilion, glowing with fulfilment. 'The
sound of cheering in front of the pavilion,' as Bernard Darwin
beautifully says, 'has scarcely died away yet.'

Indeed, those cheers have tended to obscure the historic fact
that the game itself had an exciting finish, for Middlesex, forced
to follow on, made a fighting recovery, set Gloucestershire 43
runs to win and gave them the fright of their lives in getting
them.

III

In this golden season there were five more centuries to come, all
of them good and some of them grand; these were in addition to
a vigorous 91 at Brighton, which with a little luck might have
been his 103rd. He scored 125 at Lord's for M.C.C. in the
return game against Kent, a game to which the Kentish bowlers
must have looked forward with dread. Though he had scored
centuries for the Gentlemen at the Oval, Scarborough and
Hastings, he had not made one on their behalf at Lord's for
nearly twenty years. He was to make one now, sharing a first-
wicket partnership of 151 with Stoddart in characteristic
fashion. The other nine batsmen did not raise 50 between them.

Later in the season he hit 119 against Notts on a wicket so

inimical that nobody else made a third of his score, and a game that must have given him acute pleasure was the match played at Lord's for the Gentlemen of England against the I Zingari Club to mark its jubilee. The Club put a side into the field that included some tremendous fellows, such as F. S. Jackson, A. E. Stoddart and A. G. Steel, while the Gentlemen had W.G., Arthur Sellers, father of Brian Sellers, W.G. Junior, and a young fast bowler from Oxford named C. B. Fry.

Rapid scoring by both sides went on practically all the time and, after W.G. had raced to a first innings top score with 79 and Stoddart for the Club had just missed his hundred, the Gentlemen were set 172 and made them in the briskest possible time without loss. The score read: W.G. 101; Sellers 70; and the proportion could not have been better arranged.

Finally, at the end of the season, there was his ninth century in a South v. North game at Hastings, where he and Stoddart had another picnic. In another hundred-and-fifty partnership the two of them not only treated the bowling of Mold, Pougher and Johnny Briggs with disrespect but scored runs off practically every ball.

The Varsity match of 1895 marked the zenith of this royal season and the Champion's biographers have lovingly lavished their descriptive powers on W.G.'s frock coat and effulgent silk topper as he presided like a benevolent Jove over these ritual revels. When he appeared in the pavilion, arrayed like Solomon in all his glory, A. E. Stoddart favoured him with a stony stare.

'Pardon me,' inquired Stoddart, who was sitting on the table in the Long Room, 'would you tell me whom I have the honour of addressing?'

This was exactly the kind of unsubtle humour that W.G. enjoyed most. 'Ah, you old rogue,' he chuckled, 'there will be one or two here that I shan't be knowing later on.'

He had been anxious that the young W.G. should get a Blue and, now that, in his second year, the Blue had been awarded, W.G. Junior had the chance of winning his spurs. He went in first with the rugger-playing Yorkshireman Frank Mitchell and in each innings his batting was both sound and attractive. His scores were 40 and 28 and there was no doubt that they helped

to lay the sure foundations of a Cambridge victory. C. E.
Green, to whom W.G. introduced Mrs. W.G. on the first morning of the match, invited them to his private box over the grand-
stand at lunch-time and the Champion beamed out in kindly
delight on all the world, because Bert had made an excellent 40.
It is probable that this 40 of his son's in an important game gave
W.G. a greater amount of pure pleasure than any one of his own
hundred hundreds. At the interval Green and his friend went to
join the usual parade of fashion on the turf and when they returned they could scarcely get in at the door of the box, for they
found that W.G., still glowing with universal, and genuine,
benevolence, had taken charge of operations and invited most of
the Oxford and Cambridge elevens in to join in the celebration.

IV

I have always regarded with awe the pronouncements of up-to-
the-minute psychological novelists, ever since one of them told
me that Nelson had an inferiority complex, and there is no
doubt that these powerful intellects could go all the way to town
over the father-son relationship of W.G. and W.G. Junior. Here
were the ideal ingredients for their favourite witches' brew: on
the one hand the big, bluff, earthy extrovert, whose arrested
mental development was demonstrated by his inordinate love
of schoolboy games, schoolboy arguments and naïve schoolboy
jokes. On the other hand, here was the natural introvert, the
shy, spectacled student, the sensitive mathematical scholar to
whom parental philistinism must bring constant pain and who,
in a thousand novels, is rendered sour and sick by the fact that
his father will never attain an adult outlook. Here surely was
matter for misunderstanding, frustration, and for all those
stresses and tensions which make psychiatrists happy.

Now the facts are different. W.G. Junior was as fond of
cricket as his father and, from the age of six, had learnt to sit
in the pavilion with a scorebook of his own, marking down the
family runs. He won two scholarships by the time he was twelve
and went to school as a day-boy at Clifton, where he was good
at work and an excellent if rather inelegant performer at games.

Some fortunate boys have talents for both work and games and
W.G. Junior was one of them. It may well have been more
embarrassing for the son of a famous father to display a
moderate talent than to have possessed no talent at all, but
W.G. Junior does not seem to have suffered, for, without being a
nonesuch, he had a first-class athletic record all round. He and
his younger brother used to walk every day from Stapleton
Road to school, a distance of three and a half miles. It seems
hardly credible that, for a time at least, they came home for
lunch, thus walking fourteen miles a day, but this was so. Later
they took sandwiches and walked only seven miles. W.G. was
most anxious that 'Bert' should excel, as he had himself done, on
the running track and prevailed on one of Bristol's leading
athletes to pace him for the Public Schools quarter-mile. When
the athlete slowed down around 350 yards, W.G., pelting along-
side, yelled: 'Come on, lazybones!'   In the field of family
athletics there is a further endearing picture of W.G. rushing
madly through the rain at the side of the track as his second son,
Edgar, runs in the school quarter-mile. It was a fighting finish
in which the future admiral came in, a plucky second, and
W.G., wildly waving the boy's coat and waistcoat, was an
excited third.

No coaching could endow W.G. Junior with a graceful batting style but, both at home and at school, he practised his
cricket assiduously without, so far as anyone knows, neglecting
his more academic work. He was a member of his school eleven
for three years and in 1893 his batting average was excellent,
while his bag of over fifty wickets constituted a school record.
At Cambridge he made a flying start in the Freshman's match
with a score of 88 but he did not keep up this form and was not
awarded a Blue until the following year, with the excellent
results in the Varsity match which we have seen. His first
innings in this game was really his best for the University and
we have seen how it brought delight to W.G. and a host of his
friends.

The University match of the following year lives in cricket
history as the game won for Oxford by the batting of G. O.
Smith, a last-minute substitute and more famous as a Corin-

thian footballer. On the other hand, it brought misfortune to
W.G. Junior, the supreme misfortune of a duck in each innings.
The disappointment to both father and son was deep and
natural but, though they differed greatly in temperament, they
were at one in their freedom from brooding reproaches, or self-
pity. Indeed, one might well have pointed out to the other that
in the 1895 match even so great a prodigy as C. B. Fry was dismissed for 1 and 0. Horrid as the thought of a pair of spectacles
might be, it was all in the game. Nothing was here for tears and
in a county game played very shortly afterwards W.G. Junior
made 62 against Notts in confident, hard-hitting style. Neurosis
was hard put to it to find a foothold in the Grace family.

W.G. Junior did not cling to the county cricket in which,
despite a few excellent innings, he had failed to make a particular mark, but he clearly enjoyed himself, in his quiet way, in less
serious cricket, sharing a first-wicket partnership of 337 in a
college match at Cambridge and an even bigger one for London
County in a minor match. He always played in spectacles and
was in style what the critics called a 'stiff cricketer' with little
ease of movement but a capacity, as his occasional big scores
showed, for hitting the ball extremely hard.

After coming down from Cambridge he became a schoolmaster first at Oundle and later at the Royal Naval College,
Osborne. In 1905, just ten years after the Varsity match which
brought such delight to his father, he died of appendicitis for
which the operation was not performed sufficiently promptly.
That he died at thirty, the same age as his youngest uncle, Fred,
was a tragedy involving the loss of a valuable young life, and of
a fine character of unchallenged integrity. There was tragedy in
his early death but there was no tragedy in his relations with
W.G., for no father and son ever loved and respected each other
more deeply.

v

Besides praise, there were for W.G. money rewards in 1895.
These came through natural outbursts of generous feeling from
the British public whose heart is frequently in what used to be
called the right place and whose head is not so often in the

wrong place as its detractors allege. It is difficult in the present
age to imagine a flood of admiration that is completely natural.
Today the idol of the moment is supported like the ping-pong
ball in the fairground shooting gallery by a jet of pumped-up
publicity which can be turned on or off as with a tap. Turn off
the tap and the idol falls, because it has no vitality or character
of its own. This may be necessary or indeed inevitable in a
world of competitive screaming for recognition but, by the
beard of the press agent, it is not spontaneous.

The tributes to W.G. that poured in were natural and instinctive and were couched in language which may sound
sententious to the modern ear but, in its context, was wholly
sincere. Such praise expressed, it was said:

> 'the general love for those outdoor sports and pursuits which,
> free from any element of cruelty, greed or coarseness, most
> and best develop our British traits of manliness, healthy
> training of the mind and body; and at the same time giving
> pleasure and amusement to the greatest possible number.'

The words are flowery, but the facts are well rooted enough.

There were many suggestions in the newspapers, some
facetious but most of them serious and sensible, that W.G.
should be knighted and among the more surprising trophies
awarded to him was the gold medal of the Balloon Society of
Great Britain.

The promoters of the material tributes to W.G.'s prowess
did not have to whip up enthusiasm: they merely distributed it.
The flood of admiration was canalized into four main channels.
There was the *Daily Telegraph's* National Shilling Testimonial
which amounted to £4,281 9s. 1d.—who gave the odd penny?
—and which the newspaper's proprietor, Sir Edward Lawson,
later Lord Burnham, regarded as 'a manifestation by classes
and masses alike of their abiding preference for wholesome and
honest amusements in contradistinction to sickly pleasures and
puritanical gloom . . .'

In a letter sending five pounds to the fund, Lord Salisbury,
one of the least nonsensical of Britain's Prime Ministers, wrote:

'I beg to enclose a centenary of shillings, to use the current phrase. I have not touched a cricket ball for more than fifty years—so I am afraid that I can only claim a "locus standi" as owner of a village cricket ground. You are kind to refer to the cricket of my sons. I regret to say that it is wholly despicable.'

Imagination toys respectfully with the reactions of Viscount Cecil and Lord Quickswood to this paternal libel. The newspaper did not suffer for its generosity.

A contemporary cartoon, showing a large W.G. receiving the cheque from a small newspaper proprietor, makes Sir Edward say:

'Don't mention it, Doctor. Look what you've done for my circulation.'

This fund formed a firm foundation. *The Sportsman*, the paper to which W.G. was to write his famous wartime letter, collected a second fund and agreed to its amalgamation with a third started by M.C.C. A fourth fund raised by the Gloucestershire county club, of which the Duke of Beaufort was president, brought in an additional sum of nearly £1,500 and the total handed over to W.G. was £9,073 6s. 5d.

Mr. A. G. Powell, the veteran authority on the Grace family, regrets that, beyond the bare notification of £100 presented to the Fund, there is no mention in the county club's records of the culminating triumphs of their own favourite, and cricket's most illustrious figure. He can only attribute this odd omission to the fact that E.M., as the club's secretary, was inclined to frown on all this fuss about a member of the family. The modesty of the old-fashioned Englishman can seem to the outsider to have a touch of arrogance in it and E.M. was very English. His attitude may possibly have been: 'It is well known that we Graces are good, but we don't need everyone in England to go around shouting about it, dash their eyes!'

Amid all the applause and rejoicings of the year there was one sad event. In November, Henry, the eldest of the Graces, died

suddenly at the age of sixty-two. It was Henry, we remember,
who took the young W.G. to play in his first game in London
and insisted, as temporary chieftain of the clan, that the boy
should play in the next match at Brighton, an insistence which
started W.G. well on his mighty career in first class cricket.
Henry was a sound if not brilliant cricketer, and, by his very
nature, a devoted if not brilliant doctor. There was in him his
full share of the family character. The Graces could conduct
their family quarrels very prettily. In the famous game in
which W.G. was caught by a fieldsman leaning back over the
boundary, Henry was on the fielding side. When W.G. raised
his historic heart-cry, 'How many times have I told you,
Oliver', Henry shook his fist in the harassed umpire's face and
shouted: 'Be a man, Oliver; be a man and give him out!' Out
went W.G. at length, which proved that Henry was also a
formidable character. It also shows that a stranger might well
misunderstand some aspects of the Graces' family fun.

Like his father, Henry loved his cricket in summer and his
hunting in winter and he filled the unforgiving minute with
sixty seconds' worth of duty done and sport enjoyed. He would
have claimed that he worked hard and played hard and, though
the precept has an old-fashioned ring, it remains true that its
fulfilment stands high among the simpler human satisfactions.

VI

It would hardly have been possible for any cricketer of W.G.'s
age to improve on his achievements of 1895. This was his peak
year and no man of forty-seven had ever risen to such a peak.
What is remarkable is that 1896 was only a little less glorious in
achievement. The rocket had by no means come down like a
stick, but remained long in a glow of its own to light the sky.
He had an aggregate of over 2,000 runs, which was only a
couple of hundred fewer than the previous year's heavy total,
and higher than any other yearly aggregate of his long career,
except for those three mightiest years of the eighteen-seventies.
In 1896 only two other batsmen, Ranjitsinhji and Abel, rivalled
him in reaching the 2,000 mark. Even among the brilliant

younger men, only the two at the top of the tree were fit for his company.

The Australians were in England again and it was in the first game of their tour, played against Lord Sheffield's Eleven at Sheffield Park, that Ernest Jones bowled the unforgettable ball through W.G.'s unforgettable beard. Jones was the fastest Australian bowler before Cotter and the ball proceeded over the wicketkeeper's head for four byes. For once the lightning had defied Ajax. 'Whatever are ye at?' demanded W.G., or, as some report, 'What's this, what's this?'

Trott, the Australian captain, said: 'Steady, Jonah,' and Jones murmured the classic apology: 'Sorry, Doctor, she slipped.'

Lord Harris says that this occurred in the first Test at Lord's but I am more inclined to trust the recollection of F. S. Jackson and C. B. Fry, both of whom were playing in the Sheffield Park game and were good judges of Jones's pace and power, if only because they received more than their quota of bruises. Jackson, never a complainer, got a cracked rib, Fry took some nasty knocks and W.G.'s chest was battered black and blue and red. Bruised to the colour of a Turner's sunset though he was, the Old Man made an imperturbable 49. Asked how he endured such a hammering, he replied: 'Well, he did rap me a bit sharp, but I don't mind even now how fast they bowl to me. It's the slow ones I don't like.'

In the same innings Shrewsbury and Gunn, it was whispered, unvaliantly got themselves out to dolly catches in the slips, while Ranji, whose footwork was like a leopard's, made a lovely but perilous 80 by 'flicking them off his nose'.

The Tests of that year were won by England after a close struggle. Tom Richardson, nearly as fast as Jones and far more accurate, settled the game at Lord's by taking six Australian wickets for 39 in their first innings. W.G., who made 66, helped Abel to supply a backbone to the English batting. The second game, played at Manchester, is known to history as Ranji's match, though England lost by three wickets, and rarely can so dazzling an artist have found himself on a losing side. In the first innings he and Lilley, the wicketkeeper, were the only bats-

The picture known as *The Champagne of Cricket*—the England team in the Oval Test of 1896, a superb eleven of W. G.'s late period. J. Phillips (umpire) T. Hayward, A. A. Lilley, T. Richardson, J. T. Hearne; A. C. MacLaren, K. S. Ranjitsinhji, W. G. Grace, F. S. Jackson, Capt. E. C. Wynyard; R. Abel, R. Peel

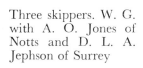

Three skippers. W. G. with A. O. Jones of Notts and D. L. A. Jephson of Surrey

Centenary tablet erected outside the county ground, Bristol

From the caricature at Lord's

W. G.'s 'hundredth hundred' Banquet. The menu on the back embraces turtle soup, salmon, pigeon pie, sirloin, roast lamb, chicken and duckling. Sherry, port, hock and claret were all 5s. a bottle and brandy 6d. a glass

men to reach fifty and when England followed on Ranji played, in his 154 not out, what must have been one of the two or three most brilliant innings ever played in a Test match anywhere. Imagination calls up Jessop at the Oval in 1902, Trumper at Sydney in 1904, Macartney at Leeds in 1926 and McCabe at Nottingham in 1934, but the lone splendour of Ranji may well have outshone them all.

In the third game the wicket was evil and there was deadly bowling on both sides, England's being slightly the deadlier. W.G. with a small but valuable score—his 24 on that pitch was worth many a century in easier conditions—rallied England's batting in the second innings. Thereafter, an act of skilled judgment helped him to settle the matter for good and all by putting Peel on after a maiden over from Richardson. Tom may have been surprised at being taken off, but Peel captured six wickets for 23 and the change was justified. The Australians were out for 44 and if the last man had not staged a wild hitting display, wielding his bat like a battle-axe, they might have made no more than 28.

W.G. consistently reached the top of his form whenever he was pitted against the attack of this strong Australian side. For a South of England eleven at Hastings he showed his mastery over superlatively good bowling with a half-century which was easily the highest individual score on either side. Even when Gloucestershire at Bristol were out for 17, he held to his principle of contributing more than half by scoring 9. In the other Gloucestershire game against the Australians his scores of 27 and 66 were small mountains, among the molehills of his colleagues, who did little against bowling that was much too good for them.

This was the year in which there occurred what we should now call industrial *malaise* among the English professionals. They were, by present-day standards, extremely ill-paid and their grievances came to a head in the belief, based on fairly ill-natured rumours, that certain amateurs, and especially W.G., were being paid excessive expense allowances. The feeling was so strong that before the Oval Test of 1896 the professionals who had been picked for it threatened to go on strike if their grievances were not remedied, and so many insinuations were made that the Surrey County Committee felt obliged to deny the most damaging of them.

'During many years, on the occasions of Dr. W. G. Grace playing at the Oval, at the request of the Surrey Committee, in the matches Gentlemen *v.* Players and England *v.* Australia, Dr. Grace has received the sum of £10 a match to cover his expenses in coming to and remaining in London during the three days. Beyond this amount Dr. Grace has not received, directly or indirectly, one farthing for playing in a match at the Oval.'

One sympathizes strongly with the professionals' demand for better pay and conditions, but the belief that W.G. had been making money out of his games at the Oval was genuinely refuted, for nobody could reasonably contradict the Surrey Club's statement.

There were four centuries this year: 102 not out against Lancashire, 186 against Somerset and a roaring cataract of runs against the lordly Sussex of Ranji and Fry, 544 'home and away' for once out, including a 243 not out and the third three-hundred of his career—301. By the very laws of nature it was clear that a man of forty-eight could not go on riding the whirl-wind in this fashion for ever but it almost seemed, in these two innings, as though time had run back to the years of the glorious 'seventies and acknowledged his claim to immortal strength. It was as though he had cast off the years with his sweater when he went out to bat.

VII

In this year E.M. retired; not from cricket, you understand, for he cannot be said to have retired from cricket until he died, fifteen years later, at the age of seventy. In 1896, however, he gave up playing regularly for his county. E.M. was, always excepting W.G., the most remarkable of the Graces, and his early impact on cricket was just as striking. Indeed, even W.G.

did not burst so flamingly upon the fields of Canterbury as did E.M. at the age of twenty and in the capacity of an emergency man. In this game he virtually exploded like a bomb, just missing a score of 200 not out and capturing all ten wickets in the enemy's second innings. He was fifty-five when he retired from first class cricket and had played in quite good class cricket from the age of thirteen. Like his brother, he had irrepressible energy; he wanted to be doing something every moment of the game. He liked to go in first; then, by quickness of foot and eye and a punitive unorthodoxy of stroke, he would demoralize the bowlers. At the wicket he would never keep still; nobody knew till the last instant what kind of a stroke he would attempt and, even then, it was generally something wholly unexpected. Often he would bamboozle the field by pretending to start off on an impossible run and he gained many an overthrow in that way. 'A proper comedian,' said my old Downend cricketer. 'He could have gone on the Halls . . .'

He believed not merely that attack was the best form of defence, but that cricket was no fun without it. When warned of the difficulty of the bowling and the urgent need for steadiness, he would flare out: 'A fat lot of good you fellows have done by your steadiness. F.U.N.K., that's how it's spelt and I'm going in to stop it.' And, as W.G. commented, stop it he did. A bowler who has lost his length knows that he will be punished, but there are few who could stand up to having good length balls on the middle or off stump consistently pulled straight over the square-leg boundary. That is what E.M. loved to do. He was born a breaker of enemy morale. His brother Alfred once said that nobody could bowl a bad enough ball to get him out.

It is said that E.M.'s earliest bowling was the old round-arm stuff, but that, having hurt his shoulder in a hunting accident, he took to cunningly flighted lobs which tempted and deceived. As a fieldsman he carried out his attack on enemy morale by standing close in at point. This policy of intimidation by propinquity was highly successful and he was acclaimed as by far the most dazzling point of his period, even bolder and more brilliant than W.G. was to become later. E.M. fielded at point, not, as some veterans do, because he was too slow to field anywhere else but because he would have liked to snatch every ball straight off the blade of the bat. His friends sometimes asked him ironically if he were not afraid of getting splinters from the bat in his hand. His was the post of peril that a later generation saw claimed by the formidable Yorkshireman, Emmott Robinson. ('Thee get on wi' thi' lakin', Mr. Foster, and I'll get on wi' mine.') He once actually caught Stoddart, a man utterly unintimidable by close fielding, in a position so near to the crease that he was able to hand the ball to the wicketkeeper without moving a step.

One of John Wesley's more imaginative biographers felt obliged, for reasons that escape me, to find a family villain for the sake of the story and was pleased to cast Charles Wesley for the part. If such a foolishness were attempted with the Grace family, perhaps the award might go to E.M. All the Graces were keen on winning and E.M. was the keenest. If the rights of the clan were threatened, all the Graces protested and E.M.'s protests rang out loudest of all. If the clan charged into battle, E.M., so to speak, waved the claymore and sounded the pibroch simultaneously. He enjoyed, perhaps even more than W.G., the rigour of the game. He played harder and rode harder than any of the others. He suffered few fools gladly and was seldom tempted to offer the soft answer that turneth away wrath. It may even be that some of the legends of super-keenness attributed to W.G. really originated with E.M. It is true, too, that we owe the gaps in our knowledge of what happened at vital moments in the earlier history of Gloucestershire cricket to E.M.'s honourable but exasperating reticence. But, by any standard, E.M. was a splendid cricketer, a fine gentleman of the old school and an intensely vital human personality.

He was, even a little more than his brothers, a rugged individualist and a fanatical devotee of the game. His physical vitality was colossal and it was truly said of him that he overflowed with cricket at every pore, 'full of lusty life'. In contrast to the tall W.G., he was comparatively short. As against W.G.'s six feet two inches his height was only five feet eight and a half, but he was immensely strong and agile and, if put to it in pursuit of his horse, he could leap over a five-barred gate in hunting kit, top-boots and all. There are stories of his dealing faithfully with barrackers and indeed of his chasing them all over Clifton Downs. There are two sources for the legends. One came from a Somerset game in which Sammy Woods hit E.M. on the hand with a venomous shooter. E.M. dropped his bat and a voice from the crowd shouted: 'Hold an inquest on it, Coroner!' E.M. whispered to the Somerset captain: 'May I go after him?' Then he set off in pursuit of the barracker and did not give up the chase until his quarry had fled from the ground. Then E.M. came back, resumed his innings, and hit up a hearty 70. The other story concerns an authentic incident which happened after the match in 1896 between Gloucestershire and the Australians at Bristol. In this, as we have seen, the county were heavily defeated and, as the match finished all too early, E.M. challenged H. Donnan of the Australian eleven to a single-wicket match without fielders. The game was begun but never finished, because a presumably intoxicated spectator kept shouting rude remarks from behind the bowler's arm. Stung to fury by the interruption, E.M. dashed towards the interrupter, who fled for his life. How far E.M. chased him and what induced E.M. finally to break off the chase, it is difficult to ascertain sixty years later. When questioned on his return, E.M. said: 'He's still running!' I have seen a letter from Mr. Donnan, now an extremely hale old gentleman nearer ninety than eighty, who remembers the incident clearly and regrets that the single-wicket match was never finished.

A third barracker ventured some critical observations on E.M.'s batting one day when he was leaving the field of play. Reaching over into the crowd, E.M. seized his critic by the collar, but the man wriggled clear and shouted from a safe distance: 'Look yer, Coroner, you can sit on a dead man with twelve men to help you, but you can't sit on a live man!'

Of his slightly fantastic doings with his own club of Thornbury the stories are countless. He once, with C. J. Robinson, put on 357 for the first wicket and at one time all the available balls were out of the ground. The Thornbury umpire, who was also the local postmaster, always went on the field with his pockets crammed with cricket balls. This time he conceded nine and they were all 'put away'.

E.M. would never abandon a fixture merely because he could not raise an eleven. One Saturday afternoon in July 1888 he turned up at Dursley with a side consisting of C. J. Robinson, F. L. Cole to keep wicket, and his redoubtable self. 'We'll give you a good game,' he announced to the Dursley captain and went on to

(1) pick up eight non-cricketing rustics;
(2) win the toss;
(3) score 147 with Robinson for the first wicket.

Cole and the rustics added nine more and then Dursley were quickly tumbled out twice. Thornbury won by an innings and E.M. took fourteen wickets in the match.

In a game against Sneyd Park, E.M. refused to let Thornbury bat unless the wickets were re-pitched north to south instead of east to west, because of the powerful effect of the sun in the batsmen's eyes. Neither the umpires nor the opposing captain would agree and the match had to be abandoned.

Once at Thornbury he indulged in a big hitting match, challenging the bowlers to get him out. He watched a mighty lofted hit which did not quite clear the fence, slowly descending into long-on's hands, shouted: 'I declare!' stalked back to the pavilion and commanded the scorer to set him down as 'not out'.

E.M. married four times, his second wife being the lady who had once been engaged to Fred. His humour had a touch of the sardonic. His reputed reply to the prepaid telegram, asking him to hurry back to an inconvenient inquest, *Put corpse on ice till close of play*, was a sign more of his fun than of his fury, and it might be claimed that modern refrigerative science has long since adopted his suggestion.

A man may give devoted service to a cause in return for the pleasure he gets out of it, but nobody could derive selfish pleasure out of being a club secretary. From its inception till two years before his death, E.M. was secretary of the Gloucestershire county club and he carried the bothersome burden lightly, without staff and without grumbling. Mr. A. G. Powell has given an unforgettable picture of E.M. jogging along among the spectators scattered round the county ground and stuffing their proffered subscriptions into his pockets. He continued, laughing and joking, on his way, without jotting down a single note, but every member got his ticket and receipt in the morning. This forceful character did not fail to give his opinion at committee meetings, whether it was asked for or not, and he once caused a rumpus by his insistence on his right to vote.

When he retired from the county secretaryship in 1908 he received a testimonial, raised by public subscription, which amounted to £600, an acceptable but by no means massive sum. This was presented by the Duke of Beaufort, president of the Gloucestershire club, and it showed a genuine if perhaps belated appreciation of the altruistic service E.M. had rendered for nearly forty years.

Long after he had given up turning out for the county, E.M. played good club cricket, mainly for Thornbury on its beautiful village ground, and though he no longer completely terrorized the bowlers by ferocious hooking, he continued to be a difficult man to get out. His bowling continued to have a hypnotic element. In 1905, that is in his sixty-fifth year, he was writing: 'If my knees had not been so bad, I should have had 200 wickets by now.' And the date of the letter was 5th July. He once sardonically suggested that he had three hundred catches missed off him in a season.

He died in 1911 and was buried, like his parents and youngest brother, in the churchyard at Downend. The funeral service in the church was crowded and movingly, if with a touch of unconscious irony, the congregation sang the old warrior's favourite hymn:

> '*Tell me the story simply*
> *As to a little child . . .*'

VIII

In 1897 W.G. enjoyed a tranquil year, and some people in that year of Diamond Jubilee surmised that perhaps W.G. was saving himself for his own jubilee, for he would be fifty the following July. Nevertheless, he made more than 1,500 runs, including four centuries, two against Notts, one of them against an excellent touring side from Philadelphia. He played some games on a short tour in Ireland and Patrick Hone, author of *Cricket in Ireland*, was photographed with W.G. and the slim and handsome C. L. Townsend. W.G. called out: 'Hey, Challie, come and have your picture taken!' But when the two stood together W.G. frowned. 'Challie makes me look too fat,' he said, 'so come in, boy.' And that is how young Patrick, aged fourteen, was photographed with the great man. His batting average that summer was down, but, as it was only down to 49, many a man might have envied his declension. His bowling figures showed improvement, too, and the bright illusion that he could go on for ever almost seemed to hang in the summer air of that glittering Diamond Jubilee year. The great Albert Schweitzer has said that you can burn the candle at both ends if it is only long enough, and W.G.'s candle seemed infinitely long.

This was the time when, as G. M. Trevelyan has said, 'the pageant of distant and diverse lands, all come to do homage to the little lady in grey, was displayed with startling effect in London streets . . .' Many colourful characters were to be seen, visiting Britain as members of the jewelled spectacle of Empire: Indian rajahs, Canadian 'Mounties', bearded Sikhs, dusky African chieftains in their flowing robes. . . . Yet among them all no vivider figure was on view than W.G.

It was from this time that he rose (not lapsed) into the title of the Old Man and the only Englishman who could compete with him for that title was the Grand Old Man, William Ewart Gladstone himself, who died, full of age and honours, the following year. The only figure, after the aged Queen, who could compete in contemporary renown with these names was, surprisingly enough, a fictitious character, lately created by a cricketing doctor. The character's name was Sherlock Holmes. It would make an interesting study to compare W.G. with Holmes, with special reference to their unique methods, their unchallenged supremacy in their own fields, their favourite operations in the Baker Street area and their common recognizability by the man in the street. Without doubt, the fictitious character had come near to fact and the factual W.G. had developed many of the attributes of heroic fiction. This must be left, however, until some member of the Baker Street Irregulars writes what Holmes himself would unquestionably have called a 'fascinating monograph' on the subject.

Popular enthusiasm swelled once more into a Handelian conquering-hero chorus as 1898 swept W.G. on towards his fiftieth birthday. Philip Guedalla, smiling at the English love of Grand Old Men, once said there was nothing they enjoyed so much as wheeling bath-chairs up the slopes of Parnassus. W.G. was now only half a centenarian and, though continually battling with his bulk, needed, by heaven, no bath-chair. That season he made three centuries and was well set for a fourth, when suddenly he raised his hand and brought his partner in.

'What on earth made you declare when you were 93, W.G.?'

'I just remembered it was the one score between nought and a hundred that I'd never got.'

On a broiling day at Lord's there was a palpitating finish to the Gentlemen v. Players game in which a crippled, battered W.G. played a hero's part. To be just, there was another hero, too. The Gentlemen had the worst of the wicket and suffered a minor martyrdom against the most destructive of England's professional bowlers, J. T. Hearne, Lockwood, Schofield Haigh and Brockwell. Limping but obstinate, W.G. fought them all for an hour and a half and his score of 43 was worth double. On the third day on a damaged wicket the Gentlemen were given the impossible task of making nearly 300 runs to save the game. Worst of all, W.G., who had a badly bruised hand and was dead lame, had to put himself in late. Instead of batting in the No. 1 position, which he had held by right for thirty years, he did not go in until seven wickets had fallen for 77. In point of fact he had not meant to bat at all, but J. T. Hearne's break-back bowling had forced the pace of dismissal. Even then, two more wickets fell quickly and when, at twenty minutes to six, he was joined by Kortright, a demon fast bowler but hardly a reliably defensive batsman, spectators prepared tolerantly to watch a wild, heroic hit or two and then go home.

From the instant of Kortright's arrival they found themselves watching the most enthralling game of the season. W.G., lame as he was, nursed his partner cunningly, and Kortright, resisting a natural temptation to have a go and get it over, played with resource and a truly noble restraint. Steadily the score mounted, the hands of the clock moved round. W.G., unable to ride the whirlwind, was superb in directing the storm, while the normally volatile Kortright, under the master's inspiration, remained steadfast as a rock. It was half-past six. They had batted exactly fifty minutes and Kortright gave a gulp of relief, but it was premature. He vividly remembered the crowd surging in over the boundary, while W.G. flourished his bat and yelled to them to go back. Shrewsbury, the Players' captain, had claimed the extra half-hour and the struggle had to begin again. The half-hour seemed an eternity, but at five minutes to seven Lockwood came on. The first two balls were fast and Kortright blocked them. 'Well played,' called W.G. from the other end. The third ball was Lockwood's killer, a slow, 'hanging' ball of deceptive flight. Kortright hesitated, made a Laodicean stroke and was lost. To his intense exasperation, for he knew it was his own fault, he saw the ball skim upward and forward, to be nicely caught by Haigh running back from cover. The Gentlemen had lost in what was virtually the last over, but it was one of the most gallant defeats in cricket history. Say not the struggle naught availeth . . .

This warm summer of 1898 was a gay and fruitful season and W.G. enjoyed it hugely. Though little given to introspection, he may well in years to come have looked back nostalgically upon those sunny months.

He was still to do some outstanding things, but this was his last truly triumphant season.

CHAPTER FIVE

WINTER

I

THE summer of 1898 brought pleasure, but before the year was over W.G. and his wife suffered a cruel blow. In December their daughter Bessie died of typhoid. The tragedy was sudden and medically hard to explain. Bessie was a true child of Grace, tall and strong with grey-green eyes, bubbling with humour and vitality, fond of games and, as some friends of the family said, with the makings of as good a cricketer as any of them. She was educated at Clifton High School and once made a dashing 63 for Ladies of Clifton against Ladies of Glamorgan. In the family records she was set down as 'a good bat, an underhand bowler and a splendid field'. She took turns with her brothers at scoring in county matches and, with family strength of charac-ter, forced W.G. to wear a muffler one bitterly cold May day in 1898. W.G. was stricken by the loss and his wife, quiet and steadfast as always, was prostrated with grief. One major reason why W.G. afterwards consented to accept the manager-ship of the new cricket ground at the Crystal Palace was that, following the end of his medical appointment in Bristol, he had taken up residence in Sydenham and he hated leaving his wife at night, deeply upset as she was by Bessie's death.

The loss of his only daughter in 1898 and of his eldest son less than seven years later formed the two most tragic afflictions in W.G.'s life. Another event, less calamitous but undoubtedly painful, was his break with the county of his birth. The *Memorial Biography* gives, for understandable reasons, the meagrest account of this. The older-fashioned biographer's reasons for a particular reticence are seldom as discreditable as his detractors allege. He may be unwilling to hurt living per-sons and he may find knowledge of the facts hard to obtain.

Neither of these reasons, as a rule, restrains the other, and more regrettable, kind of biographer. A decent and intelligible account, conveying what is virtually the only coherent information available on the affair, is to be found in the previously quoted triple biography, *The Graces* (*E.M.*, *W.G.*, *and G.F.*) by A. G. Powell and S. Canynge Caple. The hero of this volume was not always right, nor were the people with whom he sometimes disputed always wrong, yet it is difficult to find W.G. more than, say, a quarter culpable in the matter of his dispute with the committee. There is embarrassment in the quarrels of good men and, though there is drama in the clash of personalities, it is more edifying when seen on the field, between bowler and batsman, than in the committee room. W.G., as is nowhere hidden from us, could be 'a harbitrary gent' when crossed, but he was certainly not the only awkward customer concerned. Responsibility for the breach might reasonably be apportioned: W.G., twenty-five per cent; Committee, seventy-five per cent.

There had, of course, been disagreement before this on the question of picking the county teams. Here is a typical letter which shows the semi-feudal manner in which he summoned his warriors to service:

'Dear Francis,
   I shall want you at Gloucester against Notts July 14, 15, 16. Hope you will have better luck than you had at Cheltenham. Yours truly, W. G. Grace.'[1]

As captain, W.G. had the right to pick 'his' team, a right which had been delegated to him by the committee early in the history of the club. It was, I am sure, a right that he would have demanded in any event, but it was inevitable that there should be a school of thought both in the county and on the committee who disagreed with his methods of choosing. The argument is one of those old differences of temperament and opinion which have existed and, in some form or other, will go on existing

---

[1] Here is another: 'Dear Edmund, I cannot play, you will lick them. Ted [E.M.] has no one but himself and Nicholls. W. G. Grace.'

for ever. Broadly, W.G. preferred a side filled with amateurs and particularly youngsters from the universities and public schools; furthermore, he had a flair for discovering them. On the other hand, there were many talented cricketers in the various clubs throughout the county who felt that they never got a look in. Their grievance was genuine and their friends on the committee did not hesitate to say so. That the club cricketers should not have their chance was clearly unjust, though it is possible that, with a few exceptions, they were hardly of county standard. On the other hand, W.G.'s preference for the school and university amateur was neither merely snobbish nor perverse and he was especially anxious to have young men about him who would be able to turn out more regularly than the club players would be likely to do.

At a committee meeting in the early 'nineties the argument suddenly boiled up. Some committee members must have complained of what they considered W.G.'s autocratic attitude, while he flared out against what he felt to be their interference. Before anybody had quite realized what was happening, W.G. had resigned from the committee and from the captaincy as well. At the next meeting a request was made to W.G. to withdraw his resignation and in the dispute that followed the chairman himself resigned.

It is hard to discover what actually happened next, but wiser or at least more pacific counsels prevailed and W.G. and the chairman were both asked once more to reconsider their decisions. This they agreed to do but, while W.G. returned to the fold, he stuck to his guns and refused even to consider the notion of a selection committee.

'I will have nothing to do with it. I do not think it will help us to win matches or that it would work at all satisfactorily . . .' Arbitrary, indeed, wrongheaded, if you like; but it is what even the most amiable and co-operative committee-victim feels about committees much of the time.

For some time after this episode an uneasy peace reigned, but the grumbling went on underground and was bound to go on as long as Gloucestershire were doing badly. By 1895 W.G. had seemingly vindicated his policy, partly by the brilliance of the

young men from the schools that he had brought in, for no one
could deny the abilities of such youngsters as C. L. Townsend,
G. L. Jessop, and C. O. H. Sewell. There was also vindication
in his own astonishing personal success, which was capable of
turning aside almost any criticism.   While these triumphs
lasted, he was almost bound to get his way. Nevertheless, the
basic difference remained and in 1899 it was to arise again in a
new form. Without a hint of the gathering storm, W.G. went off
to play in the four away matches that opened the season. He
then received a copy of a resolution, passed by the committee,
demanding that he should state exactly what matches he intended playing in during the year.

   This was both an ultimatum and an innuendo. The committee had learned, though they did not say so, about the invitation W.G. had received to manage the new cricket club at
the Crystal Palace. It even appeared that W.G. was being
brusquely told to make up his mind and choose between the
two clubs. Now every single member of the committee must
have known that it was a dangerous business to point a pistol at
the head of a Grace. It is ungracious and unfruitful to seek a
scapegoat at this time of day, but surely the majority of the
committee cannot have wished to be so offensive to a man who
had loved Gloucestershire with a love passing the love of
women. Someone should have known that they were accusing
him of extreme selfishness or even double-dealing and that he
would inevitably be offended and hurt.

   W.G. was imperious, maybe far too imperious, but he was not
presuming on his reputation. He was reacting normally as any
Grace would. He roared at them but by no means like any
sucking dove and showed them, only too well, that he was not a
naughty little boy to be snubbed. He had done more for the
glory of cricket, and particularly for Gloucestershire cricket,
than any man alive or dead, and had some right to be treated
with courtesy. He treated the ultimatum exactly as he would
have treated any other bad ball : he hit it for six. This was not
the moment at which he in fact uttered the semi-fabled
exclamation : 'Won't have it, can't have it, shan't have it !' But
it might well have been. His reply stands among cricket records

as Dr. Johnson's famous letter to Lord Chesterfield stands in literature:

> St. Andrew's,
> Lawrie Park Road,
> Sydenham, S.E.
> May 28th, 1899.

To the Committee of the Gloucestershire County Club.

Gentlemen, in answer to yours of the 26th, re resolution passed on the 16th and kept back from me for reasons best known to yourselves, I beg to state that I had intended to play in nearly all our matches, but in consequence of the resolution passed and other actions of some of the Committee, I send in my resignation as captain, and must ask the Committee to choose the teams for future games, as I shall not get them up.

I have always tried my very best to promote the interests of the Gloucestershire County Club, and it is with deep regret that I resign the captaincy. I have the greatest affection for the county of my birth, but for the Committee as a body, the greatest contempt.

> I am,
> Yours truly, W. G. Grace.

A. G. Powell, who is one of the few living persons with any real knowledge of the course of the quarrel, thinks the letter shows that W.G. tried to hold himself in until the last sentence and then, patience failing, let fly. There is no doubt about that final roar of the wounded lion. That last sentence, though it has won itself a niche in the temple of invective, had better not have been written. Up to that moment, it might be said, the committee had behaved unwarrantably. From then on they made creditable efforts to retreat from their false position. While they not unreasonably felt that 'no self-respecting body could accept such contemptuous terms' and hoped that W.G. would, on reflection, see fit to withdraw them, they made their suggestion in rational and respectful tones. W.G. never nursed his wrath to keep it warm but at this point it had hardly had time to cool down from its original temperature and he refused to withdraw.

The committee, for their part, could devise no direct way out, and there the matter rested. It seems clear, however, that there might have been no quarrel at all if their earlier communication had been couched in such conciliatory tones as the resolution which they passed at their next meeting:

'That while the Committee are conscious of the great services rendered by Dr. Grace to the Gloucestershire Cricket Club as well as to cricket generally, and feel deep regret at his severance from them in spite of the efforts which have been made by them to avoid it, they feel they have no course open to them but to accept his resignation.'

It was all over. The incredible had happened. W.G. would never again play for the county of his birth. The whole world of cricket was bewildered and saddened. It is easy to be judicial (it is never easy to be wise) after the event. Plainly everyone concerned might have employed more tact. W.G. might have explained that he intended neither desertion nor neglect. He might have shown how his natural bubbling optimism had led him to believe that he could run both the Gloucestershire and London County elevens without excessive difficulty. The committee might at least have reflected that they were dealing with a man nearing his fifty-first birthday who, in the course of nature—if W.G. indeed *were* subject to the laws of nature—could not go on playing cricket for ever.

Obviously both sides could (and no doubt should) have refrained from manœuvring themselves into impossible positions. Both sides might without loss of face have submitted the matter to some form of arbitration. (Here was work for an earlier Sir Walter Monckton, cricketer, conciliator, and Member of Parliament for a Bristol constituency.) Take it for all in all, it was a sad business, and no beating of the breast can make it better. But disputants did not give way then as easily as they do now, for their beliefs, whether right or wrong, were stronger. Time has brought a gain in tolerance but a weakening in conviction.

The least distressing element in the quarrel is the fact that

W. G. with Lord Hawke in Festival mood

'The long-whiskered doctor' with a highly successful England captain

from the moment the break became inevitable, ill-feeling dimin-
ished and in a comparatively short time died. In 1902
Gloucestershire made W.G. a life member of the club, 'in
recognition of his services' and in the same season fixtures
between Gloucestershire and London County were arranged.
In these two games the last breath of animosity was blown
away. London County won both, one of them crushingly.
W.G. must have chuckled good-naturedly in his beard over
that.

II

Not only did 1899 see W.G.'s last game for Gloucestershire; it
also saw his last game for England. This was played in the first
Test match of the season against the Australians at Nottingham.
Incidentally, this was the first Test ever played at Trent Bridge.
Against these tourists he had earlier in the season played a
dominating innings of just under 50 for an eleven of the South
at Crystal Palace. At Trent Bridge in England's first Test
innings he batted far better than anyone else in the team except
Fry and Ranji, but in the second he was bowled by a swift
breakback from Howell for one. (Jackson was bowled for 0 and
Fry and William Gunn made only a dozen between them.) He
said to F. S. Jackson after the game: 'It's no use, Jacker. I
shan't play again.'

C. B. Fry has given a tantalizing account of the meeting of the
selection committee that followed. As Fry approached the
doorway of the committee room, W.G. met him and demanded:
'Would you play MacLaren?' Considering the question on its
merits, Fry said 'Yes'. To his dismay he discovered, as discussion proceeded, that if MacLaren came into the team, Grace
went out. The moment Fry scented this, he naturally tried to
hedge on his opinion, but it gradually began to dawn on him
that he had unwittingly given the decision that was required
and that the others meant it to be so. 'So,' said Fry, 'I, who
owed my place in the England team to W.G.'s faith in me as a
batsman, gave the casting vote that ended W.G.'s career of
cricket for England.'

But Fry, who had suffered acute discomfort from all this, was eventually put out of his misery by the discovery that W.G. had intended to go in any event. He did not believe that he had seriously declined as a batsman or a bowler, but his bulk had handicapped him in the field—his hands were too far from the ground—and he had even been barracked by the Trent Bridge crowd, a body of citizens not diffident in their criticism, for not getting down to the ball. He needed no selection committee to tell him the meaning of that. In the next game of the Australians' tour, he played against them for M.C.C. and, just as a reminder that the old lion could still roar, he made a splendid 50 while the other batsmen were falling like ninepins to the violently fast bowling of Jones. Finally, he clean bowled Victor Trumper, the most brilliant Australian batsman before Bradman, which was nice work for an elderly gentleman who was thinking of giving up bowling. And in the second Test match the first English team to play without him in England was soundly beaten.

III

The London County Cricket Club had a comparatively short life but a gay one. In 1899 it had not been regarded as a first class county, but from 1900 it was officially recognized. W.G. enjoyed himself hugely for most of the time, wearing the dark green London County cap with its narrow bands of yellow-red-yellow. The splendid action photographs by Beldam in the *Memorial Biography* show him in this cap. In the fictional kingdom of the Crystal Palace he was a kind of jolly monarch and he worked hard to make his realm happy and successful. The cricket was lighthearted and more often than not he put a fine eleven into the field against the counties and universities. In his first match of 1900, for example, he was able to call on the services of such outstanding players as C. B. Fry, C. L. Townsend, G. W. Beldam and Leonard Braund, and in the course of London County's five first class seasons there were many of what we should now call 'guest artists', including members of touring sides, who felt personally honoured to play for the Old

Man. Among these were C. B. J. Wood of Leicestershire, C. McGahey of Essex, L. O. S. Poidevin, the Australian from Lancashire, and G. C. B. Llewellyn, the Hampshire South African. Visiting South Africans, M. Hathorn, J. H. Sinclair, W. A. Shalders and J. J. Kotze, also played in one or two of the matches.

In the later years at the Palace W.G.'s chief companion was W. L. Murdoch, now twenty years older, if not twenty years sedater, than when he won W.G.'s sovereign with his defiant century-and-a-half in the first Test match ever played in England. These two elderly schoolboys rollicked together through the first seasons of the twentieth century. In W.G.'s London County period he scored eight centuries, seven of them at the Crystal Palace, and did some useful bowling against the Australians in 1902, against whom he took eight wickets at less than a dozen runs apiece. When you reflect that England's 1902 side has been reckoned the best of all, and yet the Australians won the rubber, this seems a tidy achievement for a man of fifty-four.

London County's cricket was great fun, but not a financial success. It is argued, and the economic side of the argument is crushing, that, however talented the sides, you cannot draw big crowds season after season with 'friendly' matches alone. We go to see our side win, or, at any rate, to see it engage in a fierce grapple with a temporarily hated foe. This does not in the least mean that we do not go to see good cricket, but good cricket, like good drama, must hold within its framework an element of sharp conflict. This at least is the northern attitude, regrettable in the abstract, perhaps, but immovable in the concrete, and that it is not absent in the gentler and more civilized south was proved by the fact that London County failed to attract a partisan nucleus.

The club staged some excellent matches; it thrashed Gloucestershire twice without ill-will, and it revealed to the world the shining talents, undiscovered by Surrey, of Leonard Braund, who was soon to go to Somerset and become one of England's half-dozen greatest all-rounders. W.G. and Rhodes were, I think, his superiors and Hirst and F. S. Jackson were probably his equals, but, even in that richly golden age, there were very few who were anywhere near him in ability.

London County also assisted in the education of that remarkable character, W. C. (Razor) Smith, who in the next few years was to cut and trim Surrey's opponents to such purpose. On one occasion at the Crystal Palace, Smith was umpiring and had the temerity to give W.G. out leg-before.

'Razor,' said the Old Man wrathfully. 'I always thought you a fool. Now I know it.'

But W.G. thought a great deal of Razor Smith, and was heard to say: 'There's a fellow, not good enough for Surrey, might play for England.'

W.G. revelled in his cricket at Crystal Palace. 'Billy' Murdoch called him the Kent Colt because one of the many small jokes between them was that the Old Man was trying to qualify for Kent. There was never any telling what those two elderly jokers might be up to next. There is one story of their playing a country game in a spot where the angling was even more delectable than the cricket. Said W.G.: 'I'll bet you, Billy, I'll catch more fish than you'll make runs.'

'Done,' said Murdoch.

W.G. got up at four in the morning and fished away till he had caught a hundred, mostly roach, which should have been enough and indeed would have been if Murdoch had not scored 103.

Another small joke was the whistle which W.G. blew to summon Bill Murch, the old Gloucester slow bowler whom he had brought with him to be a sort of sergeant-major to his ground staff. W.G. would blow his whistle as soon as he came near the ground and, as Murch was rather deaf, the entire London County staff would rush out, as from an anthill, to see if Murch had heard it. An old acquaintance, visiting Murch, was alarmed to hear the Old Man rush in and shout: 'Bill Murch, you're sacked!'

'That's all right,' murmured Murch imperturbably, 'he sacks me twice a week.'

W.G. also came to enjoy his bowls, entering gleefully into the spirit of this by no means old man's game. He was the first man to arrange international tournaments and so may truly be called the father of international bowls. All the skills that go into this sober but absorbing game were of the kind to appeal to the cunning of his hand and brain. In a short time he became as popular a figure among bowlers as he had been among cricketers. He had the gift of green fingers and his bowling and putting greens at the Palace were always in perfect order. When he was not playing or practising cricket you would find him regularly on one of the bowling greens among his bowling cronies. A young relative of his who went up with him one April to watch Bristol City play in the Association Cup Final at the Palace was awed to see the number of people W.G. knew, or who knew him; the greeting was so enthusiastic that the Old Man and his nephew very nearly lost sight of the match altogether in the crowd.

In 1901 W.G. applied, on behalf of his London County Club, for admission to the Scottish Bowling Association, a body which might then have been described as the M.C.C. of bowls. Scotland had nearly four hundred linked clubs, while the other home countries had no associations. W.G. set the ball rolling for the forming of such bodies in England, Ireland and Wales and soon there were not merely four associations but four national sides. In 1903 the first international games were played at the Crystal Palace, as a compliment to W.G., and England won a needle contest after an exciting finish. These games went on every year until, eleven years later, the war stopped them. In 1906 W.G.'s England team won the international trophy. Until 1908 he was England's captain and in that year he took his side to Edinburgh, where he spoke at a Scottish cricket dinner and told his hearers that they ought to be sensible fellows, like bowlers, and play international matches. In all bowling matches he remained immensely popular and he was described as a reasonable and congenial companion on the International Board. He may even have mischievously hoped that the committee of the Gloucestershire county club might learn just how reasonable he was.

IV

The year 1905 was a sad one, for in it W.G. lost his eldest son,
who died suddenly after an unsuccessful operation for appendicitis. This was the second loss of a beloved child and the whole
of the rest of W.G.'s life was clouded by it. He was fifty-seven
and the London County Club, where he had enjoyed so much
fun, was folding up under him. His career in first class cricket
was, in the nature of things, almost over. Yet the old flame was
to flare up once again. In 1906 he made a few respectable
scores, and, for a side raised by himself, he played two really
fine innings against his old whipping-boy, Cambridge University. Then, in July, at H. D. G. Leveson-Gower's personal
request, he turned out for the Gentlemen against the Players at
the Oval. He reinforced his acceptance with a schoolboy grin.
'Well, I've been well advertised all my life. If I fail, it'll be
passed over. If I do well, it'll be a grand exit.'

It was a grand exit. The third day of the game was his
fifty-eighth birthday and his appearance before that happy
Oval crowd crowned a near-lifetime of joyous participation in
the game. Forty-one years had passed since he had played in
his first Gentlemen *v.* Players game on the same ground. All
that time he had gone on, in happy ruthlessness, 'giving the
Players a treat'. For the Gentlemen he had made over 6,000
runs, including fifteen centuries, and taken nearly 300 wickets.
His first century had been in 1868 and his last twenty-seven
years later. None of the other players in this 1906 game at the
Oval had been born when he first played in the series and there
were at least half a dozen of the young Gentlemen whose
grandfather he was old enough to be.

In the second innings of this game he played some of the
best of England's professional bowlers with the old ease and
mastery. He was, as he had always been, happier with the fast
stuff, but none of it gave him any serious difficulty. He looked
a little tired after he had made fifty, but until that moment his
batting was, as *Wisden* said, 'good enough to give the younger
people among the crowd an idea of what his batting was like in
his prime.' It was indeed an object lesson to show that, what-

ever anybody said, there had never been, and never would be, anyone like him. Even then he had his small private joke. He had taken a fancy to a bat in G. W. Beldam's bag. 'Take it,' said Beldam, 'but if you make a century today, you must give it me back with your autograph and score on it.'

W.G. chuckled. There was not much fear of that. Yet he made an almost perfect half-century and went on as far as 74, when he was caught by Trott. It is doubtful whether he or the crowd was more delighted with his success. He returned to the pavilion amid a storm of cheering. The members in the pavilion and the crowd round the rails were happily at one in their minds. Every man felt that he had been present on a truly memorable occasion. As he flung down his bat he exclaimed: 'There, I shan't play any more.' But he spoke with no sadness of farewell. W.G. had gone out, not with a whimper, but with a bang. At the end of the season he sent Beldam back the bat, signed and bearing his last big match score: 74.

v

W.G. had not much further to go in first class games. He turned out in the first match of the season at the Oval in each of the following two seasons. For his own Gentlemen of England side against Surrey he made 16 and 3 (bowled by his protégé, Razor Smith) and in 1908 in the corresponding match, which was played in an April not yet freed from winter's grip, he did well to score 15 and 25. In the first innings of this second game he batted for two hours in a courageous attempt to stave off the follow-on. These were the last times his name appeared in the first class averages. Cricket's great stage, the centre of which he had held for so long, was his no longer. That 74 at the Oval had been his grand exit line. He did not 'lag superfluous on the stage,' but quietly moved away to the wings.

He did not brood upon his sorrows, the loss of his two children and the fading of his great career. He was indeed a 'debtor to time and fortune' and for that double bereavement there was no consolation. But, so far as his sporting life went, there were many pastimes left to him. There was club cricket, there was golf, which he and Billy Murdoch took up together with intense mock-seriousness. It was impossible for him to play any game less than well and, once he had settled down to it, he achieved mighty deeds in handicap (if not of weight) reduction. In fact by sheer will-power he brought it down to nine.

There was bowls, in which he had become something of a champion, shrewd, calculating, the cunning old skip of the side. In winter there was curling, the game he had learnt from his Scottish bowling friends. In his enthusiasm he once alarmingly crashed through the ice on the Crystal Palace pond. There was also sport with the Worcester Park Beagles—he was living at Mottingham now—for which he never failed to turn up even in the worst of weather. It had always been a joke in the Grace family that all the brothers were valiant riders to hounds, except W.G. who, when he reached seventeen stone, could not find a horse with a backbone strong enough to carry him. (One wonders what the great John Jorrocks would have said to that.) Because of his skill at 'finding' he was presented with a whistle, or perhaps he carried the whistle with which he had been used to awaken Bill Murch from his lair in the morning. Whatever the source of the whistle, he blew it with maddening frequency.

'Why don't you take it away from him?' demanded a visitor.

'Take it away?' was the reply. 'No fear, he's always right.'

Perhaps he enjoyed the golf most of all, with his many friends and especially his old comrade-in-arms, Billy Murdoch. When young, they had been rival champions in the first Test match played on English soil. At the other end of their cricket careers, they had been jesting companions and opening batsmen at the Crystal Palace, where the professional jokers called W.G. 'Father' and Murdoch 'Muvver'. Now on the Mid-Surrey golf course they amiably battered their way round with some skill, a little skulduggery (as between friends) and an immense amount of boisterous chaff. No kind of weather, however evil, could keep W.G. off the course and the characteristic portrait of him at golf would show him battling on in snow storm or thunder shower. He liked his fun, and a bit of sheer fooling as well, but he would not have been W.G. if he had not learnt to play

extremely well. He would never be a champion, but he was an
excellent performer. He drove powerfully and putted with
judgment. The wristwork of the man who had caned all the
fast bowlers of England and Australia in forty years of cricket
was bound to be supple and strong. His friend, G. W. Beldam,
cricketer, golfer and inventor of high talent and photographer of
genius, was also the man from whom he borrowed the bat with
which he made his last good score. Of the Old Man's golfing
days he wrote: 'On the links he seemed to brim over with joy;
the heath, the breeze, the sunshine, the comradeship, he enjoyed them to the full, and his happy childlike nature was the
more evident because of his huge form . . .'

Murdoch went back to Australia after the London County
Club had passed away. For a time W.G. lost touch and was
delighted when he received a postcard from him. One day in
the winter of 1910–11 in the excitement of watching an
Australia v. South Africa Test match at Melbourne he collapsed
from an apoplectic seizure and died on the ground. It is an
ironic oddity that Billy Murdoch, who had demanded that
W.G. should be embalmed, had already made arrangements for
his own body to be embalmed and brought to England for
burial. And so he went to Paradise by way of Kensal Green.
It is ironically sad that W.G. could not attend the funeral of his
old friend, for W.G. was at the bedside of his brother E.M.,
who indeed died two days later. So, within a week passed from
the scene two of the closest companions of W.G.'s life.

W.G. could, of course, never quite give up cricket, and he
enjoyed turning out for the local club. The captain of one club
has left a striking picture of W.G. running slowly but purposefully between the wickets, with 'the ground apparently shaking
beneath his feet'. There was also the solemn spectacle of W.G.
keeping wicket and C. B. Grace, his engineer son, bowling
tempting lobs. There is a photograph of him with the rest of the
Eltham team, taken just before the war; his beard is silver, his
hands and feet are quite as massive as legend has since made
them and he is wearing a giant-sized trilby hat. The centenary
of the establishment of Lord's upon its present site was celebrated in June 1914 and happy multitudes watched a game in

which a Rest of England team, beneficently treated by the weather, defeated the powerful side which had toured South Africa the previous winter.   W.G. was roundly cheered wherever he appeared on the ground and at the centenary dinner, held at the Hotel Cecil with Lord Hawke in the chair, he received an ovation worthy of a prince.   His name, along with Lord Harris's, was coupled with 'County Cricket' and Mr. C. E. Green, who proposed it, said: 'Dr. W. G. Grace is, as you all know, the greatest cricketer that ever lived or ever will live . . .'

W.G. rose and a tornado of cheering broke out such as can hardly ever have greeted an after-dinner speaker before or since. He looked round and saw them: the fine flower of amateur cricket, the Gentlemen whose almost unconquerable Champion he had been for nearly half a century.   He could not but have experienced a surge of emotion, sentimental but strong.   There may, too, have crossed his mind that mischievous suggestion which had occurred to him on one or more unsuitable occasions: 'Shall I give 'em one of my Canadian speeches?'

When he spoke, his mood was both generous and lively and he said something like this: 'County cricket is as good as ever it was.   I will only say this about cricket: the young players don't make enough use of their legs as they ought for punishing the bowling.   I have not seen much first class cricket in the last few years but I reckon that the Test match play is rather too slow.' (*Slow* . . . And the current English Test side included Hobbs and Woolley.)   A twinkle came into his eye and his voice quickened.   'I'd give 'em four days for Test match cricket and if they couldn't finish the game in that time, they had better begin it all over again.'

He played for the Eltham Club in July 1914 only a few days before war broke out and he went once more to Lord's to watch Hobbs's benefit match, which could not be played at the Oval because that ground had already been taken over by the War Department.

During history's most fateful August he was a prey to anxiety and, greatest of games players as he was, he was worried that young men should go on playing and watching games when their country was in peril. On 27th August there appeared in *The Sportsman* one of his rare letters to the press:

To the Editor of *The Sportsman*

Sir,—There are many cricketers who are already doing their duty, but there are many more who do not seem to realize that in all probability they will have to serve either at home or abroad before the war is brought to a conclusion. The fighting on the Continent is very severe, and will probably be prolonged. I think the time has arrived when the county cricket season should be closed, for it is not fitting at a time like this that able-bodied men should be playing day after day, and pleasure-seekers look on. There are so many who are young and able, and are still hanging back. I should like to see all first-class cricketers of suitable age set a good example, and come to the help of their country without delay in its hour of need.

Yours, etc.,

W. G. GRACE.

In the last game that he played for Eltham against Grove Park in July 1914, he made 69 on an 'undertaker's' pitch and he remained undefeated at the end. The last game he attended was a charity match at Catford Bridge on Whit-Monday the following year. Those who were drawn there by his name did not know that they were seeing him for the last time. An account of this game has been given by a player who made a century in it, Captain Percy Burke, who was a batsman-wicketkeeper for Kent second eleven and afterwards for Bedfordshire. The proceeds of the game were to be given to the fund for Belgian refugees and W.G. had promised to play. When he arrived at the ground, however, he felt unwell and thought it would be unwise to play. 'It's a pity,' he apologized, 'but I'll tell you what: I'll go round with one of the collecting boxes.' His unspoken thought was that the many who had come for his sake should not be disappointed. At least they would be able to tell their grandchildren that they had seen him. So this charity game gave one corner of what remained of the cricketing public its last two glimpses of the Old Man : first, when he walked round among the crowd, jingling his collecting-box, laughing, chaffing, and leg-pulling, just as E.M. had done, gathering in subscriptions in early-season days at Clifton. The last glimpse of all was of W.G. making one of his short gruff speeches, presenting congratulations (and a bat) to Burke, who had been the hero of his side's innings. Now at seventy-seven Burke is a proud old gentleman, proud of his own admirable career, proud of the talents of his great-nephew, Jim Burke, the Australian batsman, and proudest of all of having received a bat and a generous word of praise from the greatest cricketer who ever lived.

VI

There are two further pleasant pictures of the Old Man in his last days. One shows him smiling with sincere pleasure at the news of his son's promotion to captain in the Royal Navy. (H.E. continued his distinguished naval career until he retired with the rank of admiral in 1934. He died three years later.) The other shows W.G. being interviewed by a social worker who wanted a place to hold his annual sports for 500 poor London children on the sports ground at Lee. 'You can borrow the lot,' said W.G., 'ground, gear, waitresses and all. But mind you,' he added with his old schoolboy grin, 'all the crockery you smash you'll have to pay for !'

All through the summer he worked in his big garden at Mottingham, where he had laid down a matting practice wicket. He had always been a keen gardener, with a happy green-fingered touch with turf and lawns. All through that same summer the nation was less peacefully engaged. It was occupied, and justly occupied, with matters of heavier moment than the life and death of any cricketer, however renowned. In June at his home in Sydney died Victor Trumper, best loved of all Australian cricketers and, except for Ranji, most dazzling of all batsmen. But the world had harsher work than mourning.

Yet even in the savage grapple of the European struggle to save the sum of things, even after the dreadful slaughter of Loos, those who heard it could spare a pang of sadness when they heard that W.G. was ill. Working in his garden, he had a sudden stroke. He managed laboriously to struggle into the house, but, once he had been put to bed, he was unable to get up. On 12th October Mrs. Grace was pathetically writing to the author who had asked W.G. to look over the proofs of his book: 'The doctor is ill and may not do anything . . .'

Later she asked Sir Henry Leveson-Gower, whom W.G. always called 'Snipe' instead of 'Shrimp', to go and see him and W.G. said that he disliked the Zeppelin raids. (Who that was within their range did not?)

'Why, W.G.,' said Leveson-Gower, rallying him cheerfully, 'how can you be bothered by Zeppelins, seeing you played all the fast bowlers of your time with ease?'

'Ah,' replied W.G., 'I could see those beggars, I can't see these.'

A few days later he tried to climb out of bed, stumbled and fell. After he had been helped back into bed, he never got up again. Perhaps, like the Falstaff he in some sort resembled, he 'babbled o' green fields'. On the twenty-third of the month he died, dismissed, in his friend, C. I. Thornton's phrase, by 'the last bowler, Death'. And if the trumpets did not sound for him on the other side, then surely the bells of every heavenly pavilion pealed out a welcome. German papers said that he had been the victim of a Zeppelin raid, which was, in a sense, indirectly true.

He was buried at Elmer's End Cemetery, not far from the Crystal Palace, on 26th October, an afternoon of winter rather than autumn weather. The cemetery chapel was packed with mourners, most of them cricketers, in or out of uniform. There they were, the men bred in Gloucestershire: J. A. Bush, the wicketkeeper who had been his best man, O. G. Radcliffe, who had shared many partnerships with him, R. F. Miles, Frank Townsend and the rest of them. With them was C. E. Green, who had played for several counties and a year before had proudly proposed his health. There was the Jam Sahib of Nawanagar, once known as Ranji and now in staff officer's uniform, and with him were those civilians in khaki, P. F.

Warner, H. D. G. Leveson-Gower and the Somersetshire hitter, H. T. Hewett. Many professionals were there too: not those rugged warriors of W.G.'s golden days, James Shaw, Fred Morley, Tom Emmett and Happy Jack Ulyett, for they had died before him. These were the working cricketers of a later time: Alec Hearne, Huish, the Kent wicketkeeper; Martin, the left-hand bowler who had rattled the Australians in 1890; Razor Smith ('I always knew you were a fool') and Philip Need, the Lord's dressing-room attendant, whose benefit match was the last in which W.G. had turned out to play.

When the procession wound from the chapel to the graveside, the massive coffin was followed by members of the family, by C. L. Townsend, most brilliantly apt of the Old Man's cricketing pupils, and by Lord Hawke and Lord Harris, those two great captains of the north and south, who had been his admiring coevals and were to live on into an age that knew not Grace.

They laid him under a hawthorn tree, beside his son and daughter. There are other trees nearby: a horse-chestnut behind and a sycamore on the right. In forty years of sun and rain they have grown in girth and spread their branches. On that melancholy day they looked shabby and forlorn. Ended was cricket's great age in which he had played and laughed with schoolboy gusto. And as that great company melted away into the darkening shadows of the October evening, there was hardly one among them who could fully realize the bitter truth: never again would they hear that jolly high-pitched chuckle or see that mighty figure at the crease.

> *From quiet homes and first beginning*
> *Out to the undiscovered ends,*
> *There's nothing worth the wear of winning*
> *But laughter and the love of friends.*

The laughter was stilled. The love of friends, valiant and abiding, remained and will remain as long and 'as sure as God's in Gloucestershire'.

CHAPTER SIX

THE CHAMPION

'No monument, no portrait, no book can adequately represent either the vitality of W.G. or his superb skill in the game he loved.'

LORD HAWKE.

I

In the celebrated oil-portrait that was painted in 1888 by Archibald Stuart Wortley and now hangs in the Long Room at Lord's you see W.G. in characteristic stance. His cheeks are bronzed and his beard dark and bushy. His right foot stands squarely along the popping crease, his left well forward, the toe of his brown boot raised. (Billy Murdoch said he raised his toe to tread on a yorker but, in fact, it was next to impossible to bowl him a yorker because he could automatically convert it into a full toss.) The bat, which looks small in those huge hands, is raised in a high back-lift. The pose is easy, balanced and, most clearly and plainly, poised for attack. ('But, Dr. Grace, would you stand as easily if the game were in a tight place?' the artist asked. 'Certainly,' said W.G., 'because, after all, I should only be facing the next ball.')

All his life he was facing the next ball. He was not 'the greatest batsman the world has ever seen' merely because in his career he scored just under 55,000 runs, including a thousand in a season twenty-eight times. Four batsmen—Hobbs, Woolley, Hendren and Mead—have surpassed the first of these feats and Woolley has equalled the second. W.G.'s records are immensely impressive by any standard of any time, and by those of his period stupendous, but records do not tell the whole story. Mere figures do not tell his stature among his fellows or explain that he was a giant among giants, an Everest, not above the foothills, but above the Himalayas. Figures do not depict the dramatic hostility of the bowling, or show that during the whole

of his career, from 'Fearful' Jackson and 'Tear-'Em' Tarrant
to the Demon Spofforth and Ernest Jones, it was hostile to the
point of physical violence; they do not tell how evil many of
the pitches were, even (and indeed especially) at Lord's and the
Oval; and they do not tell you that, unless you had hit the ball,
say, into St. John's Wood Road or its territorial equivalent,
everything had to be run out.

His supremacy rested on two foundations: the first was his
superb physical health from which he drew his quickness of
eye, strength of arm and, above all, his unquenchable energy.
There is a story from fairly unimpeachable sources that he had
only one lung, but medical friends are apt to be disrespectful
when the supposition is mentioned. The man who made 282 on
a bitter-cold day towards the end of his forty-seventh year and a
gay 74 on his fifty-eighth birthday was unlikely to be a lung
short. The second basis of his mastery was the inspired early
coaching of Uncle Pocock in the orchard at the Chestnuts,
coaching which insisted above all things on sound defence and
the straight bat. It is not genuinely paradoxical, when the
question is reconsidered, that the methods of this hard-hitting,
swift-scoring batsman were built on the rock of solid defence.
He thought nothing of the two-eyed stance. 'These fellers,' he
said, 'don't know how to hold their bats.'

W.G.'s batting had grandeur and not elegance. It was
massive and ingenious. W.G. was not a 'beautiful' bat, as were
R. A. H. Mitchell in his earliest and L. C. H. Palairet and R. H.
Spooner in his later days. He would seldom dazzle the eye with
sheer witchery and enchantment, as did Victor Trumper and as,
to this day, Denis Compton can sometimes do. He was not a
subtle magician like Ranji, some of whose leg-glances came
near to sorcery and were as far removed from credibility as the
Indian rope-trick. He was not so polished as Hobbs or so
elementally roof-wrecking as his county colleague, Jessop. He
did not create the game of cricket or invent the elements of
batsmanship. There were handsome batsmen before him, such
as Silver Billy Beldham of Hambledon and William Ward and
Fuller Pilch; there were, as we know well, imperial batsmen
after him: Hobbs and Hammond and Bradman and Hutton

and Compton and a few, but not many, more. His career was immensely long and at each end of it there were great batsmen. They were, however, considered great only as coming near to himself. For all the years of his playing life, then, he was cricket's overlord.

I have already quoted Ranji's metaphor of the single-stringed instrument and the many-chorded lyre. He also said: 'W.G. discovered batting; he turned its many straight channels into one great winding river.' W.G. played all the old strokes with greater force than had been known before and, indeed, as a rueful Kent bowler observed: 'There's only one thing the Doctor has to learn and that is to hit 'em up high.' He also brought in one stroke which he made peculiarly his own: a hard push to leg with a straight bat. This was the stroke of which it was said: 'Oh, yes, he blocks the shooters but he blocks 'em to the boundary.' Of this stroke, too, he is himself reputed to have said (no doubt apocryphally): 'I don't like defensive strokes: you can only get three off 'em.'

'There is something monumental in his stance at the wicket,' said Andrew Lang, 'wholly free from a false refinement, without extraneous elegances. His is a nervous, sinewy English style, like that of Fielding.' He could, and did, hit all round the wicket and he could keep this hitting up all day. His superb skill as a batsman can never be dissociated from his energy, stamina, and quick clearness of eye. There were few firework displays but every ball was regarded as something that could be hit. He hit the ball hard and he did not relish the thought of failing to score off any ball sent down. 'Leaving the ball alone,' he said, 'never won matches.' He would have scorned the half-hearted modern habit of leaving alone any ball outside the off stump. Indeed, he felt it somehow immoral that a ball should be allowed to pass his bat. Old Parson Wickham, who kept wicket in his brown-topped pads in the game when W.G. made his hundredth hundred (and then another hundred-and-eighty more), said that in all that time W.G. let only four balls go by. Some commentators have said it was five and some have said six, but Wickham should be allowed the last word. He was there all the time.

10

One of the hardships that drove W.G.'s opponents to admiring exasperation was the extreme difficulty of setting a field for him. His power of placing, gained in the hard school of batting against Eighteens and Twenty-Twos, seemed uncanny. As soon as you moved a fieldsman, the ball went whizzing past the spot he had just vacated.

Not merely did W.G. hit almost every ball: he hit it in the middle of the bat. Critics of style have claimed that that was his highest distinction. In 1884 the Australian tourists complained that English bats were wider than they ought to be. Some English players conscientiously measured and even planed the edges of their bats. But W.G. only laughed and said he didn't care how much they shaved off *his* bat. 'All I want,' he said, 'is the middle.'

It was, of course, part of his character and of his devotion to the game that he hated not making the best of every single innings. What else did you have a bat for? Almost everybody who batted with him grew tired as time wore on, but W.G. never. His imperviousness to fatigue made him seem relentless, for the bowlers grew weary so long before he did. In the golden 'seventies it was said that he 'made all the bowling plain and all the bowlers desperate'. The professional bowlers were so overjoyed to see the back of him that when one of them finally got rid of him he would fling his cap in the air with delight. Once Tom Emmett missed him off a simple caught-and-bowled and was so mortified that he flung his cap on the ground and danced on it. He then kicked the ball to the boundary.

'Kick it again, Tom,' said W.G. 'It's always four to me.'

At the end of each over throughout the day Tom apologized. 'I weren't mad with thee, Doctor. I were mad with my-*sen*.'

You had only to look at W.G.'s brown, hairy, massive forearms to see the power which he could put into a stroke. In his earliest period he never retreated from his maxim of the firmly fixed right leg. He even advocated that the beginner's right foot should be pegged down until he gained ease and confidence in playing back and forward. He disagreed with the notion that the weight should be equally distributed on both legs. 'The weight should be chiefly on the right foot and kept there when you raise your bat to play the ball.' Watching an early Test match, A. G. Steel said of him : 'Other men keep their right foot steady, but W.G. never moves it during the actual stroke, and that is what I have always envied in him most.' He would cut, as E. D. H. Sewell said, 'off the right foot the long-hop which others often cut off the left foot.'

Twenty years later when told that his methods were out of date he stuck to his guns, but maintained that the policy of the firm right leg was not aimed at the correct disposal of the body's weight but to prevent the novice from drawing away his foot, and therefore his body, from a rising ball towards short-leg. (This was what Patsy Hendren afterwards called 'kicking the square-leg umpire'.) 'And,' W.G. added, 'I have always believed in footwork, but pulling away from the wicket and footwork are two different matters. Footwork comes with experience, after a batsman has learnt to take up a proper position.'

There were critics who half-humorously approved of W.G.'s firm-footed stance because, as they maintained, if he had added to his own princely gifts the star-twinkling footwork of a Ranji, it would have been impossible even to hope to get him out. If he had learned and practised the quick-footed backstroke thirty years before in the orchard at Downend, then, they argued, 'an intervention of Providence would be required to shift him.'

He loved, and chastised, the fast bowlers and their medium-fast colleagues, though he greatly respected George Freeman and Tom Emmett. A fifty against those two on a difficult wicket, he reckoned, was as good as any hundred scored in any condition against anybody else. He respected Spofforth, too, if only because the Demon was not crippled by reverence for him. Morley was a fierce fast bowler, too, but he said of W.G., after being sadly hammered by him on a rough pitch at Trent Bridge : 'He hit me for a couple of sixers off his eyebrows and then I bowled him through his flaming whiskers !' There was a memorable occasion when, on an appalling wicket at Lord's, W.G. blocked four venomous shooters in succession from the same bowler. They would so obviously have bowled any other living batsman that the crowd rose and cheered him as though he had just completed a century. It is also a fact that he hated the bowling that was called 'slinging'. His method of dealing with slingers did not include appealing to the umpire against an unfair delivery, as was his undoubted right. His way was to subject them to retributive chastisement. There was another memorable occasion when W.G. was savagely hit about the body by Crossland, to the vocal anger of the large crowd. Limping haughtily to the boundary, he told the spectators to mind their own business. He then went back to the crease and subjected the bowlers, and especially Crossland, to a positively sadistic century.

With the slow bowlers he was perhaps not quite so happy, but happy enough. Alfred Shaw clean bowled him twenty times, Barlow thirteen, Briggs ten and Peate nine times. Here were fifty-two separate feats spread over many years. But nobody has calculated how many of his 55,000 runs were scored off the slow bowlers. 'I love 'em all,' he once said in an expansive moment. Broadly, this was true and certainly none of them had any serious terrors for him, not even Wilfred Rhodes, who played his first Test in 1899 when W.G. played his last. 'I never saw such a fellow for hiding the ball,' said W.G. 'He kept the ball out of sight such a time and didn't seem to let you have a look at it until it was almost upon you . . .'

Though his technique was masterly, he did not surround it with a smoke-screen of pretentious nonsense. I once heard J. M. Barrie tell how he came upon Thomas Hardy, sitting among a crowd of people, all talking at once, about Art. 'He was the only one who knew anything about it and he never said a wor-rd.' W.G.'s attitude to his undoubted art was similar. When asked what was the best way to play a particularly awkward ball, he replied thoughtfully: 'I should say you ought to put the bat against the ba . . all.' And as he said it, his vowel was as broad as his bat. The reply was neither facetious nor pompous. It was both simple and profound, because, however clever the techniques you might invent for dealing with a difficult kind of ball, they would come to naught if you failed to observe the elementary precept of putting the face of the bat squarely against the ball. There is no substitute for first principles.

He was no great believer in an anxious watching of the bowler's hand. He preferred to watch the ball and not to anticipate the break. This, he argued, applied especially to googly bowlers who in his later days had begun to bowl an off-break with a leg-break action. He quoted with strong approval the counsel given on this problem by Arthur Shrewsbury, whom he considered the next best batsman in England to himself. 'If this kind of bowler,' said Shrewsbury, 'pitches a ball outside my off stump, I expect it to break in from the off and I'm ready to play it that way. If it breaks the other way I leave it alone. But if it pitches on my legs or between my legs and the wicket, I expect it to break in from leg; if it does, I play it, if it doesn't, I leave it alone. And what's more,' added Arthur shrewdly, 'I bide my time, because I never saw one of those chaps who didn't bowl one or two bad balls in an over, and I'd get a four off those . . .'

That was the principle—it was no secret—on which W.G. batted. Everything that could be hit he hit hard and straight. For a kind of sunlit magic he could not be compared with Ranji and Trumper, but for sheer dominance of the scene there was none to compare with him before and only one after : Sir Donald Bradman. Similarly, one may say of Bradman that his batting was not so lovely a spectacle as that of his contemporary, Stanley McCabe, but of his absolute subjugation of the bowlers on the field of play there is no shadow of doubt. Wilfred Rhodes, who took more wickets in first class cricket than anybody else and had as richly varied an experience in taming batsmen as W.G. had of battering bowlers, had no doubt in his own mind who was the greatest batsman he had ever bowled against. This man who had bowled against Trumper, Jessop, Ranji, MacLaren, Fry, Hobbs, Hammond and Woolley told me : 'Why, Bradman, of course. I once saw him come in and put his first ball past the bowler for four. And the second. And the third. Just like that. Without getting his eye in or anything. You should have seen the power of it, and every one a defensive stroke off a good ball . . .' This was a true description of Bradman's dominance and, by the same token, it could have stood as a description of W.G.'s as well.

Each of these great batsmen towered above his age, with the difference that Bradman's age was shorter and that he retired on health grounds, as Hutton retired later, before his powers had waned. There was a striking difference in the physical presence of the two men, the difference between the heavy hunter and the racehorse, the bulldozer and the Bentley. Grace's height and reach were commanding, even before he began to put on weight, and his limbs were long and sinewy; Bradman was neat, not obviously muscular, and almost a little man, achieving the opposite effects of looking both dapper and dynamic.

Both practised with almost fanatical concentration when young. Grace was master on bad wickets and on good. The wickets of his stupendous triumphs in the 'seventies were, by modern standards of groundsmanship, almost uniformly bad; indeed, they were literally lethal, as in the fatal match at Lord's in 1870 that killed poor Summers. Bradman shone less often on bad wickets, but I have always felt that the reason for this was no reflection on his competence. Bad wickets were, in his view, outside the realms of serious cricket. He believed that a great batsman should no more be asked to perform on ruined wickets than that, say, Walter Lindrum should have been called on to play on 'a cloth untrue with a twisted cue and elliptical billiard balls'. W.G., not to put too fine a point upon it, was not so fussy. Philosophically or perforce, he put up with whatever wickets he could get.

W.G. had astonishingly keen eyesight at the age of fifty-eight, so that in the years between twenty and thirty his vision must have been more than remarkable. Watching Bradman, you would have said that his eye was equally matchless. You would have been wrong: his eyesight was normal rather than super-normal. His jet-propelled speed in moving to the pitch of the ball came not from eyesight but from his footwork, to which not even Ranji's was superior. This is another reason for believing that Bradman was contemptuous of, rather than inadequately equipped for, play on a bad wicket. A cricketer

who combined Grace's eyesight and forearms with Bradman's
footwork would have been even further outside the limits of
human achievement (and credibility) than either of these great
men in fact was. Both were massively effective in execution,
not in any dull or mechanical way, but in the sense that their
batting was potent far beyond that of any of their contemporaries and almost invulnerable.

I was once in company where the venerable question was in
its perennial process of being tossed about: how much had
cricket methods changed since the time of W.G. and how would
the Old Man get on today? The opinion was rather freely
expressed that, with the advance of bowling techniques and the
increased concentration on a tight leg field, he would have been
hard put to it to survive. My own view, offered without dis-
respect to anyone, was that the Titan would not, so to speak, be
tamed by a Titmus. He might pull his beard over the first ball
or two and have a good old-fashioned look at the bowling for
the first over or two, but all the time he would 'put the bat to
the ball'. Then, having taken its measure, he would settle down,
as he had done any summer day in forty years, to play the new
bowling comfortably.

The question came round to a very old cricketer who had
played against W.G. in his London County days and, as a boy,
had watched him in the eighteen-nineties. His tone was
courteous and almost compassionate.

'Why,' he said, 'he'd *murder* 'em.'

II

You will remember that W.G. began his career as a round-arm
bowler of medium pace with an action as high as the laws would
allow at the time. Gradually he adopted the slower, guilelessly
guileful delivery, well remembered today by elderly Gentlemen
who saw it when they were boys. His success in his first
Gentlemen *v.* Players game was with the ball rather than with
the bat and nobody doubted his worth as an all-rounder. It
may have been a pardonable exaggeration when Bob Thoms,
whom we might call the Frank Chester of his day, asserted that

if W.G. had not been the best batsman of all time, he would have been the best bowler. There are many candidates for that hypothetical honour. It depends on your period and your allegiance: David Harris, Alfred Mynn, Alfred Shaw, F. R. Spofforth, Sydney Barnes, E. A. Macdonald, Harold Larwood, 'Tiger' O'Reilly. . . . For myself, I should plump for Wilfred Rhodes, whose figure of more than four thousand wickets over a period of more than thirty years is fantastic and almost unanswerable.

But while W.G. could hardly be considered among the greatest half-dozen bowlers, he was well worthy to march in their company. He was a great—the greatest—natural batsman. His contemporaries agree that he was a 'made' bowler: that is, by resource and perpetual practice, he made himself into something far more than a creditable performer. One thing is certain: if he were not a 'great' bowler, he was an almost maddeningly successful one. You cannot take nearly three thousand wickets in first class cricket without being a formidable attacker. These wickets were taken in a career during the greater part of which first class matches were far less frequent than in a modern season. Counties were few and in the other 'big' matches the opposition was formidable. Yet he took 2,864 wickets in first class games. How many he took in games that were less, some only a little less, than first class, only God and Mr. Neville Weston know.

It is an added wonder that many of his most stupendous bowling feats were performed immediately after he completed some big innings, lasting four or five hours. And without doubt he was the most ineluctably persistent of bowlers. 'Just one more over.' 'I'll have him directly.' Or, as when his captain suggested a change: 'All right, then, I'll go on at the other end.' These were phrases cherished and remembered by those who had been with him on the field. His bowling figures were remarkable and good judges surmise that, had he been content to bowl a little less, they would have been more remarkable still.

A. G. Steel left a pretty picture of the Old Man in action: an enormous ogre of a man rushing to the wicket with both elbows out, great black beard blowing on each side of him, red and yellow cap on top of a dark, swarthy face. . . . Thus confronted, the batsman expected something more deadly than a gently lobbed-up ball that actually arrived; he could hardly believe that this milk-pudding sort of bowling was really the great man's.   Consequently he became flustered and lost his wicket.   W.G.'s bowling looked difficult when it was easiest and easy when it was genuinely tricky.   There is evidence, too, that he had a firm command of length.   Nearly every bowler of W.G.'s era, in contrast to some in our own, kept a reasonably consistent length; otherwise he would not have found a place in a county side at all.   W.G.'s length was unexceptionable and though no wizard as a contriver of break, he could turn the ball sufficiently to bother an inexperienced batsman, particularly when, as has been noted, he was looking for non-existent terrors in an innocent delivery.   To a newcomer he would murmur blandly: 'I'll get you out, boy; I always get young 'uns out.'   And he usually did, but if you looked downcast, he would say: 'Come along to the nets in the morning, and I'll show you how to play that ball.'   W.G. at all times used his height and used his head.   It was his heart that prompted him to suggest the nets in the morning.

He got many of his wickets from catches at long-leg, for even an experienced batsman found it difficult to resist having a swing at a slow ball on the leg side, apparently sent down for the purpose of offering a bonus in the shape of an easy and satisfying six.   This hit did not as a rule quite go for six.   Instead, it came down after a period practically in the stratosphere, descending into the safe hands of cousin Gilbert or of brother Fred, the most predatory and prehensile of long-legs.   W.G. was once heard to say: 'You saw old Mary Ann (Ephraim Lockwood) look round to see how the field is placed?   I'll make him put one right into Fred's mouth.'   And, as by some act of hypnosis, that is exactly what he did.   Everything happened as if the ball had been on the end of a long piece of string.   But although he took many wickets in this way and loved to tempt the demented to destruction, he did not like it to be thought that this was the sole weapon in his armoury and he would not have been pleased to hear that E. V. Lucas called this his 'bread-and-butter ball'.

There was far more than bread-and-butter on W.G.'s plate. In the famous match against Notts in 1877 he took seventeen wickets for about five runs each : the last seven of these fell to him in seventeen balls for no runs at all, three of them in one over. It is no compliment to the batting side to call it bread and butter. It was, in more modern phrase, a piece of cake.

W.G. believed in trying every form of cunning attack. He even believed that, in the last resort, a bad ball would sometimes steal a wicket, particularly from a good batsman who treated it with contemptuous carelessness. In the Gentlemen v. Players game at Lord's in 1896 he had been audaciously hit about by Frank Sugg. Imperturbably placing every fielder except himself and the wicketkeeper out in the deep, he saw Sugg caught at long-on in the next over. He sometimes even bowled the googly, as M. Jourdain spoke prose, without knowing it. The lumbering sway of his body as the ball left his hand with a slight leg-break could, if the wind was blowing across the wicket, achieve an off-break with a leg-break action.

He seemed to sum up every batsman's weakness and he would play on it as a dentist plays on a hollow tooth with his drill. Most of all he took an impish delight in bamboozling you out.

III

When he was young, W.G. was a notable outfield, though, in fact, in his first Gentlemen v. Players match, he fielded brilliantly at cover-point; in later years he was a sturdily courageous point, but his most spectacular fielding was done in none of these positions. At his most brilliant he regularly took catches—hard and low or hard and high—off his own bowling somewhere between cover and silly mid-off.

In 1866, in his eighteenth year, W.G. was reckoned outstanding in the long-field, and especially at long-leg, the position in which young Fred was to achieve even more sensational renown. W.G.'s throw-in on the run was one of the sights of the period. The ball seemed to be bowled rather than thrown. It had, according to the records, a peculiar spin that often baffled the wicketkeeper. Sympathies go out almost auto-

matically to the wicketkeeper, for W.G.'s throw-in at this time
when he was at his fastest as a runner and hurdler, must have
been a formidable affair. His record for throwing the cricket
ball was 122 yards, set up at Eastbourne. At the athletic sports
held at the Oval in 1868 when the team of Australian aborigi-
nals were paying their solitary visit to England, he threw the
cricket ball 116, 117 and 118 yards in successive throws and,
although these came nowhere near the absolute record of 140
yards 2 feet, achieved by R. Percival sixteen years later, it was
an impressive feat, especially as, when he had finished, he threw
the ball back a hundred yards in sheer exuberance.

W.G. gave up fielding in the deep fairly early in his career
because of a damaged shoulder and took up a position near the
wicket. He disliked fielding at slip but, as we have observed,
he never minded keeping wicket. (There is a record, late in his
life, of his keeping wicket in a club match at Eltham, joyously
whipping off the bails as the batsman missed the insidious lobs
bowled by his youngest son, C.B.) He was never as hostile and
thrusting a fieldsman at point as E.M., who was an almost
sinful performer in this position, but he was a point to be feared.
It was not true, as E.M.'s admirers alleged, that W.G. was 'not
within streets of E.M.'; he was practically in the next street.

Even when older and bulkier, he never lost a certain degree of
agility. When the ball collided with either of his huge hands,
there was a sound like a smack on a board, and the board was
extremely hard. The ball went into those hands, as C. T. Studd
said, like a pea into a top hat. On his American trip a startled
critic wrote: 'It would seem as if the ball were fascinated by
Mr. Grace's basilisk eye, for it seems to jump into his hand.'
When on his first trip to Australia, he and his friends were
afflicted in the small back-blocks town of Stawell by a plague
of Egyptian dimensions. Smiting a fly-covered table with one
mighty hand, he slew seventy-six. It was the hand of fate and
the hand of a master-fieldsman.

But the form of fielding he enjoyed most was a gallop towards
silly mid-off directly he had delivered the ball. He always had
his mid-off straight behind him to cover the empty space.
There was something mesmeric about this action which was not

wholly dependent on the subtlety of the delivery. Without any good reason within the laws of physics, the ball would get itself cocked up, as if under some malign influence, in his direction. Some of the catches he made off balls of this kind were easy, some were brilliant, but almost all of them were willed and dictated by a personality stronger than the batsman's. In the Old Trafford Test match of 1888 he took four of these catches, none of which, in the ordinary conceptions of fielding, might have been regarded as catches at all.

Once, in a country game, a ball sent down by W.G. was skied high and hard above square-leg. Yelling to square-leg to get out of the way, W.G. came pounding forward like a charging buffalo. As, with one hand stretched out in front of him, he seized an astonishing catch at full gallop, the bewildered batsman was heard to mutter: 'That chap won't be satisfied till he's keeping wicket to his own bowling.'

In his first class career W.G. took 871 catches. It is usual in such comparisons to leave out wicketkeepers, and if this is done, the only fieldsman with a greater number of catches to his credit than W.G. is the long-armed Frank Woolley.

W.G.'s unconquerable might as a batsman, his craftiness as a bowler and his agility as a fieldsman, need no emphasis. These qualities in combination comprise the most striking phenomenon that has ever appeared on the cricket field. Added to this concentrated wealth of talent was the natural confidence that he possessed and with which he inspired the rest of his side. If W.G. was with you, the game was not lost until the last ball had been bowled. Conversely, if he was against you, the game was never won till the last moment. He revelled in a crisis but did not approach it, 'grim and pallid'. His determination was strong; it was also cheerful. Being human, he occasionally failed with either bat or ball, but failure instantly became a thing that had to be redeemed and redeemed handsomely. Think of those two first-innings ducks for which the misguided James Shaw dismissed him. The retribution exacted in the second innings of each of those two games was overwhelming. You literally never knew when you had him. His consistency over the years was unique.

When someone ventured the opinion that W. L. Murdoch was as good as W.G., Alec Bannerman scornfully replied: 'Murdoch?   Why, W.G. has forgotten more than Billy ever learnt.'

As for Murdoch himself, hero of the first Test match played on English soil, he had no illusions about the comparison, and his own tribute was sincere in the Murdoch manner.

'What do I think of W.G.?   Why, I have never seen his like and never shall.   I tell you my opinion, which is that W.G. should never be put underground.   When he dies his body ought to be embalmed and permanently exhibited in the British Museum as "the colossal cricketer of all time".'

CHAPTER SEVEN

THE DOCTOR

'He was a good gentleman, with no pride whatever . . .'
UNKNOWN PATIENT OF DR. GRACE

I

C. B. FRY says that, according to a wholly unfounded witticism, W.G. was the only man who ever received a medical degree because of successful operations on the cricket field. This was one of the many quips aimed, but without malice, at W.G.'s professional qualifications. He took such jokes in good part and, when they were running short, was always happy to replenish the store himself. Speaking of a difficult maternity case, he said: 'Well, the baby's dead and I don't think there's much hope for the mother, but I do believe I shall pull the father through.'

It is just as probable that he said this as it is improbable that it ever happened. He was himself the sponsor, if not the inventor of many slightly outrageous stories of the kind and delighted in such highly fictitious sallies as the reply alleged to have been given to a patient inquiring timidly at the surgery door:

'Is Dr. Grace in?'

'Of course he's in. He's been batting since lunch-time on Tuesday.'

Or in his imaginary injunction to the anxious mother of twins suspected of measles:

'Put 'em to bed and don't bother me unless they get up to 208 for two before lunch.'

He said of his eldest brother Henry: 'He was a good doctor, he was.' My own belief is that W.G. was a good doctor, too, and that hundreds of patients in the poorer part of Bristol would have gratefully agreed. He may have progressed towards his qualifications at a more leisurely pace than he would have advanced towards a century, but in the end, as the most venerable of all the W.G. anecdotes relates, he 'got his diploma'.

The medical registration examination he passed was that of Durham University. He then studied, as his father and brothers had done, at the Bristol Medical School and afterwards did his practical training at St. Bartholomew's and Westminster Hospital. For two years after his return, with his bride, from the extended honeymoon of his first Australian tour, he studied at Bart's under Howard Marsh and A. E. Cumberbatch. For a short time after that he stayed with his brother Henry at Kingswood and acted as his assistant. When the young couple returned to London they lived first in Earl's Court and then in Acton and W.G. 'walked' the wards at Westminster Hospital under the famous Dr. Allchin. It was the work done at the Westminster which enabled him to qualify for his L.R.C.P. By the end of the year 1879 he had become a Licentiate of the Royal College of Physicians at Edinburgh—this was the diploma of the Tom Emmett story—as well as Member of the Royal College of Surgeons (England).

For the greater part of the next twenty years, he followed his profession in Bristol both as parish doctor and as general practitioner to a large working-class practice. This practice was large enough for him to employ an assistant all the year round and a locum during the cricket season. Without labouring the point, it may be said that he did not neglect his patients for his cricket. Summer's lease hath all too short a date and the official cricket season is not a long one. If W.G. practised batting in his garden on a cold February morning or played an occasional Saturday afternoon game in October, no patient suffered. Even in the height of the season, he always liked to be home from his cricket for the week-end. Once he was back in Bristol he could not keep away from his patients, and he put in a great deal of work on Saturday and Sunday evening. The county club made him an allowance towards the expense of paying a locum. The allowance, which was at first fixed at £20 and afterwards increased to £36 as fixtures became more frequent, is hardly evidence of a grasping nature in its recipient.

Whatever his bedside manner may have been, his crease-side

manner was unexceptionable. Once E. M. (Joe) Hadow made a running catch at deep square-leg to dismiss W.G. and, unable to check his career, stumbled forward to fall with his head against the projecting metal edge of a stand. On his way back to the pavilion W.G. paused and administered first aid with a gentler firmness than he could reasonably have been expected to display towards a man who had just caught him off a hit that should have been a six.

Palmer, the old Kent wicketkeeper, was badly cut over the eye by a fast bumper which had just whistled past W.G.'s head. Efficiently if painfully, the batsman stitched up the wound. When play was resumed, W.G. stepped out of his ground to hit a slow ball for six, missed it and was stumped. He gave the wicketkeeper a reproachful parting frown.

'After all I've done for you,' he growled, 'that's what you do to me . . .'

The most famous example of W.G.'s cricket doctoring involved the undoubted saving of life. The patient was A. C. M. Croome, the old Gloucestershire cricketer and cricket writer, who in the county's Lancashire match in 1887 had gashed his throat on one of the spiked railings in front of the pavilion at Old Trafford in a vain effort to save a four. The laceration was deep and while messengers were scurrying round Stretford to find a surgical needle to stitch it, W.G. held the jagged edges of the wound together. It was a matter of life and death that the injured parts should be kept perfectly still and the Doctor's hand never shook for one instant. He literally held the victim's life in his hand for nearly half an hour and such a feat would only have been possible to a man of his iron nerve and fantastic stamina. It would have been remarkable at any time but W.G. had been in the field all day and done a good deal of bowling, as he always did. That he should have held on without the slightest twitching of finger and thumb was something near a miracle.

The nerve and endurance displayed on that day were of greater value to the individual patient than any amount of tact and suavity, and there were few men and women among W.G.'s large working-class practice in the Stapleton Road district of

Practice makes perfect with net results

W. G. in his aptly glittering setting at the Crystal Palace

Left: W. G. starts a cycle race at a Bristol sports meeting and *Right:* with C. J. Posthuma, the 'grand old man of Dutch cricket, who played successfully with both bat and ball for London County. He called his three dogs after cricketers: 'W. G.' 'C. B.' after Fry and 'Archie' after MacLaren'

'There was also sport with the Worcester Park Beagles. . . .'

Bristol who did not enjoy the advantages of these qualities and many others. Nothing seemed to tire him on his rounds any more than at the wicket. In the middle of a big innings against Middlesex he was up all night wrestling with a confinement. In the morning he came back to the Clifton ground to take his score to 221, at which point his No. 11 left him with the total at 348. Anyone else in the world would then have felt entitled to a rest, but not W.G. Bowling at one end with Woof at the other, he helped to rattle Middlesex out in time to win the game by an innings. In the match he took ten wickets for a song. Perhaps he had a good sleep on the third night.

Occasionally the emergency treatment given on the field was drastic rather than delicate. There was a young Kent amateur, C. J. M. Fox, who had an extraordinarily unfortunate experience of what we may term the rougher end of the Grace osteopathy. Fox, fielding at point, stooped sharply to stop a hard hit and pitched heavily forward, putting his shoulder out. E.M., backing up at the bowler's end, ran to him, at the same time waving his bat towards the pavilion. Out bustled W.G. and the next scene presented to the astonished spectators was that of E.M. sitting on the head of his prey while W.G., grabbing an arm, began to pull, with his foot as a fulcrum. There was an agonizing pause. Then a loud crack, as the shoulder went back into place, announced that the Graces had done their job. 'You're a very lucky young man!' cried W.G. It was a rough bit of Bob-Sawyer-like surgery, but it worked.

This slightly macabre incident had an unbelievable sequel. Two or three years later the thing happened again, like a second performance of a Grand Guignol play. The unfortunate Fox fell and put his shoulder out. E.M. rushed to the rescue. There was only one absentee, and that was W.G. himself, who did not happen to be playing. Two Kent colleagues were called on to sit on the patient's head, while E.M. performed the ferocious pump-handling. Desperate ailments need desperate remedies but the Grace remedies were seldom as desperate as that.

II

Rough-and-ready as such incidents may occasionally have been, W.G. did not gain the respect and affection of a large part of the working population of Bristol by mere rough-and-ready methods. His physical strength, his unshakeable confidence, his steadiness, as experienced by Croome and, above all, his buoyant, boyish humour: all these qualities are desirable in any man; in a doctor their worth is untold. Without exaggeration it is possible to think of him as almost the ideal doctor for this kind of general work: big, bluff, cheerful, imperturbable, friendly but not too sympathetic; widely experienced in every-day ailments. He was frankly no specialist, but an admirable general practitioner.

Since W.G.'s day medical science has made enormous strides in drugs and radiological treatment, but not in the personal responsibility of the individual doctor, who tends to pass his patients into hospital with all the nervous haste of a scrum-half menaced by wing-forwards. The attitude of modern medicine towards the general practitioner is one of amused condescension. There is a specialist for most ailments, and if we cannot fit our ailments to the available specialists, we are made to feel that we are somehow culpable. A friend of mine, an architect, joined the army in the second world war and was placed on fatigue duty, chopping wood in the cookhouse. Being the sort of man he was, he clumsily cut his wrist with his hatchet and was hauled, bleeding, before the regimental medical officer. This officer gave my friend one horrified glance and ejaculated: 'Take him away, I'm a brain specialist.' He then fainted away. And if my friend's wound had not been bound up with a puttee by his fellow-cook, a lecturer in theology, he would probably have lain, like Dryden's Darius, weltering in his blood to this day.

Now W.G., whatever his shortcomings in specialization, would not have fainted at the sight of a cut wrist. If you were in his hands, you were in his hands, not dainty but immensely capable. His patients admired him without hysteria. He had neither the passion for healing nor the saintliness of character which gave a man the title of Beloved Physician. But he was

magnificently equipped with the middle virtues: kindness,
patience, good humour and that general practitioner's standby,
common sense. He was to his patients, as to his cricketing
opponents, something outside nature, a genuine nonesuch.
Tom Emmett said W.G. ought to have a 'littler bat'. There is no
record of any of his patients demanding that he should have a
smaller stethoscope, yet, as has been frequently recorded, he
seemed to many of them a kind of outsize Santa Claus. The
people who afterwards recounted tales of their doctor were
mostly simple, unsophisticated folk and their stories often ended
with a typical line: 'He was a good gentleman, with no pride
whatever.'

The stories of his doctoring are almost as many as of his
cricket, but they are not so varied: running through them all is
a thread of gruff kindness and unsentimental competence.
Dressed in a roughish tweed suit with his blackthorn stick under
his arm, he would walk briskly along the streets of his 'parish',
sometimes reading his newspaper and sometimes pausing
gravely to converse with stray children and dogs. If a family
was short of fuel or food, he would rather grumpily produce a
bag of coals or a basin of soup, as though out of a conjurer's hat.
He would also take delight in bullying some friend of his into
giving an unemployed man a job. If he went into a house where
an ample dinner was on the table he would sniff the air
appreciatively and murmur: 'By jove, that smells good,' and
sit down to eat with the family. In winter weather, when snow-
balls were flying, his top hat was an inevitable target, but, as
you might imagine, he deemed attack the best form of defence
and gave as good as he got. His pick-up was swift, his return
deadly, and he always seemed to have plenty of ammunition.
Roaring with laughter, he volleyed and thundered.

His practice lay in a district of Bristol subject to periodic
flooding and when he saw the waters beginning to rise, he
shrugged his shoulders, put on his fishing waders and set off on
his rounds. When he found patients in bed on the menaced
ground floor he picked them up without ceremony and carried
them upstairs to the first floor. In the wild winter of 1888 the
whole of the Frome Valley was a swirling torrent. W.G. was

determined to visit a patient on the far side of the Monk Street bridge, which had become perilously impassable. He hailed a water police boat which, with a crew of a sergeant and four constables, was patrolling the flooded area, and managed to extract from them a promise to take him across. The very thought of crossing was frightening, because there was every risk of the boat's being dashed over or against the coping of the bridge but, 'Now, boys, for it,' cried W.G., and over they went. When you think of the extra weight of bone, muscle and determination they had taken aboard, you will agree that all five policemen merited a medal.

He was occasionally eccentric in his prescriptions. Throughout the course of an influenza epidemic he was called out at all hours of the twenty-four and there came a time when he was feeling extremely short of sleep. An anxious husband threw stones at his window in the middle of the night, and, when the window was opened, described his wife's symptoms at great length. 'Go away!' W.G. called out at last; 'I'll see her in the morning. She'll be all right till then if you'll warm her half a pint of old beer!' Then the great bearded silhouette retreated from its frame and the window was banged down.

To a mildly drunken sweep who had beerily demanded a tonic, W.G. replied: 'What you want, my lad, is exercise, not medicine.' He then called out to the maid: 'Mary, fetch me those boxing gloves.' At that the patient rushed out of the surgery in terror, crying out as he ran down the street: 'The great big b—— wants to fight me!'

To the surgery in the Stapleton Road which is now part of a block of shops, he would walk every day. During his twenty years of practice in Bristol he lived in several houses, some of them near, and some of them a good distance from the surgery. What he wanted as an adjunct to his house was a garden which, like the old orchard at the Chestnuts, could provide a reasonable cricket pitch. We do not know how early in the morning W.G. started his practice or if it was as early as the hour at which his father had carried bat and ball to Durdham Down sixty years before. But we do know how early in the year he began.

Thrissel House,
Stapleton Road,
Bristol.

Dear Sir,—I hear from . . . . . that you are a fast bowler. If you can get down here on Saturday at 3 o'clock I shall be pleased to see you bowl. I have a good wicket here.

Yours truly,

W. G. Grace.

The year was 1884 and the day, 17th February. The 'good' wicket, which in fact sloped a good deal, was about thirty yards square, and some of the Gloucestershire players would come along for practice on early mornings and Saturday afternoons long before the official opening of the season. From that moment, whatever the weather, the summer had begun.

Thrissel House was the second of his Bristol houses. The first had been the smaller Thrissel Lodge and both were close to the surgery in Stapleton Road. The third house was in Victoria Square, Clifton, and the fourth was a 'rather grand residence', Ashley Grange, which stood some distance out of town and nearer the county ground. W.G.'s eldest son was a day boy at Clifton and the second boy was undergoing regular coaching for entry into Dartmouth. From Thrissel Lodge the two boys walked the three and a half miles to Clifton every day, and neither they nor their father thought anything of it. When the family moved to Clifton, W.G. regularly walked the same journey in reverse to the surgery.

This is not the place to write the history of 'the Robinson matches', games between local teams and an Eleven of Robinsons, the great Bristol firm of printers and papermakers. It is a fascinating narrative, well worth a book in itself, but it only concerns us here in so far as it touches the story of the Graces. When an Eleven of Robinsons met an Eleven of Graces their corner of Gloucestershire resounded with the clash of mighty opposites. It was during W.G.'s Stapleton Road period that these games reached their heyday. The Robinsons, with almost religious conscientiousness, held to their self-imposed rule of fielding a family eleven. The Graces, on occasion, were not so particular. In one of these games Henry Grace, who by this time was growing a little stiff in the joints and slow in the field, went in early and, shortly after he was out, received a telegram urgently summoning him to attend to a patient. A substitute in the field was asked for and chivalrously granted. The substitute happened to be, as it were by sheer chance, the young and agile Jack Board, who cheerfully fielded in the deep at both ends and cut off innumerable fours. Dr. Henry, who had now returned from the imaginary bedside of his hypothetical patient, sat coolly and gratefully out of sight in the shade, watching his family register another victory. It was one of the most successful combined operations ever performed by the Graces. All of them looked innocent, but W.G. looked innocent beyond all human belief.

W.G.'s first biographer was deeply impressed by the contrast between the splendour of W.G.'s fame on the cricket field and the modesty with which he carried out his work among the poor. Shorn of the slightly high-falutin' language of the period, this is what he said: 'Here is a man at the top of the tree, the most famous cricketer in the world, better known by the crowd than any other Englishman; and when the season is over, often when the day's play is ended, he goes quietly on with his work for his poorer neighbours and often enough he does not get paid for it.'

When W.G. parted from the county club and went off to manage the London County Club at Crystal Palace, all cricketing Gloucestershire was shocked and cast down; when he gave up his practice on the amalgamation of the Bristol Poor Law Unions, his patients had the same deep feeling of loss.

'For years after he left Bristol,' said his friend, F. S. Ashley-Cooper, 'poor people would relate how, after a tiring day in the field, he would visit them, not in a professional capacity, but as a friend, doing much to alleviate pain and spread cheerfulness. Is that nothing in our times?'

It is something in *anybody's* times.

CHAPTER EIGHT

THE IMMORTAL ANECDOTES

W. G. Grace
Had hair all over his face.
Lord! How the people cheered
When a ball got lost in his beard.
                    EDMUND CLERIHEW BENTLEY

I

SYDNEY SMITH, Oscar Wilde and James McNeill Whistler were not personally and individually responsible for all the quips and cracks attributed to them. The fact is that a witticism, even if it came out of a cracker, will attach itself to the wittiest person in the vicinity, on the general grounds that, even if he did not say it, it was the sort of thing he would have said. It is similar with a reputation for 'character'. When evidence of richly rounded character arises, it automatically attaches itself to the richest 'character' in sight.

A thousand and one stories, at a conservative estimate, go to building the foundation of the W.G. legend. Some are well documented, some are probable, some are wildly improbable and some frankly impossible, but even the last of these are received with a knowing chuckle: 'Just the sort of thing the Old Man would have . . .'

There is a wide borderline where the authentic shades off into the apocryphal, but one thing is certain: such a luxurious growth of anecdote never spread over a nonentity. The first type of story is the 'nonesuch' story and it mainly came from the professional bowlers of W.G.'s early days who at first had been unable to believe the rumours they had heard of his extravagant scores. When they met him in the flesh, they found that the wildest of the rumours were in fact mild understatements and that they themselves were instantly mesmerized by his per-

167

sonality and prowess. Tom Emmett was frequently the stooge in these happy little dialogues—honest Tom, that open-hearted son of the West Riding, who was paid half a crown for his first professional engagement, to which he proceeded in clogs, using the local newspaper as a cricket bag. When he first heard of the Grace exploits, he was patronizingly incredulous:

'It's all very well making these scores against south country bowlers, but wait till we get him up in Sheffield. Me and George'll show 'im . . .'

(George Freeman was the handsome fast bowler from Thirsk whom W.G. thought the finest of his period.) As it turned out, W.G. made a joyous 122 at Bramall Lane against the most hostile attack that Yorkshire could bring, and Tom, suffering under the flail of wrath, wilted visibly. 'I call him a nonesuch,' he exclaimed. 'He ought to have a littler bat.'

In the middle of W.G.'s wonderful week in August 1876, an awe-stricken Tom Emmett heard from the Notts players that W.G., riding on the crest of his 344 at Canterbury, had not let the bat sleep in his hand, but had hammered Alfred Shaw, Morley, Selby and the rest, England bowlers to a man. Gritting his teeth, Tom muttered: 'Afore we'd let him do that to us, we'd shooit him!'

But the next game was the one in which W.G. made 318 not out. As we have seen, he practically drove the Yorkshire bowlers to mutiny, and at the same time he drove Tom to rueful head-shaking: 'It's Grace before meat, Grace after meat, Grace all day, and I reckon it'll be Grace tomorrow.' Of the manner in which W.G. meted out the punishment, he murmured just as ruefully: 'The better I places 'em, the better he pastes 'em!'

If Tom Emmett had not been a tremendous character in his own right, he would have come down in history as the author of the 'diploma' story. Returning to London after his historic visit to Edinburgh to receive his L.R.C.P.—this would be in 1879—W.G. overtook Tom Emmett walking along St. John's Wood Road. 'Is it all right, sir?' asked Tom. 'It's all right, Tom,' said W.G. 'I've got my diploma.' M.C.C. won the toss and when Yorkshire came out to field, the ground was wet and slippery. Tom Emmett was fielding at cover-point and W.G.

cut a furious slash straight at him. It struck Tom full in the
midriff, bowling him over like a ninepin. There he lay, clutch-
ing the ball and gazing at the sky.

'Are you hurt, Tom?' demanded W.G.

Tom slowly rose, turned and exhibited a large green moon
on the seat of his trousers.

'No,' said Tom, 'but I've got my diploma.'

The best known of the tributes wrung from reluctant bowlers
was the venerable dictum of James Shaw, who was also a fast
left-handed bowler of ripe, nutty character, and came from
Nottinghamshire. He made, as the *Dictionary of National Biography* demurely states, 'an epigrammatic comment, divested of
some adverbial adornment.'

'I puts 'em where I likes,' said James, 'but that beggar, he
puts 'em where *he* likes!'

James once missed W.G. off what looked like a comparatively
easy caught-and-bowled and, when someone remonstrated,
James replied: 'I like to see the beggar bat.' Sometimes under
the lash he would reach a point of exasperation when he felt
his only hope was to bowl W.G. a nice ball to be hit so that he
could get him to the other end and have a go at somebody who
could be got out. Even when he attempted this strategy, W.G.
would hit him for four or six and not change ends at all. When
a critic jeered at James: 'You can't get the long 'un out' he
retorted: 'You don't want me to, do you?'

He occasionally got his own back, for he once broke W.G.'s
stumps, but this was a familiarity that had to be paid for. The
worst fate that befell James was to get W.G. out for a duck, for
that meant that he would hit something like 200 runs in the
second innings. W.G. was not completely infallible. Ducks
were for him a possibility, as with lesser men, but the better the
bowling, the better he liked it.

II

The great Duke of Wellington, who died when W.G. was four
years old, was acclaimed by the Poet Laureate as 'rich in saving
common sense' and 'in his simplicity sublime'. W.G., though

not given to reading odes, had more than a touch of the same qualities. His unsubtle mind went as directly to a problem as the middle of his bat went to the ball. Playing in a west-country game, he was bowled neck and crop by an unknown bowler. The batsman who followed him was also clean bowled and, as he came in, he grumbled about the bad light.

'I could have played it if I could have seen it,' he complained.

'I was just the opposite,' said W.G. 'I could see it all right, but I couldn't play it.'

There was an occasion when Sir Leonard Hutton showed much the same 'saving' common sense in our own day. Several sympathizers who had watched him clean bowled by an awkward ball ventured to speculate upon its semi-supernatural qualities. Did it shoot? Did it turn from leg? Did it go with the bowler's arm? Did it . . .?

'It didn't do anything,' said Hutton. 'I missed it.'

W.G. carried his common-sense attitude right through to the end of his career. There was a young club batsman playing for the first time for London County. W.G. asked him politely what number he would like to bat.

'I don't mind,' said the young man. 'I never made a duck in my life.'

'What, never made a blob?' growled the Old Man. 'Then Number Eleven for you. Not enough experience.'

He had a literal mind and was glad of it.

Batting against a Colts' Eighteen, W.G. wrote down their qualifications on a piece of paper and, in the middle of an innings in which he was being particularly severe on one of the bowlers, he dragged the bit of paper out of his pocket. Waving it to his partner, he grinned: 'I rather like these bowlers who break both ways—to the boundary!'

But for the most characteristically 'sensible' of all W.G.'s sayings we have to return to his counsel for playing a difficult ball: 'I should lay the bat against the ball.' If this is considered in all its implications, literal and metaphorical, it is probably the most profoundly wise counsel ever given to anybody on any subject whatever.

III

The most frequently quoted of all the W.G. stories concern W.G.'s artfulness. Some have called it more, and worse, than artfulness. But these have been finally silenced by Neville Cardus's old cricketer.

'Did the Old Man cheat?'

'No . .o. He was too *clever*.'

That is the truth, if not the whole truth. Of course he was artful. He was artful, because he was a countryman, with all the countryman's inherited resource in getting the better of nature. In the same way he liked to get the better of his opponents, and he liked to have his joke, too. 'The long-whiskered Doctor,' Francis Thompson called him, 'that laugheth the rules to scorn.' But he did not in fact mock the laws. He kept them faithfully, with an innocent smile for their occasional flexibility. As for 'cheating', he was so full of craft within the rules, it would have been absurd to go outside them.

Sometimes he would do something well within the rules and still be criticized. Fielding at point, he kept a lynx eye open to see whether a batsman carelessly strolled out of his ground. He did not run many people out in this way, but he kept them on their toes. At a critical moment of the famous Ashes Test Match of 1882, he nipped in from point and ran S. P. Jones out with a ball that the wicketkeeper had darted after and returned. Jones claimed that the ball had been dead and that he was only 'gardening'. But old Robert Thoms, fairest of umpires, gave him out. Jones, in the heat of the moment, felt outraged, but, when tempers had cooled, it was generally agreed that W.G.'s action had not been in the least outrageous and one of the Australians—it sounds like Spofforth—admitted that he would have done the same thing. There was a feeling that the man who had been a victim of W.G.'s artfulness should have been grateful rather than angry, because he had had the privilege of learning an unforgettable lesson, even if he had learnt it the hard way.

A good deal of the Graces' alleged misfeasance was schoolboy larking and no more, only reprehensible to those who sometimes forget that cricket is a game. W.G.'s side in the field, whether it was Gloucestershire or M.C.C., was seldom a silent service. He and E.M. were continually chipping and ragging each other. Once in a Gloucestershire game against Surrey, E.M. crept in so close to the batsman that he could hardly move his bat and E.M. added insult to injury by appealing for obstruction.

'Obstruction be blowed!' shouted W.G. 'Catch the ball and never mind bamboozling the umpire.'

As captain of Gloucestershire, W.G. was once criticized for dropping his two regular bowlers on the morning of a county game. He explained with a chuckle that the wicket was too good, anyhow. 'So I thought us bad bowlers were just as likely to get 'em out as the decent ones.' He also thought it good for bowlers to be dropped occasionally if they ever began to think themselves indispensable.

As captain of England, he put A. A. (Dick) Lilley, the famous wicketkeeper, on to bowl in the 1896 Test match at Manchester. Lilley bowled five overs—the first of them yielded 14 runs and a wide—and then broke the big stand by getting one of the Australians caught. (Oddly, it was J. T. Brown, keeping wicket for Lilley, who caught him, just as W.G., keeping wicket for Lyttelton, had caught Midwinter in 1884.) After his one success Lilley thought a career as a Test bowler was opening to him, but W.G. shattered his dream.

'Put those gloves on again, Dick,' said W.G. 'You must have been bowling with your wrong arm.'

The tales of W.G.'s tussles with umpires are many, and have increased in size and quantity with the telling. He would claim, sometimes with a wink and sometimes with extreme seriousness, that he was educating them. Without doubt some of the country umpires needed a good deal of education. There is no need to be over-solemn in defending W.G. on this point or to pretend that he did not like to have his own way. But it must not be forgotten that the present high standards of umpiring did not spring up overnight. Like so many English excellences, they were of slow, and even painful, growth. Today one would as soon argue (in church) with an archbishop on theology as with an umpire on his decision, but umpires were not always worthy of the respect they now rightly receive. Some of the early umpiring in country matches was partial and much of it was wildly incompetent. It was not unreasonable that W.G. should sometimes step in and teach them the elements of their job. One of his most frequently repeated heart-cries relates to a catch made by a fieldsman standing on the boundary's edge and leaning back over the wall.

'Oliver,' shouted W.G., 'how often have I told you that if he catches me after the ball has gone out of the ground, it's six to me?'

This occurred in one of those slightly ferocious family games, with Graces on both sides, and it is only fair to add that Henry, from point, adjured the umpire with equally strong emotion: 'Be a man, Oliver!' cried Henry. 'Be a man and give him out!'

Once more I would wish to avoid over-solemnity. There was a good deal of amiable fooling and the ragging that went on among the Graces, particularly between W.G. and E.M., who was a much more constant appealer, was, in the current phrase, just nobody's business. Sometimes, on a particularly loud appeal from E.M., the umpire would look round with a bewildered expression and W.G. would explain: 'Take no notice of *him*. It's when I appeal that it's out!'

Once Fred Roberts, Gloucestershire's fast left-hand bowler, hit a batsman hard on the leg. W.G., moving across from square-leg at the end of the over, demanded: 'Why didn't you appeal, Fred?' 'Oh,' said Fred, 'I was waiting for *you*.'

As for the professional umpires, the retired county players who became the spiritual ancestors of the unimpeachable umpires of today, they were a horse of a different colour. There was no need to 'educate' them, but there was no reason why he shouldn't have his fun with them. The cream of the joke, however, was that the umpires frequently got the better of him. They knew his tricks and manners and, indeed, had a fine selection of tricks and manners of their own. If an umpire's decision went against him, he could somehow look astonished, indignant, *grieved*, but the umpires were ready for him. They had known him of old. Their admiration and affection for him were unbounded, but did not in the least extend to letting him get away with anything. Here, for instance, was Luke Greenwood, the canny, grumpy old Yorkshireman from Lascelles Hall, who gave W.G. out to a wickedly deceptive ball from Spofforth. It had been going to 'break a mile' but did nothing of the sort. Instead, it hit W.G. on its way towards his leg stump. 'Out,' said Luke, raising a firm if reluctant finger. And as W.G. passed him, deep in lamentation, Luke muttered—and I can just hear his flat West Riding voice: 'I can't help it; no, not if you was the Prince of Wales his-*sen*.'

There was Pooley, the gnarled old Surrey wicketkeeper, who in his heyday had played for and against the Champion many a time. He knew his man and was ready for anything. Once W.G., when Pooley gave him out, advanced down the pitch, indignantly demanding: 'Which leg did it hit, Pooley, which leg?'

'Never mind which leg,' retorted Pooley. 'I've given you out and out you've got to go.'

And there was Richard Barlow, of 'my Hornby and my Barlow long ago', the shrewd, cunning, bearded old Lancashireman, one of the most serious-minded men who ever played cricket. Above the doorway of his house at Blackpool a bat and wickets were set in terra cotta and in the glass panel of the vestibule there appeared, like saints in a church window, figures of himself and Hornby with Pilling keeping wicket and an eye on both of them. Dick Barlow knew the Old Man, too. After giving W.G. out leg-before-wicket, he waited stolidly for violent repercussions. 'Barlow,' complained W.G., with all the air of a good man wronged, 'I played that ball.'

'Yes, I know, Doctor,' said Barlow, 'but it was after it had hit your leg.'

The umpires, that is, the real umpires, were firm and, if they gave him out, he had to go. But his artfulness and their firmness were both part of a gigantic game of spoof that they were playing all the time. He knew them and they knew him, but they got the better of him far oftener than he got the better of them.

One of the most outrageous of the stories came from C. J. Kortright, the Essex amateur fast bowler whose reputation was for a time almost as prodigious as W.G.'s. His pace was terrific and his contemporaries claimed that he was the fastest bowler who ever lived. These things remain matters for conjecture. Jones, Knox, Cotter, Larwood, Tyson : who can tell which was the fastest? If the speed of fast bowlers can be scientifically measured at the present day, it could certainly not be measured then. Without doubt Kortright was one of the very fastest. He was also a gay, carefree character and no respecter of persons. He might well, by temperament, have been the bowler, rather than Ernest Jones, who put the ball through the Old Man's beard. It was in an Essex *v.* Gloucestershire game that he made several appeals which the umpire turned down, to the bowler's disgust. Finally, with a terrific yorker, he sent W.G.'s middle stump cartwheeling out of the ground. As the dismissed batsman passed him, Kortright murmured in mock incredulity : 'You're not going, Doctor? There's still one stump standing.' W.G. said he had never been so insulted in his life, but I will wager that he laughed afterwards and indeed, that those two incorrigible jesters laughed together. And there is always a chance that Kortright invented the story off his own bat.

If we were working to the thesis that W.G. was a cunning old rogue who made his runs by foxing the umpires and built up a reputation for smartness by cozening the innocent, our research would bring us sad disillusionment, for there are far more instances of people scoring off W.G. than of W.G. scoring off anybody. What is more, he would recall stories against himself with gusto and relish. They would all come under the heading of what Mr. Punch of the day would undoubtedly have called Collapse of Elderly Gent.

There was the small boy at Lord's who demanded his autograph.

'But I gave you my autograph at Brighton a month ago,' said W.G.

'I know,' replied the boy, 'but I swopped you for Dan Leno and a couple of bishops.'

A dozen urchins were playing cricket on Clifton Down while the bearded gentleman, pausing in his walk, gazed benevolently on the scene. A demand went up to heaven for leg-before-wicket, the infant batsman roundly refused to go and an appeal was lodged with the only adult present.

'You were out, old man,' said W.G. 'Better go like a sportsman.'

'Garn,' retorted the boy. 'What's an old buffer like you know about cricket?'

There was even the servant girl who, on her first visit to London, paid a visit to Madame Tussaud's.

'Ah, Mary,' said W.G., when she got back to Bristol, 'did you see me there?'

'Oh, no, sir,' she replied, 'we'd have had to pay sixpence extra to go into the Chamber of Horrors.'

Even his inquiry regarding Phil May's delightful *Punch* caricature drew an amiably dusty retort. The artist in depicting his cockney sportsman, 'Arry, ridiculously disporting himself at cricket, had shown the fieldsman at square-leg wearing stumping-gloves. 'Why, oh, why?' W.G. demanded. 'To keep his hands warm,' said Phil May.

He liked best to tell of the wild Highlander who was a member of his bowls team. W.G., who was skip, was excitedly shouting advice to his colleague.

'Play to my foot, man, play to my foot.'

'Play to your foot?' retorted the Scot. 'Why, your foot's all over the green.'

Collapse of Stout Party indeed.

Even his famous tossing trick, the evidence for which has truly Irish reliability, could not be successfully tried twice upon the same victim. Before the game with Trinity College, Dublin, on one of W.G.'s early Irish tours, J. M. Meldon, the Irish captain, tossed up and W.G. called: 'Woman . . . Good, we'll bat.' And it was some time before the captain realized that W.G. would broadmindedly have accepted, under the fair mantle of femininity, either Britannia or Queen Victoria. But the next time they met, Meldon, whose initials should surely have been J.J., not J.M., was ready for him.

'Go on,' said W.G., 'toss up.'

'No, Doctor,' said Meldon, 'you toss up this time and *I'll* call.'

W. G. with the Eltham Cricket Club, 1914

The last picture taken of the Great Cricketer. *Left to right:* a nephew of Ranji, A. C. MacLaren, W. G., K. S. Ranjitsinhji and W. G. Heasman. This photograph was probably taken in W. G.'s garden in 1915

W. G.'s grave at
Elmer's End cemetery.
'They laid him under
a hawthorn tree beside
his son and daughter.
. . .'

The Grace Gate at Lord's. 'To the Memory of William Gilbert Grace,
the Great Cricketer'

Even the classic ejaculation: 'Shan't have it, can't have it, *won't* have it!' with which W.G. greeted his dismissal by a doubtful decision was capped, at least in the authorized version, by Walter Read who, fielding in front of the Oval pavilion, replied with a sunny smile: 'But you'll *have* to have it!'

Considering the number of rebuffs he received, the picture presented might almost be made to seem a sad one, but the very thought is ridiculous. The anecdotes show W.G. as what would now be called a super-keen type, ready to take any legitimate advantage, but accepting with reasonably good grace if the law did not allow anything more. But, more than all, he was an incorrigible humorist.

IV

And now we approach the patently apocryphal. There are three instances that I find particularly endearing. A country wicketkeeper made a strident appeal for a catch-at-wicket while W.G. was batting.

'Don't you mind him, Doctor,' said the umpire affably. 'We none of us think much of him in these parts.'

The burden of county captaincy fell temporarily upon a young amateur, who shall be nameless for the best of reasons: I do not know his name. He was keenly anxious to do his best against the formidable county of the Graces and on the first day of the Gloucestershire match he had his men out early at the nets, bowling, batting and fielding away for dear life. So absorbed was he in the task of rehearsal that he took insufficient note of, and indeed lost all sense of, the passage of time. A bell rang and, as the young captain led his men back to the pavilion he was met by the redoubtable pair, W.G. and E.M., padded, gloved and eager to be at the bowling.

'Come along, young fellow,' said W.G. severely. 'Can't play about here all day.'

So the young captain led his men back on to the field and then, on a beautiful shirt-front wicket, those two unconscionable jokers proceeded to flog the bowling from the very first ineffectual over. At lunch-time the scoreboard showed about 150 for none, and the youthful captain, as his fieldsmen trudged wearily back to the pavilion, was troubled by a disturbing thought. Just then it occurred to him that they had never tossed up.

There are two stories, or perhaps two versions of one story, about another captain in a north country game who was convinced that the only way to shorten a W.G. innings was to lush him up with champagne at lunch. In the first version the champagne was offered and politely declined, 'Thankee,' said W.G. blandly; 'keep it cool. I'll drink it when I'm out.'

In the second version, the lushing was offered and accepted by an apparently willing victim. This suggests that, as W.G. claimed that he would never drink champagne except on a special occasion, some appropriate occasion must also have been offered and accepted. Perhaps it was to celebrate the death of Queen Anne or the signing of Magna Carta, who knows? (He once, under mild protest, celebrated the Battle of Bannockburn.) The champagne was of happy vintage and generously supplied. A bottle and a half is the quantity mentioned. At or about tea-time, standing muzzily at square-leg, the fielding captain watched the fourth four of the over whizz past his vaguely outstretched hand.

W.G. looked round and caught his eye.

'Ho,' said the Old Man wickedly. 'I'll champagne yer.'

A final episode of some charm comes from W.G.'s early medical days. He was staying at the Chestnuts and was awakened in the middle of the night by a loud thud and a yell of dismay. Going down to investigate, W.G. located the sound. A somewhat villainous tramp had been seeking to raid the larder and had met with misfortune, for the heavy window-sash, which he had managed to raise, had suddenly fallen back with the spitefulness of its kind on his hands, like a man-trap, damaging his fingers and holding him prisoner. 'And what did you do?' demanded his brother when the adventure was over. 'Why didn't you hand him over to the police?'

'Medical etiquette,' said W.G. solemnly. 'I dressed his wounds. First-class job, too. But hand him over? Oh, no, not my patient. I just went round and gave him a running kick and let him go.'

CHAPTER NINE

EMINENT VICTORIAN

I

It is a poor thing to bestow excessive praise upon the past at the expense of the present. *Punch* is not what it was. It never was. Cricket is going downhill. It always was. Such assumptions are harmless if known to be relative and if an old gentleman thinks there is no one like the heroes of his boyhood he is following a natural, if irrational, impulse. For the man who as a boy stood by the fringe of a Kentish meadow to watch the Lion of Kent roll back the sleeve of his leg-of-mutton arm and pound up to the wicket with the full weight of his eighteen stone and deliver his swift round-arm ball so that it hummed through the air—for that man, I say, there would never be anyone like 'kind and manly Alfred Mynn'. Let a man say that there has never been anyone like Hobbs (or Hammond or Hutton) and you can gauge almost the time and place of his birth. It is just as likely that at a future date some elderly gentleman, now a lad, will pilot his grandson round the Long Room to show him the bat with which Peter May scored his 198th century and the ball, suitably silver-mounted, that Tyson bowled through Ian Craig's beard. It is a good thing to praise famous men but it does not need an Einstein to point out the essential relativity of most of these matters.

Yet while heroes and hero-worship pass on from generation to generation in a normal undulating line, some periods and persons stand out in high relief. The illusory nature of the Golden Age that was every man's boyhood does not mean that there never was, or could be, a Golden Age. Some men and some periods are absolutely, as well as relatively, of transcendent quality and it may be amiably, if categorically, asserted that the Golden Age of cricket covered the years around the turn of the century: that is, not the age when W. G. Grace flourished as an overwhelming champion, but the age immediately succeeding, which brought to fine flower the tree that he had planted. I refuse to go round, chalking *Ichabod* on pavilion walls and running away, for I believe that of the present age at least Hutton, Compton, Bedser and Evans are clearly of the company of the great and that May, Cowdrey, Statham and/or Tyson may well attain that stature. But this is not to deny the existence of the Golden Age. The enchantment of Ranji, the darting sword-play of Trumper, the elegance of Palairet, the happy violence of Jessop, the cool mastery of Fry, all the courage and craft of those ten-talented all-rounders, Hirst, Rhodes, F. S. Jackson, Braund and Lockwood: these were gleaming splendours in themselves, but they were even more inevitably part of the glorious edifice of which W.G. had been the master-builder.

Grace, then, lived on into the Golden Age he had done so much to create, but, strictly speaking, his own was not this, but the Victorian age that had just ended. Born in 1848, he lived through the second half of the nineteenth century and his age straddled the middle and late Victorian eras. Not only was he the greatest cricketer of his age, he was also a great figure of his age. Furthermore, I believe that this was itself a great age.

II

No nation, social group or period in history has a monopoly of virtue or vice and nothing is either good or bad because it is old or new. I hold these truths to be self-evident, but dull. They are fatally style-cramping to the champion of any country, class or era who wishes to make a dive-bombing attack upon another. Like the famous Captain Shaw, on fire that glows with heat intense they turn the hose of common sense. On the other hand, if you ignore these truths, swashbuckling is easy and satisfying. The Victorian age has taken heavy punishment in this way. Some time after the first world war it was virtually put up against a wall and shot. The advance-guard of the denigrators was Lytton Strachey, who wrote of the Victorians with brilliant malice. Like Lucrezia Borgia, he was a poisoner of genius; his successors, who had less than his brilliance and more than his malice, were merely in the Neil Cream class. Now thirty-five years later an exhumation order has been tentatively issued. On that Victorian age, at which the critical barrow-boys of the 'twenties threw their rotten oranges, the literary tic-tac men of the 'fifties are now feverishly beginning to hedge their bets. It has taken them a long time to feel safe in doing so.

Edmund Burke expressed diffidence about indicting a nation but there have been many who feel no shyness about indicting a period in history. It is easy for one age to condemn another. It is ever a favourite sport of elderly gentlemen to praise the time of their boyhood and abuse that of their younger contemporaries, as if they had not lived in, and made their contribution to, both. This kind of attack is tempting but irrational. The Victorian age, we might say, was an age of humbug, snobbery, complacency, dullness, Forsytes, whatnots and other evils. To which a surviving Victorian might retort that the present age is an age of aspirin, automation, inflation, football pools, detergents, absenteeism and double-talk, an age poised indelicately between Hollywood, Kinsey and commercial television. The Victorian age had humbug, but no monopoly of it. Humbug, like love, is universal and, on the whole, more amusing. One or two elderly Victorian spinsters might drape their piano legs in the interests of propriety, but they were babes in humbug compared with an age which can call a ratcatcher a rodent operative or can for six months solemnly conduct a ruinous strike of several thousand adult males to discover whether wooden-hole-borers or metal-hole-borers should bore holes in wooden-and-metal plates. Mr. Pecksniff would have turned green with envy to hear a B.B.C. discussion on a vital subject, while the pot so solemnly calls the kettle white, and the clang of soap on flannel resounds through the ether. Intersecular sniping, if that is the correct expression, is a barren thing but, if it were started, the Victorians might follow the example of Voltaire's wicked little animal and defend themselves.

Were the Victorians snobbish? If they were, at least they had a Thackeray to tell them so. They did not believe they had abolished the thing by standing it awkwardly on its head nor did they ululate about U and non-U. Were they all complacent in the face of poverty and social evils? The Tory, Lord Shaftesbury, was not, and the complacency of the Radical, Charles Dickens, towards the Poor Law, the old Court of Chancery and the Circumlocution Office was of a peculiar kind. We have, following his lead, abolished the Poor Law and spring-cleaned the Law Courts, but the Circumlocution Office flourishes like a forest of green bay trees, and has been permanently enlarged into our way of life, while the contemporary worship of the new blessed word, technology, indicates a daily increasing tenderness towards Mr. Gradgrind. And we have leapt from the lukewarm frying-pan of stilted Victorian speech into an unquenchable forest fire of quasi-technical jargon. Mr. Polly's 'sesquippledan verbojuice' was nothing to it.

Was the lot of women wholly dull and conventional in an age that produced (to name only a few) Florence Nightingale, George Eliot and Marie Lloyd? (I doubt if the last of these three ladies draped her piano legs.)

The indictment goes briskly on. The Victorians were without wit, like W. H. Mallock, W. S. Gilbert, Samuel Butler, Oscar Wilde and Bernard Shaw. They were without humour, like Jerome K. Jerome and W. W. Jacobs, not to mention Dan Leno. They were pale, thin-blooded rationalists like Cardinal Newman, Charles Haddon Spurgeon and General Booth. They were smug optimists, like Hardy, Housman and Gissing. They were coarse philistines, like Matthew Arnold and Walter Pater. They were respectable. This is the final disgraceful charge and it is a little harder to rebut, though no doubt Charles Peace would have done his best. The respectability was there, it must be admitted, but who shall say that Victorian virtue was more boring than Georgian vice against which the young Queen and her Consort, in their happy family life, so notably reacted?

And if it is objected that the men and women named were exceptional, the answer is that they were also representative— exceptional in being more vigorously and effectively what the best of their contemporaries aspired to be. An age is entitled to

be judged by its heroes, as perhaps ours may be by the Battle
of Britain pilots, the climbers of Everest and the lone navi-
gators of the seven seas.

But if in the Victorian age, as in any other, great men were
rare, good men were not. The Victorians believed in goodness,
without which, as Bacon says, man is a busy, mischievous,
wretched thing, no better than a kind of vermin.[1] These heroes
of theirs were good men. Superficially no men could have been
more different in character than, for instance, Shaftesbury,
Livingstone, Gordon and Gladstone: what linked them in
common service was their unswerving loyalty to their duty, as
they understood it, and to their Christian faith.

This faith they expressed most readily in action and, as a
result, the age saw more beneficent changes in its sixty years
than had happened in the previous six hundred. The advances
made in education, health and in the welfare of the poor were
enormous. Many of the grosser evils of the industrial revolution
were progressively mitigated through the efforts of Lord
Shaftesbury and other nobly enlightened men on both sides of
the political curtain. In the latter half of the Queen's reign the
country's political life, so far from being a stagnant pond of
complacency, was a continual ferment of reform. There were
successive widenings of the franchise in the second and third
Reform Acts, buttressed by the Ballot Act. In the public schools
and universities, in public health, in a remodelled civil service,
in the conditions of army life there were immense betterments,
the original drive for which came from such forceful characters
as Thomas Arnold, Edwin Chadwick and Edward Cardwell,
and behind them in all their efforts were numbers of devoted
men dedicated to selfless causes.

In 1868, when W.G. was first appearing for the Gentlemen,
Gladstone's first great administration came into office, to carry
out more reforms in 'the condition of the people' than any other
before the Liberal government of 1906. Gladstone's government passed the first of the great Education Acts, reformed the
army from top to bottom and gave the first legal recognition to
trade unions. Disraeli's Conservative government that followed,

---

[1] Have we here unearthed an even more noble and beautiful quotation?

though it had criticized Gladstone's measures, carried on the work of reform, placing on the statute book legislation which improved the previous acts dealing with education and trade unions, and consolidated many previous progressive measures in the massive Public Health Act of 1875 which was the greatest of the early blows struck for England, home and sanitation.

The country's commercial prosperity, now something of a wistful memory, owed much to the energy, and rested firmly on the genuine honesty, of most British merchants as men of business. Furthermore, among these great merchants were men who thought it not shame to be scholars, historians, scientists and theologians as well.

A wise historian of today has said: 'The Queen's Jubilees of 1887 and 1897 were celebrated by all classes with real pride and thankfulness, due in part to a sense of delivery from the conditions endured at the beginning of her reign, for the Hungry 'Forties were still remembered. Manners were gentler, streets were safer, life was more humane, sanitation was improving fast, and working-class housing, though still bad, was less bad than ever before . . .'

III

The beneficent energy of the Victorians expressed itself in play as in work. Right through this period the English love and enjoyment of games grew beyond all knowledge. 'England,' said Emil Cammaerts, 'has never ceased to be merry. She is the chosen land of games, practical jokes, comic songs . . .' The germ of the thing had always been there but the later Victorian age saw its growth and development on an increasingly scientific basis and, without question, on a vast scale. The two codes of football, after some spirited bickering about rules, sorted themselves out to draw up their own codes on their own diversely excellent lines, so, with the Football Association formed in 1863 and the Rugby Football Union in 1871, there were two fine winter games instead of one.

Cricket itself was a game that had come long before from English fields, sponsored by English gentlemen and played by

Englishmen of all classes with implements subtly evolved by English craftsmen. During W.G.'s lifetime the game grew from a simple rural pastime to those enlargements of technical skill and popularity that have lasted into our own time, so that now it has become, on the one hand, the background of Test Match big business and, on the other, and far more importantly, for countless Englishmen and members of the Commonwealth, an image and symbol of the good life. In this mighty development W. G. Grace played a part unchallengeably greater than that played by any other man, not only by his unparalleled skill in batting, bowling and fielding, but by his personality, his dominating simplicity and by his devotion to the game for the game's sake.

He was a great figure because of his robust integrity of character to which his striking presence, beard, bulk and all, gave the readiest clue. He was the true inhabitant of the England of 'games, practical jokes, comic songs'. Many of his best innings were comic songs in themselves. He was not a rebel against the conventions of his age, as some great Victorians were. He could fulfil himself and be his happy self by playing his game to the best of his superlative powers. He was freer from self-consciousness than it is possible to imagine anybody being today. Because of his almost unbelievable eminence, the people who came in yearly increasing numbers to watch him regarded him as the national symbol of their game, and almost as their own private property. Such was their pride in him that they congratulated each other on his exploits as though these were somehow to their personal credit. They chuckled over his artfulness as though his tricks and manners were their very own.

This English love of sport, like any other quality, had, and has, its defects. It could be argued that the passion for playing and particularly for watching games, drew men's attention away from social and political duties which, if performed conscientiously, would have immeasurably improved their own, and their country's, lot. No doubt this ought to have been done and it would have required only a complete change of human nature to do it.

On the other hand, it could be even more fairly argued that this English love of games, and especially of cricket, taught Englishmen that highest of principles, the rule of law, which no lawyer would ever have taught them. It helped to canalize the unreasoning violence of men's natures into comparatively harmless channels, encouraged a spirit of good humour and tolerance, and not so much softened the asperities of the class war, as kept an ugly thing from the island shore.

After all, W.G. had been born in 1848, the year of the Communist Manifesto, and on his native soil Disraeli's two nations existed in sombre fact. It would be idle to deny the dire poverty and hardship of that 'other' nation, but there were elements in English character that militated against direct collisions. There were men of good will in all classes and both political parties who dedicated themselves to the breaking down of barriers and, without claiming too much, it may be said that the common love of games, and particularly of cricket, played at least a part in bringing members of the two nations together in bloodless combat and preventing the kind of head-on crash that occurred in Continental countries.

IV

As with politics, so with the thing called culture, a word of which Matthew Arnold knew the meaning when he used it. Today the meaning is less clear. Large masses of Victorian English people, of all social ranks, were philistines, though at least they had a Matthew Arnold to lambast them for being so. Yet were they all so insensitive as a sensitive soul thought them? Poets and painters made a better living than at any time before or since. *Somebody* must have read the great Victorian novelists and the crowds who waited breathlessly for the next great instalments of *Bleak House* and *Dombey and Son* had some interests in their lives other than money and gloomy mahogany furniture. In every provincial town there was a live theatre, in large cities two or three, and when the great actor-managers toured the country they played to packed houses.

W.G. was frankly unliterary, though by no means illiterate, but, as with so many of the English, his non-bookishness took

the form of amiable neglect and not of aggressive dislike. It was
at least devoid of pretence. His little joke about reading—'Bad
for your eyesight, you never see me at it!'—need not be taken
too seriously. Like so many of his remembered observations, it
was uttered with a wink of the eye. Doubtless he ought to have
studied electoral reform, secrecy of the ballot and Irish Home
Rule, and worried about troubles in Egypt and South Africa
as he in fact afterwards worried, and worried sadly, about the
first world war which, even in his shortening lifetime, carried off
so many of his young companions. But in early days he feared
for none of these things and we might say that his neglect, and
that of his countrymen, was highly culpable. Yet have we of the
present time, who worry daily and duodenally about international politics and economics, made an overwhelming success
of our worries?

W.G. lived his life as an individual in an age of individuals,
when people were permitted to be people and not mere groups,
indices or cyphers in some bracketeer's erroneously calculated
statistics. He followed his profession honourably and brought
up his family with firm affection. The rest of his heart and soul,
his astonishing skill and his abounding energy he gave to the
game he loved.

In many ways life in the Victorian age was real, life was
earnest, even if it was an American poet who noted the fact.
W.G. was a true heir of Victorian earnestness in that he played
cricket with the single-minded purpose of playing the game as
well as it could be played both for his side and for himself. He
took the matter seriously, but not over-solemnly. Cricket was
never 'only' a game; all the same it *was* a game, with a game's
rigour but also a game's true lightness of heart.

v

W.G. was a true Victorian in his delight in family life. Every
novelist of the nineteen-twenties has written at least one powerful work on the horrors of the Victorian family. It was a com-
pulsory subject at the time. Yet the picture, if true (and it
seldom was) was infinitely less than the truth. Victorian family

life was not necessarily dull, tyrannous or a torture to a sensitive soul. The ideal of the family seemed to countless Victorians to find its happiest expression in the family life of the Queen herself. The dear old joke about the dear old lady's comment on the last act of *Antony and Cleopatra*—'So different from the home life of our dear Queen'—was poking fun at something good enough to stand a joke. The home life of many thousands of the Queen's subjects was in its modest simplicity similar to her own. They had the same kind of family holidays, the same family readings, the same overcrowded drawing-rooms or parlours, the same immense clan-gatherings.

In thousands of middle-class homes, particularly those of the country parsons, doctors and schoolmasters, of whom the Graces were typical, family life was a rough-and-tumble democracy, an unsentimentally affectionate society whose members comported themselves with a general healthy dis-respect but would close the ranks and rally to the family banner wherever it was menaced. Such was Dr. H. M. Grace's family at Downend and such was Dr. W. G. Grace's at Stapleton Road. Let no man say they were not happy families.

A typical Victorian occasion was that Sunday ritual, the family walk to see Grannie Grace at Downend. W.G. and his wife had four children: William Gilbert, born in 1874, who became a Wrangler at Cambridge; Henry Edgar, born in 1876, who had a most distinguished career in the Royal Navy; Bessie, their only daughter, born in 1878, who was to die tragically young; Charles Butler, born in 1882, who grew up to be a noted electrical engineer, lived to the age of fifty-six and dropped dead from heart-failure at the wicket in the act of making the winning hit in an exciting local cricket match. But the future lay far out of sight as the Graces made their weekly pilgrimage. Along the road was a ridge where, as a boy of seven, W.G. had watched Lord Raglan's funeral procession go by. Regularly at this point they would meet the old lady in her pony carriage. Old Mrs. Grace would take young Mrs. Grace and the youngest child in the carriage and so the cavalcade would proceed to The Chestnuts for tea.

All the Graces in their Victorian way were family-minded

and proud of it. Twice a year—once at Christmas and once at midsummer—there would be a gigantic gathering of the clans, when the resistless Graces would converge on Downend. Sister Ann, Mrs. Skelton, was their hostess and sometimes they would number as many as seventy. If this seems an exaggeration, photographs undeniably exist in which you can count up to at least fifty souls, including Henry, Alfred, E.M. and W.G. (with as many of their sisters and their cousins and their aunts as would have satisfied the captain of the *Pinafore*), not forgetting old Uncle Alf Pocock and all. It must be one of the most formidable family groups that ever existed between the brass-clasped leather covers of a Victorian album.

At Christmas there was gargantuan eating and drinking and at midsummer there were nutting parties in their neighbouring woods and cricket matches between the Grace boys and the Grace girls, in which Bessie was often the star. Family life was vivid and varied and, whatever else it may have been, it cannot have been a bore.

W.G. was especially a Victorian in his love of children. Outside family priorities, it did not seriously matter whose children they were. Children were to be played with, cosseted a little (but not too much) and gently cuffed if they were naughty. The second curate of Downend, who wrote a fascinating volume on the annals of Mangotsfield parish, has left a pleasant picture of W.G.'s Sundays with the children at The Chestnuts after those family walks from Stapleton Road. He speaks of W.G.'s 'wonderful love and admiration for his mother', which is what we should expect; he also speaks of his 'great affection and gentle condescension with regard to children'. W.G. would have said: 'Condescension, my foot!' Condescension is a pale word to describe the awesome spectacle of W.G. galumphing round The Chestnuts lawn on all fours as a buffalo or bear, while the children shrieked in terrified delight. No real bear could ever have been quite so gloriously grizzly. Sometimes you would see him solemnly playing cricket with the children; bowling left-handed because his right thumb, wounded in battle by Crossland or some other 'slinger', is tied up in an enormous poke.

The grandmother of a Bristol friend of mine told him that, when she and her sister were little girls over sixty years ago, they would pass The Chestnuts on their way to Sunday school. One day they met outside the garden wall an elderly gentleman with a top hat and a big black beard who was practising with his umbrella what the two little girls would not have recognized as on-drives. They, for their part, were kicking a large round stone along in a manner they ought to have recognized as most unladylike in the eighteen-nineties. 'Come along,' said the bearded gentleman abstractedly, 'lob it up, lob it up.' As they took it in turns to pitch up the round stone, he solemnly played it from the middle of the umbrella, to cover, to square leg and all round the wicket. 'Thank you,' he said at last with grave courtesy and two innocent little girls went on their way to church, all unaware that their experience would have driven every boy in the kingdom frantic with envy.

But the abiding Victorian memory of W.G. is of a June day at Lord's, an English sun shining in benison on English turf; a cool breeze ruffling the red and yellow flag and the Union Jack that fly from the mastheads of the new terra-cotta-faced pavilion and, more significantly, the great black beard in the centre of the picture. There is decorum but there is also colour. The parasols of the ladies form a mosaic of pink and blue and lavender; the silk hats of their escorts gleam like knightly helms. There is no Mound stand and no Father Time, but there are coaches and brakes in front of the Tavern. From far down St. John's Wood Road comes the tinkling tittup of the hansoms, answering the whispered call that the Champion is 'in'. A red ball is speeding towards the Tavern boundary, unavailingly pursued by an equally red-faced fieldsman. The Champion raises his bat, which looks a little thing, though Tom Emmett said it should have been littler. He has just reached his fifty, his hundred, or his hundred-and-fifty. . . . Benignly he acknowledges, with a wave of his sceptre, the homage of his subjects. Summer is golden and seemingly endless. There is no cloud in the sky to tell us that it cannot last for ever.

CHAPTER TEN

THE OLD MAN

'A man among men with a boy's heart to the last.'
AN OLD CRICKETER

I

W.G. CHANGED greatly in appearance between the time when he first took cricket by storm and when he retired, an indubitable Grand Old Man. Yet he had almost always been a commanding figure. From about the age of fifteen, after his first serious illness, he shot up suddenly in height and was from that time about six inches taller than his elder brother E.M. In the eighteen-seventies he filled out into a magnificently massive structure of bone and muscle. He was in his prime of manhood as a cricketer and as a superb physical specimen. He would have amply answered Falstaff's specification: 'Care I for the limbs, the thews, the stature, bulk, and big assemblance of a man? Give me the spirit . . .' He had them all and especially the spirit.

By the end of the golden decade, when he settled down, first to fairly hard medical study and then to regular practice, he had to battle with his increasing weight, but it was by no means a losing battle. Not till the Nottingham Test of 1899, when he was fifty-one, did he admit that 'the ground was too far away'. When the Trent Bridge crowd barracked him for not getting down to the ball, he did not say they were behaving unfairly, as well he might have done, but acknowledged that he was not so supple as he used to be. When he went out to open the innings with Fry, he said: 'Now steady, Charlie, I'm not a sprinter like you.' But he did not let his partner down in running between the wickets.

His beard, that banner with the strange device, was for nearly forty years part of the English landscape. It was dark as

191

Erebus, until it became flecked with grey. Among the portraits
at Lord's there is one which shows him with a beard of lightish
brown. This is an erroneous attribution. Brown boots, maybe,
but never a brown beard. When his beard first began to grow,
and it began early, he did not shave. Early authorities agree
that at seventeen his chin was covered with a bristly stubble.
Round about 1870, when he was rising twenty-two, he must
have shaved regularly for a short period, for there is an old
photograph taken of him, at an early Canterbury Festival
which shows him with unwontedly smooth cheeks, but he must
soon have abandoned the bristly battle which daily shaving
involved.

In the portrait of 'The English Twelve in Canada', dated
1873, the beard appears as firmly established, though not yet of
luxuriant habit. From then on it went on flowing, as inevitably
as and more decoratively than the Poet Laureate's brook. In
Beldam's lovely golfing photograph, taken when W.G. was
over sixty—a true artist's portrait if ever I saw one—the beard
is more grey than black, but still proudly flowing. Throughout
his career it was like a meteor flag of England that for so long
had braved the battle and the breeze. When things were going
well, he would stroke it gently; when things were going badly,
he would tug it thoughtfully and then the enemy had better
look out.

A very old acquaintance has spoken of his 'rugged physio-
gnomy characteristic of the Graces, which made them all look
more like farmers than doctors, and was full of life and vim'.
This may well have been true of most of them in later life. It
was not surprising that the Graces should look like farmers,
because they were countrymen before they were anything else—
it is the major clue to their characters—but, with respect, it is
not true to say that W.G. as a young man had rugged features.
On the contrary, the lines of his face were rather fine and delicate. If you will look at the portrait of W.G. at the age of about
twenty-three, and cover up the luxuriant beard and moustache,
you will see that the upper face bears a remarkable resemblance
to that of the best of today's young batsmen, Peter May.

The brightness of the young W.G.'s eyes seems to have struck

many of the cricketers who played with him. Sir Walter Scott
said of the eyes of Robert Burns that they were like coach-lamps
alight on a dark road at night and W.G.'s eyes had the same
luminous brightness and depth. 'His eyes,' said C. T. Studd,
'were about the finest you ever saw. It was worth going a long
journey just to look into them . . .' He spoke with the normal
west-country accent of his clan, enriched by a pleasant, un-
exaggerated west-country burr, such as he had learnt in child-
hood from his father and brothers and west Gloucestershire
neighbours. It was an accent formed long before the days
which saw regional colour drained from spoken English. His
voice would rise to the upper register in moments of excitement
or to a high-pitched chuckle when he was mightily amused, but
it was emphatically not the tedious falsetto with which some
writers have saddled him. His voice may sometimes have given
the illusion of sounding a little lighter than it really was, issuing
from so big a frame.

His hands were huge. All the better to catch you with, my
dear. (Think of the seventy-six flies of Stawell, swatted at one
blow.) A ball went into those gigantic paws, as Tom Emmett
might have said, like 'an old coal box'. When he shook your
hand, it was with a bear's grip. You might even have felt that
you would rather have had him hit you for six. His feet were
the biggest that ever pounded a cricket field, bigger even than
those of the heroic Maurice Tate. His boots had caused
admiring amazement in Australia—'two pounds and his tucker'
—and there is an authenticated story that he and E.M. once
ironed out a bumpy local pitch, in the absence of a heavy roller,
by patrolling it with solemn tread for an hour or two. One day,
the young boot-boy at brother Alfred's house was discovered
gazing in fascinated amazement at the boots of W.G., who was
staying in the house. The boy was almost hypnotized by the
fact that he could place his fingers in the toe of the boot and his
elbow in the heel.

'Canoes' . . . he breathed to himself in awestricken tones,
much as young Art Kipps ejaculated : 'Chubes!'

'I'll give you canoes, you young scoundrel!' rumbled W.G.

W.G. was a non-smoker, as were all the Graccs except Alfred

who, incidentally, lived some years longer than any of the others. W.G. believed that smoking took the fine edge off the eyesight. 'You can get rid of drink,' he said, 'but not of smoke.' When, during the M.C.C. game with the 1899 Australians, the teams were presented to the Prince of Wales, W.G. declined a cigar offered by the Prince with a momentary pang, and saw Joe Darling, the Australian captain, snap it up. Even despite this sad deprivation of a souvenir he remained a non-smoker.

He was a moderate drinker with occasional expansive moments, catholic in taste if reasonably modest in capacity. During the cricket season he enjoyed a double whisky and soda with angostura bitters at lunch and at close of play. There was a notable occasion at Fenner's which involved, and, for all I know, may still involve, the pleasant ceremony of entertaining the visitors to sherry and cake. In London County's game against Cambridge in 1904, W.G., with the utmost geniality, took sherry and cake with each individual member of the Cambridge eleven, and then went out and rattled up a gay half-century in double-quick time. In winter, when out beagling, he thought home-made cider an ideal cooler for those 'heated in the chase'; he also drank cider more regularly in later life in the hope of reducing his weight. He loved champagne and though he only drank it on special occasions, he reserved to the last his personal right to say how special an occasion might be. As we have already observed, his life did not pass by without a momentous occasion or two. In his Crystal Palace days he would cheerfully split a bottle at lunch with his crony, Murdoch, and one of his chief delights was to entertain gatherings of old friends and foes at festival week-ends, enriching the invitation with the mysterious promise: 'It's down the well!' This was a motto presaging hospitality, laughter and an infinitude of good fellowship.

II

If W.G. had one characteristic as a man above all others, it was his complete naturalness, which had its roots partly in his country upbringing and partly in his professional competence.

Those who met him met a frank and open personality, utterly free from self-consciousness and the desire to make an impression. He could look on self-conceit and mock-modesty and treat those two impostors just the same. He stood up to bad or good luck as to fast or slow bowling. If luck was bad, he would accept it, though he liked to growl a bit and get it over, in his own rumbling way. Popularity, which came to him in immense waves and might have made a vain man impossible to live with, left him unmoved. It did not unbalance him or fill him with illusions of grandeur, even though he could enjoy a reasonable amount of it enormously. Moreover he had a way of communicating this enjoyment to others which made for good feeling and good humour everywhere.

Thackeray believed, and indeed demonstrated in Colonel Newcome, that the good grow simpler as they grow older. W.G.'s later years were full of simple kindness. It would be possible to fill many pages with tributes to his personal benevolence, especially towards the young. In the simplest but richest of phrases, he was 'the kindest of men'. He acted like a gruffly affectionate father to many young players and the younger he found them the better it pleased him. C. L. Townsend, the Clifton schoolboy, was his ideal pupil, the brilliant youngster, highly talented and readily teachable. In the midst of W.G.'s concentrated struggle to achieve his hundredth hundred he called out to the score-box: 'How many has Charlie got?' He was not being publicly altruistic. His preoccupation with his own attempted feat was strong and serious, but he wanted the boy to make a century, too. Nor was 'Charlie' the only one to benefit from the Old Man's mildly autocratic kindness. Throughout W.G.'s career a succession of able youngsters appeared, some of whom became first-class cricketers and some of whom did not. But every one of them received help, encouragement, good cheer and, on sad occasion, much-needed comfort, as when W.G. would pat the shoulder of a boy who had just been bowled by a shooter and murmur, almost apprehensively: 'By jove, I'm glad I didn't have that one.'

His sympathetic outlook did not extend, and he never meant that it should, to those who were slack or showy in the field. If you were not quick and sure in your returns you might suddenly find yourself fielding long-leg at both ends, purely in the interests of a little more practice. He might shout at you if he thought you were lazy in the field; he might occasionally shout at you if you missed a catch he thought you should have held. But these were almost reflex actions. Usually his disapproval, if not the sharp expression he sometimes gave to it, was right. Sometimes he recognized, on reflection, that it was wrong. Then you would get the sort of warm-hearted apology that he once sent to Jack Board:

> Dear Jack,
>   We all miss 'em sometimes. You less than most of us.
>   Yours truly,
>   W. G. Grace.

Jack Board treasured that letter to the end of his days and felt in his sentimental heart that it made the Old Man's thunder worth enduring.

There was once a country lad named Ernest who, to the general dim-wittedness which is an occupational disease with some fast bowlers, added an impediment in his speech. Ernest had some cruel practical jokers among his friends and one summer morning he received a post card, purporting to come from W.G. and asking him to attend the County Ground to play against Yorkshire. When he arrived, his stammer made it difficult for anyone to understand what he was after but finally he was conveyed to the presence and presented his post card. W.G. regarded him gravely.

'Never mind, my boy,' he said, 'we shan't want you today, but get that blazer off and give me a ball or two.'

So Ernest bowled to W.G. at the nets, hit his stumps with a wild full-toss and lived happily ever afterwards, boasting that he had once nearly p-p-played for Gloucestershire and b-b-bowled W. G. Grace.

Much of W.G.'s temperamental poise, like his cricket prowess, lay in the first place on his superb physical strength, which rose to its prime about the time he was twenty-eight,

remained at its height through at least the first half of the
eighteen-eighties and gave way slowly, not to any kind of weakness but to increasing weight. It came back resurgently in the
middle 'nineties and never completely faded. He had, as we
know, his share of ailments, including pneumonia, scarlet fever
and mumps, but his normal day-to-day health was splendid,
furnishing him with unquenchable energy, with which friend
and enemy found it difficult to compete. Tales of his kindness
are mingled with odd stories of his physical strength. Passing
on his rounds along the Ropewalk at Bristol he heard an old
man cursing his donkey which had gently sunk to rest with its
load of coke. (An old man with an old donkey harnessed
between the shafts of an old cart was practically the commonest
sight in the streets of any Victorian town.) When W.G.
uttered a few amiable words of advice, the stream of profanity
was instantly switched from donkey to Doctor.

'You're the big lout that plays kids' games,' jeered the old
man, 'but what else can you do?'

'Not much,' agreed W.G. Then, tipping back his 'sawn-off'
top hat, he gripped the ends of the cart-shafts and lifted the
donkey on to its reluctant feet.

Another time, while following the beagles at full tilt, he
brushed through a light hedge and hurtled with a prodigious
splash into a pond that the hedge had momentarily masked.

'Serves you right,' guffawed the farmer who stood grinning
on the bank, 'for bashing my hedge about.'

W.G.'s reaction was inexcusable but understandable. Grip-
ping the farmer's collar, he gently lifted him from the bank,
deposited him in the water, and made off, splashing purposefully, in the opposite direction. And there the dazed and
martyred victim sat, muttering aloud to himself over and over
again; 'Lifted me up, he did . . . lifted me up as if I'd been a
new-born baby . . .'

III

W.G.'s character was all of a piece and, though it contained
some opposite qualities, they were firmly knitted together within

the whole. With his naturalness and kindness went a powerful native shrewdness which never failed him at work or play. Along with the rich common sense of which it was an integral part, it came from his country birth and breeding. It was a kind of rural sixth sense, learnt, not from poetic pastorals but in the hard school of country life, a life lived in the vicissitudes of wind and weather, where victory in the constant battle with natural forces could never be wholly assured. In that country life, as a wise historian has said, there was 'contact with nature, which in all previous ages had helped to form the mind and imagination of the human race . . .'

W.G. never ceased to be a countryman. Sporting dogs would refuse to leave him. Turf would grow for him as it would not grow for the ordinary groundsman. Even the reprehensible story of the wild duck at Fenner's becomes less reprehensible when it falls into place as a country story. While W.G. was bowling to Fred Wilson, of Cambridge, a skein of wild duck came streaking across the summer sky.

'By jove !' exclaimed W.G., 'look at those ducks !'

The batsman peered into the eye of the sun, resumed his stance completely dazzled and was clean bowled. The tale is quoted as an example of W.G.'s amusing smartness or, alternatively, his abominable tendency towards sharp practice. Neither example, I think, is correct. A member of the Grace family assured me that it would have been physically impossible for E.M. or W.G. to have seen birds in flight without going through the motion of whipping an imaginary sporting gun to the shoulder. It was for them one of the most clearly instinctive gestures of country life, and, if W.G. naughtily profited by it, he did not cunningly plan it. In point of historical fact, the batsman made no complaint, for he recognized that, whether W.G. had been crafty or not, it had been his own duty to concentrate.

W.G.'s country common sense helped him to diagnose his patients' ailments or to judge the state of a wicket damaged by rain. His knowledge of earth and weather left him with major suspicions about the wisdom of putting the other side in. 'If you win the toss, and the wicket's good,' he would say, 'go in and

bat. If the wicket's doubtful, go in and bat. And if the wicket's
bad, think it well over and . . . then go in and bat.'

A talented modern biographer has asserted that often a public
character is a mere bundle of attitudes and has no private
character at all. W.G. had both a public and a private character and each of them was an admirable one. His public
character was open for all to see, twenty-thousand at a time, and
he was known to his countrymen, not by empty phrases or pious
pronouncements, but by incomparable skill in what may without pomposity be called his art. His name stood for cricket in
his lifetime and has so stood ever since, even in days of sophisti-
cation and newer, if inferior, skills. His private virtues were the
humdrum virtues of a good husband, a good father, a good
doctor, and a good man. These were not bigoted and persecut-
ing virtues, such as some virtuous men use, but plain, russet-
coated virtues that did their duty and minded their own
business.

IV

There is another side to the ledger, and its entries, though
negligible compared with those on the credit side, should not be
ignored. At various times we have allegations of his tendency
towards autocracy, and of his occasional flares-up. He is also
accused of not writing his own books and of being a paid
amateur.

Certainly W.G. knew what he wanted and liked to get it. He
had much in his make-up of the stuff that made the cabman
call Mr. Dickens a 'harbitrary gent'. Certainly he could be
sometimes imperious, but that is an almost invariable con-
comitant of strength of character. If he occasionally flew off the
handle, he could apologize handsomely, as we have seen from
his letter to Jack Board.

His artfulness was genuine enough, goodness knows, but
examples of it, like Mark Twain's demise, have been much
exaggerated, partly by amiable people who enjoy pointing,
adorning and inflating a good story about a great man, and
partly by a minority for whom detraction is a hobby. He liked
to get what he wanted and he particularly liked his bit of

boisterous fun; moreover, as has been unquestionably shown, he more often than not got the worst of the battle of wits with hard-bitten opponents who knew him and cheerfully pitted their skill and intelligence against him. He was master but did not become master too easily. When he said (apocryphally) to the country umpire: 'These people came to see me bat, not to see you make a fool of yourself', he was saying (even though he did not say it) what everyone knew to be true.

As for his not writing his own books, a modern reply, cynical or tolerant, might be: 'Who does?' It is true that four books— *Cricket* (1891), *The History of a Hundred Centuries* (1895), *W.G.* (1899) and *W.G.'s Little Book* (1909)—were at various times published under his name. All these are works of some merit and it may be as well to remember Neville Cardus's warning never to be rude about cricketers' autobiographies: 'You never knew who wrote them.' (Some of them, eccentric souls, may have even written them themselves.) We know who wrote W.G.'s books, or at least helped him with them: authorship was shared by his friend, W. Methven Brownlee (who also wrote the first *Life*), William Yardley, Arthur Porritt, and E. D. H. Sewell, who played a good deal for London County and wrote voluminously on cricket and rugger. It is probably true that W.G. could not have written a whole book to save his life. As if it mattered. . . . All these gentlemen, in their varying degrees of talent, could. None of the published volumes, therefore, is without interest of some kind. Those who regard the act of 'ghosting' as disreputable would probably have looked on it as even more reprehensible in W.G.'s time. But ghosting has now become so almost universal a practice—the field is indeed full of shades!—that, if it were made a punishable offence, who should escape whipping? At least W.G.'s books were written by writers, which is more than can be said of the works of some modern 'ghosts'.

One of the most frequent allegations against W.G. is that he was always taking large sums of money as an amateur. Apart from the admittedly large sum received for his services during the second Australian tour, of which I have never been able to find an explanation, his normal dealings were the reverse of avaricious, and the sums that were known to be granted to him for expenses were peculiarly modest according to the standards of the day and highly reasonable by any standards. I have seen a letter from him in answer to one from an author who was seeking some way of reimbursing W.G. for information supplied by him towards a book he was writing. 'I should not think,' W.G. wrote, 'of receiving any payment for it . . .'

Almost his chief delight on the cricket field was to play in a benefit match for one of his friends among the professionals and the delight was increased when he could augment the gate, and therefore the gate-money, by contributing a huge individual score.[1] On at least two occasions he made a duck in the first innings, apologized profusely to the beneficiary and then, in the second innings, proceeded to amass the sort of huge total which brought the crowds hurrying back again. When Morley's benefit game was ruined by rain, W.G. offered to let him have the takings of his own testimonial. None of these actions were those of a grasping man and the last of them seems to have been reasonably generous, when you reflect that Morley, a fast and erratic bowler, had frequently submitted W.G. to heavy battery.

There are two derogatory suggestions which I find delightful. In Sir Charles Tennyson's *Life's All a Fragment* there is a vastly amusing passage, interpolated, I think, by George Lyttelton, which attributes to the eighth Viscount Cobham, irreverently termed 'Chob', a statement as superbly outrageous as it was apocryphal: 'I kept wicket behind W.G.—one of the dirtiest necks I ever kept wicket behind.' Denigration indeed! The other story concerns a night when, owing to shortage of accommodation, W.G. and A. N. Hornby were obliged to share an

---

[1] His passion to help a benefit is shown by this rather truculent letter sent to the Notts County Club in 1873:

'I have thought the matter well over and am come to the conclusion: you must give way for Rowbotham's benefit match. You may think I am using a strong expression in saying "*must*", but I think it is just to him. . . .

'If you will do this, you will greatly oblige me; if not, the only thing I can say is that I will not play at Nottingham. . . .

'If you like to play Notts *v.* Gloucester without any of the Graces, do so by all means.

'Now, I am sorry to write like this, but I can assure you that I think you ought to give in. . . . Please write me an answer as soon as you get this as I want it settled.

Yours truly, W. G. GRACE.'

hotel room.   Early in the morning W.G. was awakened by the
sound of Hornby opening the bedroom door.

'Where are you off to?' he demanded.

'To have my cold bath, of course,' said Hornby austerely.

'Oo . . . oh, Monkey,' exclaimed W.G., recoiling from the
very thought, 'you make me shudder . . .'

This makes an addition to that interesting line of research
which finds resemblance between Dr. W. G. Grace and that
other bluff, humorous, solid, commonsensical, monumental
Englishman, Dr. Samuel Johnson, for it shows that the one, just
as much as the other, had no passion for clean linen.

All W.G.'s friends, without exception, praised his kindness.
Most of them also praised his 'boyishness' and this to the modern
ear may be a hard saying. It need not be. In ordinary speech
we differentiate without tears between 'childish' and 'childlike'.
One word conveys silliness, the other innocence. W.G. was not
so much boyish as boylike.   There are in boyhood essential
qualities of innocence, simple humour, and zest for adventure
and if a man keeps those boylike qualities through his life, he is
the better man for it. It may be argued, though I disagree, that
Peter Pan is a detestable character. It can certainly be argued
that a boy *ought* to grow up. 'When I became a man, I put away
childish things . . .' Yet need a man put away boylike things?
There are great men who have kept, and will keep, their boylike
qualities till their dying day. The truly fatal act is the deliberate
avoidance of adult responsibilities. But W.G. never avoided
responsibilities. With his wife he brought up his family of three
boys and a girl and the bringing up was affectionate and
efficient. We know that he carried out his duties as a doctor
more than conscientiously and nobody will ever know how
many hours he spent of his own time with his patients. Whatever faults he may have had, the dodging of grown-up duties
was not among them. I would say that the best verbal description of W.G. as a person came, as the best pictures came, from
G. W. Beldam:

'If you had learnt to love him on the field, you loved him
even more when you saw him in his home: just the simple
natural English gentleman.'

At the end of Arnold Bennett's engaging Edwardian comedy, *The Card*, the question is asked concerning its spivvish hero: 'To what great cause has he contributed?' And the answer was: 'He has contributed to the great cause of cheering us all up.' W.G. contributed to a much greater cause: the cause of spreading innocent delight under the soft English sun among many thousands of his fellows. For, as Sir Norman Birkett has beautifully said: 'He was in truth, in the eyes of his fellow-countrymen, the great Englishman, playing the great English game in English fields.'

THE MAN IS GREATER THAN
THE LEGEND

'HE was a good man,' I said.

'Yes,' agreed my old Downend cricketer,' but he was a bit of an old devil, too . . .'

There were differing qualities in even that most uncomplicated of characters, but there were certainly no internal conflicts. He was a good man in his family and professional life, and in a more consistent sense than most of us. He was gloriously 'an old devil' in what E. W. Swanton has called his 'tinge of genial rascality': in the rich, engaging, cajoling, cozening, Falstaffian manner that now hardly any of us has the personality to imitate. He was one of the two or three best-known Englishmen in what will be known, not only as a great age, but as a solidly romantic one.

He was a countryman, rich in country wisdom, and a west-countryman at that, speaking with his own west-country accent as Sir Francis Drake and Sir Walter Raleigh spoke with theirs three hundred years before him. He was the least 'poetical' of men, but because he was born and bred a true Gloucestershire man he could fittingly have figured in that green vision that Flecker saw when, sick for home under burning Eastern skies, he sighed for the meadows of the west:

> *Oh, well I know sweet Hellas now,*
> *And well I knew it then,*
> *When I with starry lads walked out—*
> *But ah, for home again . . .*
> *Was I not bred in Gloucestershire,*
> *One of the Englishmen?*

He became and has remained a symbol of 'the beautiful but

difficult game of cricket', so that whenever and wherever his name is mentioned visions come into view of green fields and misty English skies. He is a symbol of the unsentimental, enduring things in country life, and of those elements, unsubtle but deep, in English character which are kindly and humorous but, at bottom, tenacious and, in the true old-fashioned sense of the word, tough. But, in a special and important sense, he was not a symbol of anything. He was himself. 'People loved him,' said John Arlott, 'not for the runs he made, but for the man he was.' That is profoundly true. His matchless skill in a difficult art was wholly his own. Many of the things that unpretentious English people inarticulately loved were gathered together in his large personality, but his individual self, generous, masterful, sometimes incorrigible, was his own. He was William Gilbert Grace.

His goodness was the straightforward goodness that English people recognize and respect even if they do not always practise. It was like Wycliffe's Bible, 'understanded of simple men'. His masterfulness and his guile were both qualities that his countrymen admired. They did not resent his authority, or even his occasional asperity, for their instinct told them that evil is not wrought by the masterful, but vain, weak and neurotic men. They chuckled appreciatively over his artfulness, for they recognized it as a kind of country craft, cheerfully employed in getting the better of the enemy within, if sometimes only just within, the rules. His opponents knew what the Old Man—the cunning Old Man of the tribe—was up to. They knew they must keep their wits about them to frustrate his 'knavish tricks'. Sometimes they were successful and sometimes not. The battle would as often as not end in uproarious laughter.

The people of his time knew what they loved and they took him to their hearts in much the same way as, in the words of Lord David Cecil, they took to Dickens: 'The English, the kindly, individualistic, illogical, sentimental English are, more than any other people, touched by impulsive benevolence; instinctive good nature sets a value on homely satisfactions . . .' They loved his impulsive benevolence and shared his homely satisfactions.

In one of his essays written during the first world war, A. G. Gardiner told how he walked down to his local country railway station to get an evening paper and, as he stood reading the meagre war news under the dim oil lamp, he heard a voice behind him say: 'W.G. is dead.'

'At that word, I turned hastily to another column, and found the news that had stirred him. And even in the midst of world-shaking events it stirred me, too. For a brief moment, I forgot the war and was back in that cheerful world where we greeted the rising sun with light hearts and saw its setting without fear. In that cheerful world I can hardly recall a time when a big man with a beard was not my king . . .'

Many a man felt that his king was gone. A friend of mine was in France, as most of us were in those days. The night before he was due to come home on leave he dreamed, without any apparent reason, of W.G. When he reached London, he heard that W.G. was dead and that the funeral was to take place the following day. A strong feeling impelled him to go down past the old Crystal Palace, which war had turned into a naval establishment, to the cemetery at Elmers End. There he joined the melancholy cavalcade at the graveside and as the mourners finally melted away into the cold, autumnal twilight, he lingered for a moment near the grave. There he stood and, perhaps because he was of an old-fashioned schoolmasterly type, brought up on the Victorian poets, there ran, or rather marched through his mind—absurdly, perhaps, but sadly—the slow, melancholy music of Tennyson's 'Morte d'Arthur'. He saw himself—yes, of course, it was absurd—as Sir Bedivere, watching with a sick heart the passing of the great King.

> *This day unsolders all the goodliest fellowship*
> *Whereof this world holds record . . .*

He pondered on the fevered and sombre picture of the war and its dark menace of worse to come; it might be that the old peaceful days of leisure and pleasure in the green fields of England would never come again. . . . The poem was still in his mind; he thought of the vaguely noble figure of King Arthur, the misty shadow of a poet's dream; and he thought of the wholly different 'king' who lay there in the still open grave but a few yards away, who had been so robust, so earthy, so richly endowed, not poetically, but in flesh and blood, in his own 'big assemblance', with the spirit of English laughter and the summer country scene. For an instant he thought he heard a friendly shout—'Well cot, oh, well cot!'—and the grave enunciation of first principles: 'I'd say you ought to put the bat against the ba . . .all . . .'

The leaves of the three nearby trees had nearly all gone, but in the gathering dusk a light wind swayed their branches. On the wind there came to his imagination a whisper, faint but growing, and somehow it seemed that in the whisper was a promise—a promise that 'the goodliest fellowship' would never be finally unsoldered, and that, despite war and winter, summer's world of happy days would come again, would always come again. . . . He walked down the curved path into the broad walk towards the gate. It was almost dark. The wind was still blowing and in the sound of it, the end-line of the poem swelled like a trumpet-call:

And the new sun rose, bringing the new year.

SHORT BIBLIOGRAPHY

To crib from one book is plagiarism, to crib from a dozen is research; to crib from any larger number will get you a doctorate of philosophy at one of the less exacting universities. While hopefully awaiting my Ph.D., then, I gratefully acknowledge my indebtedness to the works listed below, at the same time claiming, with some spirit, that this book's errors and biased opinions are my own.

The Memorial Biography of Dr. W. G. Grace, edited by Lord Hawke, Lord Harris and Sir Home Gordon. Constable 1919.

W. G. Grace: A Biography by W. Methven Brownlee. Iliffe 1887.

Cricket by W. G. Grace. Arrowsmith 1891.

The History of a Hundred Centuries, written by W. G. Grace. Upcott Gill 1895.

'W.G.': Cricketing Reminiscences and Personal Recollections by W. G. Grace. James Bowden 1899.

Dr. W. G. Grace by Acton Wye (Bijou Biographies). Henry J. Drane 1901.

W.G.'s Little Book by W. G. Grace. George Newnes 1907.

W. G. Grace by Bernard Darwin. Duckworth 1934.

W. G. Grace by Clifford Bax. Phoenix House 1952.

The Jubilee Book of Cricket by K. S. Ranjitsinhji. Wm. Blackwood and Sons 1897.

A History of Cricket by H. S. Altham and E. W. Swanton. George Allen & Unwin 1926. 4th ed. 1948.

Cricket: A Popular Handbook of the Game by W. G. Grace and others. Religious Tract Society 1881.

Kings of Cricket by Richard Daft. Arrowsmith 1893.

Talks with Old English Cricketers by A. W. Pullin ('Old Ebor'). Blackwood 1900.

Cricket by Neville Cardus. Longmans Green 1930.

Life Worth Living by C. B. Fry. Eyre & Spottiswoode 1939.

A Few Short Runs by Lord Harris. Murray 1921.

The Graces, E.M., W.G., and G.F., by A. G. Powell and S. Canynge Caple. The Cricket Book Society 1948.

A History of the Gloucestershire County Cricket Club, 1870–1949 by S. Canynge Caple. Littlebury & Co., Worcester, 1949.

Lord's 1787–1945 by Sir Pelham Warner. Harrap 1946.

Long Innings by Sir Pelham Warner. Harrap 1951.

Gentlemen v. Players 1806–1949 by Sir Pelham Warner. Harrap 1950.

On and Off the Field by Sir Henry Leveson-Gower. Stanley Paul 1953.

Concerning Cricket by John Arlott. Longmans Green 1949.

With Bat and Ball by George Giffen. Ward, Lock & Co. 1898.

The Complete Cricketer by Albert E. Knight. Methuen 1906.

Cricket in Ireland by Patrick Hone. Kerryman Press 1955.

History of Mangotsfield and Downend by Rev. A. Emlyn Jones. W. S. Mack & Co., Bristol, 1899.

The Book of Cricket : A Gallery of Great Players by Denzil Batchelor. Collins 1952.

The Game of Cricket, with an Introduction by Sir Norman Birkett. Batsford 1955.

Talking of Cricket by Ian Peebles. Museum Press 1953.

They Made Cricket by G. D. Martineau. Museum Press 1956.

Wisden's Cricketer's Almanack *passim* but especially the volumes for 1896 and 1916.

Sporting Campaigner[1] by M. A. Green. Stanley Paul 1956.

Victorian England : Portrait of an Age by G. M. Young. Oxford University Press 1936.

Pebbles on the Shore by Alpha of the Plough (A. G. Gardiner). Dent 1917.

English Social History by G. M. Trevelyan. Longmans, Green 1942.

---

[1] These engaging reminiscences contain an echo of the wicket-keeper's-nose-in-front theme. While Gloucestershire were playing Kent in 1912, Green sat next to W.G., watching Jessop hammering the bowling. When Jessop was given out, stumped by Fred Huish, W.G. rose in commanding wrath and called out shrilly: 'I saw you, Freddie! I saw you take it in front of the wicket!'

A FEW STATISTICS FOR THOSE WHO MUST HAVE THEM

I. BATTING AND BOWLING IN FIRST CLASS CRICKET

BATTING			YEAR	BOWLING		
Completed Innings	Runs	Average		Runs	Wickets	Average
7	189	27·00	1865	268	20	13·40
11	581	52·81	1866	434	31	14·00
5	154	30·80	1867	292	39	7·48
11	625	56·81	1868 {	–	1	–
				686	48	14·29
23	1,320	57·39	1869	1,193	73	16·34
33	1,808	54·78	1870	782	50	15·64
35	2,739	78·25	1871	1,346	79	17·03
29	1,561	53·82	1872 {	–	6	–
				736	62	11·87
30	2,139	71·30	1873 {	–	5	–
				1,307	101	12·94
32	1,664	52·00	1874	1,780	140	12·71
46	1,498	32·56	1875	2,468	191	12·92
42	2,622	62·42	1876	2,458	129	19·05
37	1,474	39·83	1877	2,291	179	12·79
40	1,151	28·77	1878	2,204	152	14·50
26	993	38·19	1879	1,491	113	13·19
24	951	39·62	1880	1,480	84	17·61
24	917	38·20	1881	1,026	57	18·00
37	975	26·35	1882	1,754	101	17·36
39	1,352	34·66	1883	2,077	94	22·09
40	1,361	34·02	1884	1,762	82	21·48
39	1,688	43·28	1885	2,199	117	18·79
52	1,846	35·50	1886	2,439	122	19·99
38	2,062	54·26	1887	2,078	97	21·42
58	1,886	32·51	1888	1,691	93	18·18
43	1,396	32·46	1889	1,019	44	23·15
52	1,476	28·38	1890	1,183	61	19·39
39	771	19·76	1891	973	58	16·77
10	448	44·80	1891–92	134	5	26·80
34	1,055	31·02	1892	958	31	30·90
45	1,609	35·75	1893	854	22	38·81

Completed Innings	BATTING Runs	Average	YEAR	Runs	BOWLING Wickets	Average
44	1,293	29·38	1894	732	29	25·24
46	2,346	51·00	1895	527	16	32·93
50	2,135	42·70	1896	1,249	52	24·01
39	1,532	39·28	1897	1,242	56	22·17
36	1,513	42·02	1898	917	36	25·47
22	515	23·40	1899	482	20	24·10
30	1,277	42·56	1900	969	32	30·28
31	1,007	32·48	1901	1,111	51	21·78
32	1,187	37·09	1902	1,074	46	23·34
26	593	22·80	1903	479	10	47·90
25	637	25·48	1904	687	21	32·71
13	250	19·23	1905	383	7	54·71
9	241	26·77	1906	268	13	20·61
2	19	9·50	1907	–	–	–
2	40	20·00	1908	5	0	–
				–	12	–
1,388	54,896	39·55	TOTALS	51,488	2,864	17·97

II. CENTURIES

1866 (2)	... 224 not out	England v. Surrey ... The Oval
	173 not out	Gentlemen of the South v. Players of the South The Oval
1868 (3)	... 134 not out	Gentlemen v. Players ... Lord's
	130 and	South of Thames v.
	102 not out	North of Thames ... Canterbury
1869 (6)	... 117	M.C.C. v. Oxford University ... Oxford
	138 not out	M.C.C. v. Surrey ... The Oval
	121	M.C.C. v. Notts ... Lord's
	180	Gentlemen of the South v. Players of the South The Oval
	122	South v. North ... Sheffield
	127	M.C.C. v. Kent ... Canterbury
1870 (5)	... 117 not out	M.C.C. v. Notts ... Lord's
	215	Gentlemen v. Players ... The Oval
	109	Gentlemen v. Players ... Lord's
	143	Gloucestershire v. Surrey The Oval
	172	Gloucestershire v. M.C.C. ... Lord's

CENTURIES—*continued*

1871 (10) ...	181	M.C.C. v. Surrey ...	Lord's
	118	Gentlemen of the South v. Gentlemen of the North	West Brompton
	178	South v. North ...	Lord's
	162	Gentlemen of England v. Cambridge University	Cambridge
	189 not out	Single v. Married of England ...	Lord's
	146	M.C.C. v. Surrey ...	The Oval
	268	South v. North ...	The Oval
	117	M.C.C. v. Kent ...	Canterbury
	217	Gentlemen v. Players ...	Brighton
	116	Gloucestershire v. Notts	Nottingham
1872 (6) ...	101	M.C.C. v. Yorkshire ...	Lord's
	112	Gentlemen v. Players ...	Lord's
	117	Gentlemen v. Players ...	The Oval
	170 not out	England v. Notts and Yorkshire ...	Lord's
	114	South v. North ...	The Oval
	150	Gloucestershire v. Yorkshire ...	Sheffield
1873 (7) ...	158	Gentlemen v. Players ...	The Oval
	145	Gentlemen of the South v. Players of the North	Prince's
	134	Gentlemen of the South v. Players of the South	The Oval
	163	Gentlemen v. Players ...	Lord's
	152	Eleven v. Fifteen of M.C.C. ...	Lord's
	192 not out	South v. North ...	The Oval
	160 not out	Gloucestershire v. Surrey	Clifton
1874 (8) ...	179	Gloucestershire v. Sussex	Brighton
	150	Gentlemen of the South v. Players of the South	The Oval
	104	Gentlemen of the South v. Players of the North	Prince's
	110	Gentlemen v. Players ...	Prince's
	167	Gloucestershire v. Yorkshire ...	Sheffield
	121	Gloucestershire and Kent v. England ...	Canterbury
	123	M.C.C. v. Kent ...	Canterbury
	127	Gloucestershire v. Yorkshire ...	Clifton

CENTURIES—*continued*

1875 (3)	...	152	Gentlemen v. Players ...	Lord's
		111	Gloucestershire v. Yorkshire ...	Sheffield
		119	Gloucestershire v. Notts	Clifton
1876 (7)	...	104	Gloucestershire v. Sussex	Brighton
		169	Gentlemen v. Players ...	Lord's
		114 not out	South v. North ...	Nottingham
		126	United South v. United North ...	Hull
		344	M.C.C. v. Kent ...	Canterbury
		177	Gloucestershire v. Notts	Clifton
		318 not out	Gloucestershire v. Yorkshire ...	Cheltenham
1877 (2)	...	261	South v. North ...	Prince's
		110	Gloucestershire and Yorkshire v. England	Lord's
1878 (1)	...	116	Gloucestershire v. Notts	Nottingham
1879 (3)	...	123	Gloucestershire v. Surrey	The Oval
		102	Gloucestershire v. Notts	Nottingham
		113	Gloucestershire v. Somerset ...	Clifton
1880 (2)	...	106	Gloucestershire v. Lancashire ...	Clifton
		152	England v. Australia ...	The Oval
1881 (2)	...	100	Gentlemen v. Players ...	The Oval
		182	Gloucestershire v. Notts	Nottingham
1883 (1)	...	112	Gloucestershire v. Lancashire ...	Clifton
1884 (3)	...	101	M.C.C. v. Australians	Lord's
		107	Gentlemen of England v. Australians ...	The Oval
		116 not out	Gloucestershire v. Australians ...	Clifton
1885 (4)	...	132	Gloucestershire v. Yorkshire ...	Huddersfield
		104	Gloucestershire v. Surrey	Cheltenham
		221 not out	Gloucestershire v. Middlesex ...	Clifton
		174	Gentlemen v. Players ...	Scarborough
1886 (4)	...	148	Gentlemen of England v. Australians ...	The Oval
		104	M.C.C. v. Oxford University ...	Oxford
		110	Gloucestershire v. Australians ...	Clifton

CENTURIES—*continued*

	170	England *v.* Australia ...	The Oval
1887 (6) ...	113	Gloucestershire *v.* Middlesex ...	Lord's
	116 not out	M.C.C. *v.* Cambridge University ...	Lord's
	183 not out	Gloucestershire *v.* Yorkshire ...	Gloucester
	113 not out	Gloucestershire *v.* Notts	Clifton
	101 and 103 not out	Gloucestershire *v.* Kent	Clifton
1888 (4) ...	215	Gloucestershire *v.* Sussex	Brighton
	165	Gentlemen of England *v.* Australians ...	Lord's
	148 and 153	Gloucestershire *v.* Yorkshire ...	Clifton
1889 (3) ...	101	Gloucestershire *v.* Middlesex ...	Lord's
	127 not out	Gloucestershire *v.* Middlesex ...	Cheltenham
	154	South *v.* North ...	Scarborough
1890 (1) ...	109 not out	Gloucestershire *v.* Kent	Maidstone
1891–2 (1) ... in Australia	159	England *v.* Victoria ...	Melbourne
1893 (1) ...	128	M.C.C. *v.* Kent ...	Lord's
1894 (3) ...	139	M.C.C. *v.* Cambridge University ...	Cambridge
	196	M.C.C. *v.* Cambridge University ...	Lord's
	131	Gentlemen *v.* Players ...	Hastings
1895 (9) ...	103	M.C.C. *v.* Sussex ...	Lord's
	288	Gloucestershire *v.* Somerset ...	Bristol
	257	Gloucestershire *v.* Kent	Gravesend
	169	Gloucestershire *v.* Middlesex ...	Lord's
	125	M.C.C. *v.* Kent ...	Lord's
	101 not out	Gentlemen of England *v.* I Zingari ...	Lord's
	118	Gentlemen *v.* Players ...	Lord's
	119	Gloucestershire *v.* Notts	Cheltenham
	104	South *v.* North ...	Hastings
1896 (4) ...	243 not out	Gloucestershire *v.* Sussex	Brighton
	301	Gloucestershire *v.* Sussex	Bristol
	186	Gloucestershire *v.* Somerset ...	Taunton

CENTURIES—*continued*

	102 not out	Gloucestershire *v.* Lancashire	... Bristol
1897 (4)	... 126	Gloucestershire *v.* Notts	Nottingham
	116	Gloucestershire *v.* Sussex	Bristol
	113	Gloucestershire *v.* Philadelphians	... Bristol
	131	Gloucestershire *v.* Notts	Cheltenham
1898 (3)	... 168	Gloucestershire *v.* Notts	Nottingham
	126	Gloucestershire *v.* Essex	Leyton
	109	Gloucestershire *v.* Somerset	... Taunton
1900 (3)	... 126	South *v.* North	... Lord's
	110 not out	London County *v.* Worcestershire	... Crystal Palace
	110	London County *v.* M.C.C.	,,
1901 (1)	... 132	London County *v.* M.C.C.	,,
1902 (2)	... 131 not out	London County *v.* M.C.C.	,,
	129	London County *v.* Warwickshire	... ,,
1903 (1)	... 150	London County *v.* Gloucestershire	... ,,
1904 (1)	... 166	London County *v.* M.C.C.	,,

III. TEST FIGURES

Matches played   ...   22

Batting		Bowling		Fielding	
Innings	36	Runs	236	Catches	39
Not out	2	Wickets	9		
Runs	1,098	Average	26·22		
Highest score	170				
Centuries	5				
Fifties	5				
Average	32·29				

IV. GENTLEMEN *V.* PLAYERS

In 141 completed innings he scored 6,008 runs with an average of 42·60 and took 271 wickets at a cost of 18·78.

V. MINOR MATCHES

Mr. G. Neville Weston, who has made a profound study of these matters, hopes shortly to publish a book on W. G. Grace's scores in minor matches. Pending the issue of precise figures, it can be roughly reckoned that in addition to his 54,896 runs and 2,864 wickets in first class cricket, he scored about another 25,000 runs, including nearly a hundred centuries, and took about 4,000 wickets in games of lesser importance.

VI. BEST TIMES IN ATHLETICS

100 yards on grass	...	10·8 seconds
200 yards hurdle race	...	28 seconds
440 yards flat race	...	52·2 seconds
Throwing the cricket ball	...	118 yards

Between 1866 and 1870 in various athletic events, including the 100 yards, the quarter and half miles, 200 and 300 yards hurdles, high and long jump, pole vault and throwing the cricket ball, his prizes amounted to 46 firsts and 12 seconds. He also received several gold medals for winning the highest number of events at different meetings.

INDEX

INDEX

If you are indexing, say, the story of Hamlet, *you run into trouble when you come to the Prince of Denmark. If you leave him out, it will look odd; if you put him in, your index will suffer from that characteristic evil of the age—inflation. So with our hero. We could get him born on page 1 and then index his every action from putting on his pads on page 12 till he finally takes them off on page 215. This would be conscientious but wearing, and would undoubtedly make the index bigger than the book. It is therefore respectfully suggested that, as an alternative to looking up* W.G. *in the index, it would be easier to read the book.*